The Love Song
of the Universe

Aug 2006

The Love Song
of the Universe

Mary Sparrowdancer

HAMPTON ROADS
PUBLISHING COMPANY, INC.

Excerpt from The Gnostic Scriptures by Bentley Layton
Copyright © 1987 by Bentley Layton.
Used by permission of Doubleday,
a division of Random House, Inc.

"Illustrations" by Oswald White Bear Fredericks,
from BOOK OF THE HOPI by Frank Waters, © 1963
by Frank Waters.
Used by permission of Viking Penguin,
a division of Penguin Putnam Inc.

Some names and personal information have been changed
in order to protect privacy.

Cover design by Jane Hagaman
Cover art by Rebecca Whitney

For information write:

Hampton Roads Publishing Company, Inc.
1125 Stoney Ridge Road
Charlottesville, VA 22902
Or call: 804-296-2772
Fax: 804-296-5096
e-mail: hrpc@hrpub.com
www.hrpub.com

If you are unable to order this book from your local
bookseller, you may order directly from the publisher.
Call 1-800-766-8009, toll-free.

Library of Congress Catalog Card Number: 00-111929
ISBN 1-57174-210-7

10 9 8 7 6 5 4 3 2 1

Printed on acid-free paper in the United States

For Emily and John,

and all Children of the Universe

who see now

—or are learning to see again—

with the eyes of a child.

Acknowledgements

I wish to acknowledge the many individuals who helped make this book possible: my parents, Mary and Charlie, who raised me to be an individual unafraid of asking questions (and who taught me to pay attention to the answers I might receive); my sisters, Colleen, Patty, and Carol who continue to touch my life in different and beautiful ways; my friends who offered their support as everything unfolded—Tom, Dove, Chenn, Linda, Mays, Raymond, Juliet, Craig, and those who cannot be named at this time. And, of course, I wish to acknowledge my son and daughter, John and Emily, without whose patience, help, and observations, this work would be incomplete.

Grateful acknowledgment is also extended to the professional staff of Hampton Roads Publishing Company, with special thanks to my editor, Pat Adler, who worked with me throughout the entire development of this book, offering her editorial guidance, insight, and suggestions on a near-daily basis.

Table of Contents

1 First Stirrings / 1

2 Visitors / 14

3 Dreamwalking / 59

4 The Awakening / 86

5 Butterfly Lessons and Storm Warnings / 108

6 Facing West / 125

7 Journey through Space / 154

8 The Great Awareness, Aware of Being Unknown / 175

9 Transition: (Let's Call the Whole Thing Off) / 194

10 . . . By Any Other Name / 202

11 The Hidden Scriptures: Let There be *Gnosis* / 220

12 Can We Try Again, Please? / 228

Epilogue / 235

—1—

First Stirrings

 I was normal until my thirty-seventh year. That was the year the Indians arrived.

The signs of their presence were very subtle in the beginning, as though they knew well that our household must be awakened gently, patiently, and quietly. They left the curious signs of their presence with unseen hands in carefully selected places throughout the house and in the yard.

First, an ancient stone medicine pestle was found lying on the shelf of the linen closet. It was an odd piece of carved sandstone, something definitely not common to Tallahassee's basin of cavernous limestone aquifers and deep layers of sanguineous clay. This was a piece of pale sandstone that hinted more of an origin in a desert.

Next, a giant, white scallop shell was found in the bathroom cabinet under the sink. This, of course, spoke its own clear message regarding origins—it had once cupped something that lived in a great saltwater sea.

While the sandstone artifact in the linen closet did seem somewhat odd, it was the giant shell lying under the sink that begged a comment. The comment, a verbal expression that something unusual was in the air, marked a starting point.

I carried the shell out of the bathroom and into the living room where Craig, my husband at the time, was reading the New Yorker.

"Why did you put this shell under the sink?" I asked.

"I didn't put it there."

Our two children, Emily and John, were both toddlers at this time and could not possibly have been suspects—it would be at least six more months before they figured out how to open the child-proof cabinets. In my eyes, therefore, the process of elimination within the household narrowed the list of suspects down to the man reading the magazine. He, of course, narrowed the list down to the woman holding the shell.

"Well, if I didn't put it there," I said, "then you must have."

He shook his head. "I've never even seen it before. Maybe you put it there and forgot about it."

Craig, a lawyer by trade and training, always sought simple, logical explanations for life's events, and my two new discoveries were no exception. When I questioned him earlier in the week about the carved sandstone in the linen closet, he simply shrugged and said that it had been there for a long time—he thought it belonged to me. Now a giant scallop shell also belonged to me. A nagging little thought of oddness trickled into my mind, but I quickly dismissed it.

Those were the first, quiet signs.

Nothing else strange or remarkable occurred in our normal, quiet household for several months following those first discoveries, thus setting into motion a pattern that would, in time, become clear. The events were to occur according to a patient and well-thought-out plan. We would be rocked slowly and gently awake by the events to come, rocked as a boat might be in the rise and fall, in the ebb and flow, of ocean waters.

Early one morning in the winter of that year, as I walked out of the house to retrieve the newspaper, I found a shard of what appeared to be American Indian pottery lying on the porch steps. I picked it up, marveling at its beauty. It was a rich brown color, striped and pierced with designs speaking to its great age. As I turned the object over in my hands, I was immediately reminded of the shell and the stone, and although none of the objects were of similar origin, I suspected that they were somehow related.

Craig was sitting at the kitchen table. I handed him the newspaper and the pottery.

"What is this?" he asked.

"I'm not sure, but it looks like a piece of ancient pottery."

"Where'd you find it?"

"On the porch steps."

He put it down on the kitchen table, and picked up the newspaper. With this simple act of being unimpressed, he seemed to dismiss the possibility that anything out of the ordinary might be occurring. "It's probably just a rock or something," he said.

After he finished his coffee and piece of toast, he left for work.

I cannot remember why I thought to look again at the porch steps that morning. I can't remember what might have compelled me to go again to the spot where I found that little piece of pottery, but I did just that.

About an hour after Craig left, I returned to the porch steps and was somewhat surprised to find a second piece of pottery lying on the same spot where the first had been found. An hour later, I was astonished to find a third piece where the first two had been found, and fifteen minutes after that, I was deeply troubled when I found a fourth piece on the same spot. All pieces were unmatching.

Clutching them, I went indoors and sat on the couch to think about the implications suddenly presented by four shards of broken pottery. It was not the pottery itself, that was so strange—so inexplicable—it was the pottery's origin. Questions such as "how," "why," and "what" flowed through my mind, followed by the inevitable, and an even more troubling question— "Who?"

A slight pinging sound caught my attention and I looked to my left just in time to see a small white stone bounce onto the hardwood floor, and then roll to a stop. I stared at it for what seemed like a long time before finally going to it and picking it up. The question of "how" had just been answered by this stone's sudden appearance, seemingly from nowhere. The other questions remained.

I placed the fragments of pottery and the stone on the mantel, not knowing what they represented—not knowing from where they came.

I was anything but comfortable with these mysteries. They created disturbing, paradoxical questions for me, since I had long abandoned all searches for anything of a true spiritual nature.

The daily routine of our household continued to proceed in a comfortable manner. Our days were filled with events typical to any American household. Bottles were prepared for baby John, diapers were changed, the grass was mowed, and there was shopping to be done at the grocery store. Quiet and not-so-quiet meals were shared, the dog slept in front of the fireplace and barked on the twenty-third of each month at the meter man, Craig left for work at the same time every workday, and arrived at home on time each afternoon.

Our normal daily routines continued. Mixed into those normal routines, however, was the on-going appearance of curious artifacts.

By the spring of my thirty-eighth year, my collection of pottery and white stones had grown considerably.

The pottery was found on the doorsteps, on the grass, in closets, on the end tables, in kitchen cabinets, on nightstands, and finally, I found a piece under my pillow.

The objects appeared so frequently that by spring I was no longer deeply troubled by finding them. I was becoming more or less accustomed to reaching for a cup of coffee while immersed in a book, and retrieving instead a fractured rim-piece of pottery. When something considered "odd" happens frequently enough, it no longer remains odd. It becomes rather normal.

And so, as I found the pieces and grew more comfortable with finding them, a long-shut, rusty hinged door began to open. The potsherds and stones seemed to be providing some sort of physical evidence that there was more to the universe than what my beliefs or disbeliefs allowed, and that the other world existed whether I personally believed in it or not.

Perhaps, I thought, there really is something out there.

Perhaps I had abandoned my search just a moment shy of really finding something rich and worthy to embrace.

Spiritual disintegration began for me at nine o'clock one cold morning in Cheyenne, Wyoming—the last of the outposts to which we were stationed during my dad's Air Force career. I was fourteen years old and in world history class the day the threads unraveled.

History, as taught in the various schools I attended, was never a subject that held my interest. It consisted of one sentence followed by another in which sometimes a century or more of mankind's past actions were summed up in a few dry understatements, and this was followed by the dates of noteworthy achievements. We were required to memorize the dates.

I learned other things during history class. I learned breath control, and that if I held my breath long enough according to the clock just over the teacher's head, I would be able to swim the full length of the indoor pool underwater during P.E. class, which was next. I polished up my drawing techniques in my notebook, changed the spelling of my name, experimented with writing backwards, and discovered that the high ceiling beyond the clock bore a water stain that sometimes grew in size after a heavy snow.

The teacher—who washed his hair sometime prior to classes on Monday, Wednesday and Friday, but wore it greasy on Tuesdays and Thursdays—appeared to be speaking, and I was in the middle of wondering what type of shampoo he used, when he said something that caught my attention. I began listening.

On this particular morning, in one forty-five-minute block of time, he lit upon the details of several dates that appeared to suddenly awaken the entire class. His talk on this day was about the activities of the Church during the Inquisition. These activities, conducted by "Christians," were carried out "in the name of God." He did not sum it up in a sentence. His description was graphic.

I was not the only one shaken to my foundations on that morning. The entire class seemed strangely silent when the bell rang, but the silence didn't last long. Several discussions broke out in the hallway, and although I was never included in the popular cliques that had a voice, I heard what they were saying: "Why have we never heard about this before?" And, I heard the conclusions: "He must be lying." And then there was more. By early afternoon, the school was abuzz with rumors about the anti-Christian history teacher who, according to some students, was a known Communist as well as a Nazi war criminal, and he was teaching Hatred of Christians and Blasphemy 101 in his nine A.M. class.

There was talk about that teacher, talk that extended far beyond the mouths of fourteen- and fifteen-year-old students. It rapidly reached the home fronts, and then spread over the telephones, and before he had time to shampoo his hair again, the teacher was called into the principal's office. There, behind the tall, closed, soundproof doors where transgressors were known to meet with harsh punishments, the history teacher met his own ill fate. He had brought it on himself with his words of blasphemy. According to the most popular narratives in circulation, after the principal was finished with him, armed guards were called in, the teacher was arrested, and whisked off to prison. There were other versions, of course—one stating that he went home sick with the stomach flu.

Nonetheless, justice was served.

After a week or so, he returned to the classroom noticeably broken, subdued, and quiet. Some said he was still recovering from the flu, but others knew better. His condition was due to unspeakable tortures inflicted in his jail cell.

He never spoke again about details of historical events, but focused only upon their dates.

All was calm again in World History class. I returned to breath control.

Forcing the history teacher into silence in order to protect our minds from history did nothing to alter what the man had already set into motion. He had planted the seeds of doubt in at least one mind in his classroom.

Raised a Roman Catholic, my next logical step was to express those doubts to the parish priest—a busy, red-faced man who sweated profusely during Sunday masses, and had a short, firecracker fuse of a temper. I confronted him with my questions in confession on Saturday afternoon, and his response was one of memorable anger. He did not speak to me in the whispers customary to the confessional chamber, but shocked me by speaking loudly. In this loud voice, he told me not to ever question the Church again because it is infallibly governed and does not make mistakes. With this public shaming, he created a fertile ground for even more questions.

I did not do the penance that he demanded of me for having questioned, nor did I beg forgiveness. I emerged from the confessional, embarrassed, to face the stares of those waiting in line. They were clearly wondering what I had done to provoke such a vocal outburst. I then did the unthinkable and simply walked out of the church—without so much as a parting genuflection. I walked out for good, and went home.

This, of course, meant certain Hell—a rather stone-cold way for God to deal with an inquiring kid—but I could not quiet the questions. All that remained of my formal spiritual training was the promise of Hell.

When I turned twenty, I found myself searching once again for spiritual harbor. No longer associated with Christianity, I converted to Judaism. I was sent to Hebrew school by my elderly rabbi, where I learned to read and write Hebrew.

The Hebrew language, which is written from right to left, came easily to me, notably so. The rabbi was summoned to the school on the third day of my training because I had already grasped the language—with one small, but conspicuous twist. I was pronouncing the language in the way that it had been pronounced prior to my birth.

The rabbi wept on that day, although I'm not sure why, and he was reluctant to discuss the reason behind his tears. On the day that my conversion became formal, he gave me a Hebrew name—Miriam—and I was known from then on in the temple as Miriam, granddaughter of the rabbi.

He remained a friend of my family—including my Catholic parents, with whom I still lived—but shortly after learning the language and becoming the rabbi's granddaughter, I also left Judaism as though it had been the Hebrew lessons themselves that seemed to satisfy some unnamed longing within.

Still in my early twenties, I could pray in three different languages—English, Latin, and Hebrew—but I never found God. The search then ended, or fizzled into a long sigh of "I give up." The only religious thoughts that were not fully unraveled remained those of Hell, and God was merely something handy to blame calamities on. Otherwise, I saw no evidence of divine existence.

Now a mature woman with my own household, a mother of two who had outgrown religious matters long ago, I was seeing unexpected evidence of something previously unknown to me. The evidence was hinting at the possible existence of a spirit world. And, I reasoned, if there was a spirit world, maybe there was a God after all. I wasn't sure. I was mainly confused as I found each piece of pottery and each white stone, and dropped them with a satisfying clink into a growing pile.

The pieces of pottery were all unmatched, the edges and hues never quite fitting or matching those of the other pieces.

These were the shards from a thousand clay pots that had somehow been beckoned forth from where they had lain buried for a long, long time. The pieces were now in plain view, quietly awaiting certain discovery. Although it seemed like a strange thing to consider, it almost appeared as though they were meant to be found.

With illustrated books that I obtained at the State Library, I was able to give tentative dates to the pottery. The shards ranged in age from shiny black pieces dating to the 1500s, to thick, heavily punctated, sand-colored pieces emerging from the darkness of centuries preceding the Common Era of Christianity.

The white stones continued to fall out of the air and land on the floor with such routine that on more than one occasion, when witnessed by the children, it was they who picked the stones up and handed them to me as casually as they might hand me the telephone, saying, "Here Mommy, this must be for you."

The shards and stones seemed to be an affirmation of sorts that the Laws of Reality—long used by wise men to measure and map the Universe—were bending in my previously normal household.

It was a strange puzzle. I gathered its ancient pieces as I discovered them.

While my stones and potsherds continued falling out of the air, several blocks away, similar artifacts were being uncovered from their resting place of 500 years by State Archaeologist, Calvin Jones.

Just up the street, and several feet under the surface of the earth, Mr. Jones had discovered the site of Hernando de Soto's winter encampment in Tallahassee. It is said that there, on that site, the explorers celebrated this country's first Christmas. Jones also said that not everyone in the village had reason to celebrate. Nevertheless, it was a monumental find for the respected archaeologist.

It also presented a rather timely opportunity for me to have my shards examined and validated by an expert.

On a muggy Thursday afternoon that spring, I selected four unremarkable shards from my admirable collection, walked up the road to the site and found Mr. Jones surrounded by student helpers, volunteers, and seekers of ancient wonders all sifting through mud.

While several people shoveled large mounds of dirt onto mesh objects that resembled screen doors, others then hosed down the dirt, creating an earthen soup that dripped through the mesh. Left behind on the mesh were acorns, sticks, stones, and fragments of history. When I approached, Mr. Jones, covered with mud, was examining the finds of his volunteers, and explaining to a group of school children the difference between pottery shards and acorn caps. I waited for a lull in the conversation before addressing him.

"Excuse me," I said, "I was wondering if you might take a look at some pieces that I've found?"

He was easy to approach, easy to smile. His manner, along with the indications of his simple pleasures present on the site—the cartons of chocolate milk and packages of sweet pastries—put me at ease. He took the pottery from my hands and studied them briefly.

"Where'd you find them?" he asked.

"Around my house," I answered honestly and with a straight face. (He was holding two pieces I had found on the nightstand, and two pieces from the spice cabinet in the kitchen.)

He nodded, turning the pieces over several times before handing them back to me, smiling again.

"Pieces like these are common in this area. This whole town's sitting on an ancient Indian village," he said.

I nodded.

"Your pieces are about 500 years old—from the time when de Soto was in the neighborhood. Very common."

He asked for my address and wrote the information down in a small notebook, noting that my house was a possible alternate site for the so-called "Happy Holidays" encampment. I put the pottery back into my pockets and thanked him.

Calvin Jones returned to his mud, and the more conventional method of obtaining historical artifacts. Theirs was a messy job.

I walked home. It wasn't until I stepped through the front door that a thought occurred to me which caused me to smile. It was safe by a wide margin to assume that the friendly and helpful archaeologist had just examined his first specimens of pottery that had apparently fallen clean and dry out of the air.

My growing calmness and acceptance of the goings-on ostensibly signaled that it was safe for the next stage of the plan to begin.

Even as dreams go, it was a strange dream.

I was standing on the parched and cracked ground of a great desert, looking to the west where a mountain range shimmered purple, in a lake-like mirage. Deep within the mirage was something white and moving. I strained to see it, but knew that I must remain patient; that in good time, what I strained to see would show itself. I watched as it emerged from the blue shimmers and approached, spectacular, and with splendor.

It was an American Indian and he was riding a white horse, and riding it hard.

On his head was a war bonnet of white eagle feathers. He was clothed in fair buckskin, its long tassels whipping in the wind from the speed of his charging horse. In his raised right hand was a long spear, and it too was adorned with eagle feathers. Its spear point glinted as it caught the reflection of the desert sun that was rising high behind me. Still riding hard, the man continued to approach, and I could feel through my own feet the thunder of four hooves as they pummeled the yellow ground. Now I could see his face. White war paint was under his eyes, and they were locked onto mine with certain intent. Terror filled me, but I knew that I must stand still, I must not do what all manner of sensibility was telling me—to turn and run faster than I'd ever run in my life. My heart was pounding as loudly as the hooves of the galloping horse heading toward me, showing no intention of stopping.

A hundred feet away, the warrior came riding. Fifty feet he came. Then twenty.

When the hooves of the white stallion touched my shadow, the warrior pulled the reins and the horse screamed, rearing up onto his back legs, his spittle and sweat flying through the billowing clouds of dust surrounding us, his front legs lashing and flailing into the empty space between us. The warrior raised the spear higher, his eyes never leaving mine, and the horse immediately stopped rearing. His hooves came down heavily upon the hard, baked desert floor, and the warrior plunged his spear into the ground next to his horse.

The horse whinnied and stomped as the warrior continued to stare fiercely at me, and trotted anxiously around in a tight circle, spinning, dancing in the dust and parched earth. As the horse turned and brought the warrior around to face me again, a change took place. The warrior smiled at me. It was a strange smile. It was not a smile that put me immediately at ease, it was more a smile that seemed to say, "I know something."

He turned his horse back to the west and rode away.

I awoke in the morning overwhelmed by a great sense of expectation mingled with a fear of the unknown. I did not tell

Craig about this dream, because discussing dreams was not normally a part of our relationship—dreams were really of no significance to either of us. Later in the day, however, still filled with strange angst, I phoned my mother who lived nearby, with the intent of telling her about it.

"I'm glad you called," she said as she answered the phone. Before I could tell her about my dream, she said, "Something happened here last night."

"What?" I asked, immediately concerned that she or my father might be ill.

"Well, I got up in the middle of the night to use the bathroom," she said, "and when I turned the light off and walked back into my bedroom, there was a large glowing light in my room near the far wall."

"You're kidding," I said. I'd never heard my mother talk like this before. Neither she nor my dad were likely candidates for witnessing unexplained glowing lights in their bedrooms. Mom was a former school teacher, and Dad was a retired Air Force officer and inspector for NASA.

"You're not going to believe this," she continued, because there was much, much more to the night's events than merely a glowing light, "but inside this light," she said, "was an Indian. He was on a horse."

My mouth went completely dry.

"We stared at each other for a moment," she said, "it was almost as though I had startled him as he sat there—and then I asked him, 'What do you want?' He raised his spear—not threatening, but more like a greeting—and then it all vanished, and the room went dark."

I could not think of anything to say, so the phone was rather rudely silent for too long.

"Are you there?" she asked.

"I'm here. I don't know what to say." But I proceeded to tell her what happened to me at approximately the same time that this had happened to her.

We spent a long time on the phone that day, and after carefully comparing descriptions of what we'd seen, we determined that the clothing and headdresses of the two Native

12

Americans indicated that they were from different tribes. Beyond that, however, we knew nothing, except that something unusual had happened.

I mentioned our coinciding events to Craig, but since neither of us had ever placed any importance on dreams, the matter was quickly forgotten.

While I continued to happily add potsherds and stones to my ever-growing collection, it would be my daughter, Emily, then almost four, who would have the first actual meeting with those who had come to visit. She would entertain her visitors with the sincere charm and honesty that only children seem capable of offering these days.

—2—

Visitors

It was a day not unlike any other summer day. A blanket of haze and hot steam rose with the shadows in the morning, and by 10:00 A.M. dissolved into clarity and blue sky. As the sun ascended higher, even the shadows seemed to retreat from its intensity.

By high noon, the heat of the day had stilled the chattering of the birds and squirrels who now rested in whatever shade they could find, and with a thrill, it awakened the cicadas. They filled the hot air with their own song—a humming, droning, summer song that one might easily mistake for the sound of heat itself.

On this day, a Friday, with the hour of noon upon us, I stood in the kitchen making tuna salad for sandwiches.

John was two that summer. He was in the den, playing. Emily, not yet four, but matured well beyond her years, was at the porch door, looking out into the front yard. She was quietly singing a song from Sesame Street about the hardships of life when one is a green frog.

The summer wind breezing through the screen was heavy with the fragrance of the red climbing roses that were once again blooming next to the porch door in their yearly crimson display.

It was while I listened to the song of Emily and the song of the cicadas that a subtle change occurred in the quiet, noon-day air. Emily stopped singing. The cicadas stopped singing. In the great silence that now surrounded us, I heard Emily speak to someone.

"Yes," she said. A long pause followed this answer as Emily listened to a voice that I could not hear, and then I heard my daughter reply, "I am."

Another pause followed, and Emily answered, "Yes, we do."

Standing very still, I strained to hear who she was talking to, but again heard only Emily's voice.

"Yes," was her next reply, "she's out in the kitchen making lunch, I'll go and ask her."

Walking the short distance from the foyer to the kitchen, Emily rounded the corner and, before I could ask her who was at the door, she said, "Mom, can I have some cookies?"

I frowned at her. "You know better than to ask that right now," I said, "you can't have any cookies until after lunch."

"But they're not for me," she said, looking slightly sheepish and pointing toward the foyer, "They're for the lady."

"What lady?"

"The lady at the front door."

"Who is she? Who's at the door?" I asked.

"I don't know," she said, "but she's there on the porch. She asked me if we had any food."

I put the celery down and washed my hands. Emily returned to the foyer. As I dried my hands on a long sheet of paper towels, I heard Emily speak again to her visitor.

"My mom says you can't have any cookies until after lunch."

I threw the towels away and, irritated at being sum-moned to the door at lunchtime, slammed shut a cabinet on my way out of the kitchen. Emily rounded the corner again, meeting me in the kitchen, this time with a slightly more urgent message.

"Mom, the lady wants to talk to you. She wants to know if she can come in."

"I'm coming!" I called. Growing more annoyed with each step, I walked around the corner with what must have been a memorable scowl on my face, and saw that there was no one at all at the door, except for Emily who had run ahead of me. Her face and hands were pressed against the screen. She hit the door with both hands and screamed, "No!"

Startled, I jumped.

"Come back," Emily yelled, rattling the door once more.

"Stop that!" I said, further annoyed by her shouting and banging.

She did not turn to look at me, but in a quiet voice, continued to address her visitor.

"Please come back," she said, "come back and I'll give you the cookies."

I glanced out the door again. There was no one on the porch or in the front yard. There was not even anyone out in the street. The air remained filled with an unearthly silence. The cicadas remained still.

"All right," I said to Emily, "please explain what's going on here."

She turned and looked at me. It was clear that she was upset, and when it became apparent that she was not going to answer my first question, I asked another question.

"Why did you tell me that there was someone at the door?" I said.

"Because there was someone at the door," she answered, frowning, "but now she's gone. You scared her away."

"What are you talking about? There's no one out there!"

"I know—because you scared them all away."

"Them? I thought you said it was a lady."

"Yes, they were here with the lady, but as soon as they saw you, they all ran away."

"Who ran away?" I demanded.

"The Indians."

I glanced out the door and at the empty lawn again.

"Oh, for God's sake, Emily," I said, "don't do this to me again."

I checked the screen door to make sure that it was locked—not because I had any fear of invisible Indians or Emily's lady—but more out of habit. One can never be sure who might come knocking. Then I stomped back into the kitchen with Emily following.

"Don't do what to you again?" she asked.

"Don't tell me there's someone at the door unless they're real!" I said, raising my voice, "I don't have time to play games right now!"

"But she was real," she said, shrugging, "they were all real. The lady was on the porch, and the Indians were all waiting out by the fence. Some of them were in the driveway. But you scared them away."

"Look," I said, returning to the sandwich making, "why don't you go play in the den with John while I fix lunch."

"She was very beautiful," Emily continued, ignoring my suggestion. She continued on for a moment about "the lady" and her beauty, but I did not pay much attention because all of her imaginary friends were beautiful. Iggy, the triceratops that had hatched one afternoon in Emily's bedroom was beautiful. Her jewel-eyed tree frogs that lived in a secret pond under her bed were beautiful. And now, the stranger at the door—she was beautiful, too.

"She said, 'Hi, darling,' and she asked me if I was Emily. She knew my name."

"Mm hmm."

"Then she said, 'Do you have any food?' I told her we did."

"Mm hmm."

"I hope they come back. They must have been hungry."

Another moment passed before it occurred to me that neither Emily nor John had ever engaged in imaginary games with Indians. In fact, I had never heard either of them mention the word, "Indian." While it is true that I had mentioned the word a few times, and while it is also true that ancestors on my mother's side were Narraganset Indians, this portion of our family lineage had been long forgotten. If one looked hard, traces of its existence might be found in our DNA, but outward traces of Native ancestry had long vanished from our modern and sophisticated lives. My life as the wife of a lawyer was filled with mauve nail polish, coiffed and sprayed hair, and an occasional cocktail party at the Governor's place. My children were being raised with equal sophistication. Their world was filled with dinosaurs, talking bears, and horses with wings. Not Indians. I doubted that Emily even knew what they might look like.

"Emily, do you know what an Indian looks like?" I asked.

She thought about this for a moment before answering.

"Yes," she said, "they look like those people in the front yard."

"Tell me what they look like."

"Well," she said, "Indians like to wear feathers. They were Indians all right, Mom. The old grandpas and the boys were down by the street, and the girls and ladies were all in the driveway."

I wondered where this strange new game was leading as I cut their sandwiches, and how the Indians would fit in with Iggy, and Shou-Shan, John's "very big dragon."

"And so this lady at the door, she was an Indian lady?" I asked.

Emily smiled. "She was the most beautiful Indian lady I have ever seen. She was too beautiful."

"What was she wearing?" I asked, wondering if she'd arrived in fringed buckskin.

Emily's eyes widened slightly, perhaps revealing a measure of delight in having succeeded in drawing me into her fantasy.

"She was wearing a long, long blue dress. It came down to her feet," she said.

I looked at her, confused.

"The sun was shining all over her. It was shining on everything. It was so bright, it was almost too bright—even the sky and the grass were yellow! But the lady's dress was blue."

I poured them each a cup of Hawaiian Punch.

"Mom?"

"Mm hmm."

"Why did the sky turn yellow?"

"Emily," I sighed, "you know very well that the sky is not yellow." I said this quietly, and evenly.

"Yes it was," she answered equally as quiet, sipping her punch and looking at me, waiting for my next comment.

"You need to take a nice long nap after lunch, young lady."

Unimpressed, she nodded, "Okay," she said, "but the sky was still yellow."

"Johnny," I called out, "time for lunch."

Emily was now staring off into space, and still talking.

". . . the sun was shining everywhere, and it was almost too beautiful to look at. Maybe yellow is the lady's favorite color. Yellow and blue . . . Maybe the sun knows that yellow and blue are her favorite colors so it turned the sky yellow for her."

I had never seen her so absorbed by a fantasy, nor so aware of its details. For reasons that I cannot now remember, I decided to ask her one more question about her lady.

"Emily, was the lady wearing feathers, too?"

She looked at me and began giggling as though I was the one asking foolish questions.

"Oh, Mom!" she laughed. "Of course not! She was wearing roses. Yellow roses."

"Wearing them?"

"Yes," she answered, "she was wearing a long belt of roses. It came down like this . . ."

She touched her left shoulder and then swept her hand downward, over her heart, and rested it at her waist.

"And what about shoes?" I asked, "Was she wearing shoes?"

"Yes," she said, her eyes widening again. The shoes in particular had caught her attention.

"Were they soft and tan?" I asked, hinting at a description of moccasins.

"No," she said, "I think she was wearing blue tennis shoes."

I rolled my eyes, a victim of utter nonsense, and carried their lunches out into the living room where we would watch Perry Mason as we did every afternoon. I noticed that the cicadas had begun singing again. Emily followed me into the room.

"I hope they come back," she said. "If they do, can I give them cookies?"

19

"Sure, sure" I said, knowing that she meant the kind of cookie that, like her tree frogs and the rest of the growing assembly, could only be seen by her, "by all means, give them all the cookies they want."

"Okay!" she said, delighted. I patted her on the head.

"Now go wash your hands."

She did as I asked.

I washed John's hands and we sat down as another familiar episode of legal drama began on the TV. It was a nice routine, culminating in a predictable victory for our hero. It lead quietly into the kids' afternoon nap time, which they accepted without a struggle.

Nap time for them meant quiet time for me, and I used the two-or-so hours to work on a piece of fiction I was then writing. I was looking forward to the afternoon's work.

After Perry won his case, the kids went into their room. I kissed them and put John in his crib, Emily in her bed. I understood, of course, that Emily would remain in her bed only until I was out of the room. She had announced months earlier that she would no longer be sleeping during nap time, because, "that is for babies." She would play quietly while John, the baby of the house, slept.

I closed their door, sat down at the computer and began the afternoon's work on my book, which I was calling *Harvest Moon*.

The afternoon steamed on, and as I typed, a strange story began to unfold in front of me. Months earlier, I'd given a curious name to my main character. I'd named him Joseph Two Horse. At around 2:30 P.M. on this day, Joseph Two Horse became a stranger to me.

The facets of his personality already seemed endless—he was a musician, a geologist, a mechanic, a biophysicist, a medic, an astronaut, a magician, a writer, a former priest, and a darn good cook. So far, I'd discovered he was part Italian and part Native American. He seemed to be everything and anything, and now he seemed also to be a stranger.

In amazement, I watched as Joseph closed the door of his brownstone apartment and walked away. This was not my planned story line.

Heading in a direction previously unknown to me, he walked away from the comfortable life that I had created for him, took a left on Canal Street, and kept on walking. He walked until he left behind the city in which he had lived for most of his life, left the state of Massachusetts, and then to my great surprise, he left the Earth itself. He escaped her orbital embrace with ease, and was now somewhere in deep space, traveling at a velocity that made the speed of light look like child's play.

The computer seemed to be tapping out swift and distant messages from him as the Universe flashed by. After a few million more miles, the messages stopped and Joseph suddenly found himself standing in awe on a distant planet.

It was early evening on that faraway world, and as the stars became visible to Joseph, he looked into the night sky and saw that the face of Heaven itself had changed. With difficulty, he located the constellation Orion and saw that the belt no longer appeared to be a straight line of stars. From where he now stood, the belt of Orion was in the shape of a triangle.

A slight noise in the vegetation behind him suggested that he was not alone. He turned, and an old man—clearly human, and dressed in fringed buckskin—stepped from behind a stand of tall ferns.

Joseph had discovered human life on another planet!

What a story! What a man!

I had no idea what would happen next but, aware of the time in my own immediate area, I would have to wait until the following afternoon to learn more.

Tiptoeing, I went to the children's room and opened the door to check on them.

The sun, filtering through leaves and vines that shaded the room's windows, filled the room with soft green shadows. A lone cicada droned on through the heat.

John was asleep in his crib. I leaned over for a moment and watched him as he dreamed. Beads of perspiration tinier than baby's breath glistened on his nose, and a wisp of light brown hair rose and fell, blown by the fan. His eyes moved under closed lids, watching an unfolding adventure. Then, as something in his dream delighted him, and with eyes still closed, he suddenly grinned. It must have been a very good dream. I kissed my fingertip and touched it lightly to his cheek.

Emily had not heard me enter the room. She sat in the green shadows absorbed in her own quiet game. Having spread a blanket on the floor and surrounded herself with the dishes from various tea sets, she spoke in whispers soft enough to leave the dreams of others undisturbed. As she whispered, I understood that she was now serving unseen cookies to her gathering of unseen friends.

"Have more," she whispered. "You can have all you want."

She offered her guests another platter that appeared empty to me, but overflowing to her. Quietly, I closed the door. The kids would decide—as they always did—when nap time would be over.

Twenty minutes later, they emerged from their room, John's energy restored by sleep, Emily's restored by play.

"Hi, guys," I said, "did you have a nice nap?"

Emily bounced through the room. "Yeah!" she said, "It was great! Come on, John!"

John was still groggy. He trailed after her trying to keep up, while also trying to comprehend everything about which he was now being briefed that had taken place in the quiet room while he slept. They bypassed their usual after-nap stop for Popsicles in the kitchen, and instead headed straight for the den.

I began preparing the evening meal, one of Joseph Two Horse's pasta dishes. When the basil, sweet peppers, and garlic were simmering in their small pool of crushed tomatoes and wine, I walked back toward the living room to watch TV.

As I passed through the foyer I noticed something unusual from the corner of my eye, something odd. There was something yellow and out of place on the front porch, but I kept walking.

Suddenly, for the second time that day, the symphony of the cicadas stopped at once, as though on cue, and the air that they had filled with summer sound became utterly still. It was this strange silence of nature that caused me to pause and listen.

The day itself seemed to have caught its breath. I turned, looking toward the porch door. Yes. There was something yellow on the porch awaiting discovery. I knew instinctively that it was something even more strange than the pottery and white stones, and as I began the slow walk back into the foyer, I tried to prepare myself. Then I looked out the front door.

Nothing could have prepared me for what I saw.

"This is impossible," I whispered, blinking several times as though blinking might restore rational order. It did nothing to alter the appearance of what was on the porch. I placed my hand on the screen door and in disbelief, pushed it open.

The bush of climbing roses, which had adorned the porch with its heady red blooms for countless years, was no longer bearing any of those heady red blooms. It was now a bush of yellow roses as brilliant and gold as the sun itself. In the center of each blossom was a blush of pink.

When my ability to think finally returned, I ran to the den closet to retrieve the camcorder. Emily noted this and followed me to the front door.

"Is the lady back again?" she asked.

I stepped onto the porch and began video taping.

"Emily, " I said, peering through the view finder, "I don't have time for that right now, okay?"

"Okay. What are you filming?"

"Nothing—just the roses. Now, go and play."

She looked out the door at the subject of my documentary.

"Why are you filming the roses?"

"Well, you wouldn't understand," I explained.

"Oh."

She remained standing there, watching me, until I finally said, "Well, you see, Mommy's roses used to be red, but they turned yellow this afternoon."

"Yes, I know," she said.

I stopped filming and looked at her.

"It was the sun," she said. "It turned the sky yellow, too."

She headed back toward the den and then paused.

"Mom?"

"Yes."

"The Indians said to tell you 'thank you.'"

"What?"

"I told them to come back after lunch like you said, and so they did. I gave them all cookies and milk. I told them that you're not really mean, you just look mean—and so they're not afraid of you any more!"

"Good," I mumbled, standing alone on the porch with the camcorder and my new bush of yellow roses. The cicadas began to sing again. I was several steps behind everyone else, and struggling to make sense of all that was happening. Joseph Two Horse had gone off in an impossible direction of his own choosing, and Emily had graciously hosted the lavish potlatch that had quite possibly opened, at last, doors that had been closed for a long, long time.

I could not explain what happened to the red roses on that afternoon. I could not explain anything that happened that afternoon. All I knew was that something other than the summer wind had passed this way, and for a while it had waited among the roses at the front door.

I don't know what was whispered to the roses as that "something" waited there, or what silent word might have suggested to the laws of nature that they bend as they had.

All I know is that by 4:00 P.M. the long journey of the climbing roses was finished. They had quietly become Peace Roses.

After nap time the following day, I watched the children play on the outdoor swings my father made for them under the dogwood trees in the front yard. The afternoon was filled with their laughter, a cloudless sky, and the expected order to be found in this homey setting—a white house surrounded by a white picket fence.

It was hard to believe that anything out of the ordinary could or ever did happen in this setting, and so, with Craig's help, life regained a sense of normalcy, and held fast to it for a few days.

The roses were still yellow, of course, and my collection of pottery and stones grew daily. But Craig had easily explained the mystery of the yellow roses and pottery.

When he arrived home from work the afternoon of the extraordinary event, he considered what I reported to him, and then he suggested that the roses had always been yellow; that we had simply never noticed. My documentary video was taken after the alleged "transformation" had occurred. Where, he asked, was my documentation of the roses in their original state of redness? Where was my proof that they had ever been anything other than the yellow Peace Roses that they now were?

He then patiently explained to Emily the difference between what is real and what is not real, and that the Indians—not to mention the lady—were not real. They were from her imagination.

I sensed his growing weariness with overactive imaginations—including my own—but I also felt a sense of frustration. We were beginning to see things differently.

For him, everything had a rational, sensible explanation. Even the potsherds could be explained—gophers were digging them up, he said, and leaving them in view.

"But we don't have gophers here," I said, and then let it rest.

The stones falling out of the air received no comment except for a quick look that indicated he'd heard enough about that nonsense.

It seemed that, as these events continued to happen, they brought with them more questions than answers, and my state of frustration was growing quickly into utter bewilderment.

Even writing *Harvest Moon* was a cause for frustration and bewilderment. I had spent the kids' nap time on this particular afternoon struggling to understand my own book.

Joseph and the old man in the clearing had formed a close friendship that seemed to border on kinship. The old man's name was Tioco. Tioco took Joseph to his village and introduced him to the other inhabitants. They referred to themselves as "the Adongohela."

Tioco then taught Joseph their native language, and it was this particular development that created a rather baffling writer's block. They began to converse in that particular language, and because I was unable to speak their language, I alone had no idea what anyone in my book was saying.

Watching the kids laughing and swinging in the shade of the dogwood trees, I wondered how much more baffling life could possibly become—and if I would witness anything further, that, regardless of logical explanations, would remain unexplained to me.

The plan was continuing to unfold, of course, and it was unfolding even on that day. I was merely unaware of it. I was unaware that I was being given a day of compassionate rest before the next afternoon's high tide was scheduled to occur.

On the following day, I attempted again to work on the book but it was a futile effort. I finally gave up and sought entertainment in front of the TV. When the kids emerged from their nap, I changed the station to Sesame Street for them, and gave them Popsicles.

Then, I returned to the kitchen and began preparing the evening's meal, listening to the sounds of their program. Sesame Street was being brought to them by the letter M, on this afternoon, and the Count was counting. Occasionally I recognized the sweet voice of Big Bird.

John finished his Popsicle first. He handed the stick to me, and headed toward the den where toys representing various epochs awaited him. Emily remained in the living room, Counting.

The den, in a wing of the house, is separated from the kitchen first by a dining room and then a short hallway. Not more than thirty feet away, I could hear John as he had a conversation with Shou-Shan, his very big dragon.

Sounds from the den then ceased as John made the discovery that there was now something other than Shou-Shan and plastic WWII warriors in the den. There was now something from an epoch previously unrepresented.

The silence lasted only for a matter of seconds.

"Blood curdling," is a phrase that one more fully understands and appreciates once it has been experienced. It is an appropriate description for the scream that issued from my son.

My recollection is that this sound propelled me several feet into the air, and that I turned toward the den while still airborne. When my feet hit the floor, I raced toward my screaming child with visions of terrible calamities flashing through my mind.

As I neared the hallway approaching the den, John left it traveling in the opposite direction, shrieking.

He ran through the dining room, and then burst into the foyer, hitting the screen door at full speed. Luckily it opened. This all happened very quickly, and I was still attempting to slide to a halt in the hallway when John left the house.

His screams were now coming from somewhere in the front yard.

Turning, I followed his path through the house and out the front door, racing after him until I finally caught him by the shoulder of his shirt, picked him up, and hugged him. I quickly counted fingers, and checked for injuries while telling him, "Shhhh, Mommy's here." I rocked him, and held him tightly, feeling his heart beat wildly as he continued to scream.

Emily, alerted by the commotion, ran out into the yard and joined us. Seeing John's distress, she, too, began crying. It was necessary for me to raise my voice so that they could hear me above the din as I attempted to find out why we were all standing in hysterics in the front yard.

"What happened?" I screamed. "Tell me what's the matter!" But John could not speak. His hands were drawn into tight fists, and he could only cry. There were no visible wounds on him, and for this I was momentarily thankful—before suspecting internal injuries. Grasping one of his hands, I pressed it against my own pounding heart, hoping that this might somehow calm him.

"Tell Mommy what's wrong," I screamed again.

He continued crying.

"John!" I screamed, startling him. "Tell Mommy what's wrong!"

He pointed toward the house, and said something I was unable to understand.

"Are you hurt?" I screamed.

He shook his head. No. This was a good sign.

"Then what is wrong?" I shouted.

"Mans," he said, between gasps.

"What?"

"Mans," he repeated pointing toward the house, "in da den."

"What is he talking about?" I screamed at Emily.

She stopped crying to interpret. "He says there's a 'mans in da den,'" she said.

"I know that, but what does he mean?"

She shrugged, "I don't know. I guess there's a man in the den."

Safe in the bright sunlight bathing the front yard, after several minutes we began to calm down enough to attempt a more normal conversation. I assured John that he was all right, that we were all right, that we were safe. I finally persuaded him to tell me about the "mans."

It seems that while he was playing, a rather tall gentleman wearing high black boots and a strange-looking hat had entered the room and joined him.

Upon discovering the newcomer, John had then vacated the area.

It was the genuineness of his terror that kept the three of us there in the front yard for the remainder of the afternoon. Whatever John had seen had been so real, at least to him, that I was not willing to reenter the house to prove that there was not, most likely, anyone inside.

We remained in the front yard for about an hour, until Craig came home. He arrived to find us in the northeast section of the yard—as far away from the house as possible—leaning against the homey white picket fence. John was still in my arms. I tried to look as normal as possible.

"What's going on?" Craig asked.

I had prepared a brief speech, but did not have an opportunity to deliver it.

"Johnny says there's a man in the den," Emily answered, eyes wide. She pointed toward the house so that her father would know that she was referring to this house, this den.

Craig looked at me, irritated. I had failed to handle the situation as a rational adult.

"Why didn't you just take him back into the den and show him no one was in there?" he asked.

I shrugged. "He was so frightened! I didn't want to make him go back in." That was, of course, only part of the reason. The rest was that I did not want to go back in there myself. Craig immediately perceived this.

"You know there's no one in there," he said.

"Well, we'll wait out here while you go in and make sure."

He sighed and went into the house in search of non-family members. In a moment, he returned to the front yard indicating his findings, which came as no surprise to him. We began walking back toward the house.

"The den window was open," he said. "John must have seen the curtain blowing in the wind."

"The den window was open?" I asked, stopping in my tracks.

"Yes. Wide open."

"But, I didn't open the den window," I said.

"Well, you must have opened it and you probably just don't remember."

The case was closed. Perpetual amnesia is difficult to argue.

In an attempt to appear rational, I allowed myself to feel genuine remorse for having reacted more like the kids than adult when John mistook the white lace curtain for a tall man wearing high black boots and a hat.

I had permitted his vision to have substance when common sense, maturity, and the Laws of Reality should have compelled me to dismiss the whole matter. It was now my responsibility to set things straight, my turn to explain to the kids the difference between people who are real and people who are not real.

"See?" I explained to John in summary, speaking as a wise adult. "There was no one in the den. You just thought that you saw a man, but he wasn't real—and so you didn't really see anything. Maybe you saw the curtains, but you didn't really see a man. Do you understand?"

Johnny looked confused, but nodded obediently as he tried to comprehend my explanation of the events. Craig, too, nodded, satisfied that I was finally conforming to established guidelines. Having spoken these words to my son, I had performed the time-honored parental duty of convincing my child that at least a part of what he had experienced was not real, and did not happen.

It would be several years before John would stumble across an illustration in an encyclopedia that grabbed his attention.

"Mom?" he would one day say to me. "Remember that man I said I saw in the den?"

"Yes, son."

"Well, here's a picture of what he looked like."

The illustration was that of a conquistador.

The expected lull following John's encounter with the curtain arrived like clockwork, and lasted for about a week. I was grateful for it, as well as for our quiet lunches with Perry Mason, and our uninterrupted daily routine. It all served to let me sink into the calming thought that, if I maintained this routine, life might stay exactly as it was forever, and never change. Everything would remain comfortable and familiar.

That, of course, was an illusion. By its own nature, life—a dance which never ends—never stops changing.

The next high tide arrived at 1:15 P.M., six days after its last peak.

With the kids in for nap time, and the noon's paper dishes thrown in the trash, the house was quiet and in order. Nothing was calling for my attention except the book. It seemed to be calling loudly.

I turned the computer on and soon found with a thrill that the conversations were once again being held in English. Joseph had taught his language to Tioco, and I was very grateful to again be able to understand what I was typing.

It was nighttime on that planet, and Joseph was sitting near the edge of a smooth-surfaced, turquoise lake. The evening air was perfumed with the exotic scent of a million flowers and the sweet, dewy breath of the rain forest. The luminous lake, whose waters were held to be sacred, was a source of light and mystery for Joseph on this night, as it had always been for the Adongohela.

By day, the lake lay upon the land in shades of clear blue eternity, as though it were a piece of sky that had come to rest in the cupped hands of the valley. By night, while its glassy surface reflected the endless, slow waltz of the stars, deep within the lake's lime-white caverns there glowed a light from an unknown source.

Joseph looked down into the glowing waters, wondering if his eyes were beholding the very nucleus of the planet, its heart, a pool of cool fire.

He remained silent, waiting, as Tioco made ready to tell him the legend of the Adongohela.

Tioco was preparing his words carefully, in Joseph's own language so that there would be nothing left unsaid, and nothing left in question. His people had waited for many years to speak these words, and Tioco was not willing to choose such words without help. He was praying.

Joseph waited patiently as the old man finished his lengthy ritual. These were a people who found delight in their traditions, and Joseph assumed that this long pause was merely the expected ceremonial requirement prior to storytelling.

He had no idea what Tioco was about to tell him, only that Tioco insisted it was of great importance, and that it could not wait until morning. Joseph was tired, and hoped Tioco's story would be brief.

The moon, a harvest moon, had seemingly just risen out of the lake to join the stars. It was easy to understand why Tioco's people believed it was this lake that gave birth to the stars each night, forming them from its eternal core of light and then sending the stars, like fireflies, up into the heavens. It would be the stars, the moon, and the strange light of the waters that would illuminate and witness the events about to occur.

"Since before the birth of my grandfather's father," Tioco began, "my people lived in the Land of the Old Sky. Some were warriors in that land, some hunters and fishers, and some planted seeds in the good soil there. In those days we were known by many different names."

Joseph nodded. This did not sound as though it would be among the shorter of Tioco's many stories, but he would be quiet and respectful.

"But sadness grew in that land," Tioco said. "There were too many wars, too many tears. Too many dead relatives. The hunters, they thought the planters were pretty stupid to live like that—hunting's more fun. The planters thought the hunters were crazy thieves. They both thought the fishermen were fools for playing in the water all the time. And the warriors hated all of them because anyone who is not a warrior is weak, and not really People.

"Each People think only they are the real People, and so they kill those who are not real People. One day, so many were dead we thought that soon there would be no one left to hunt and fish and grow food. There would be no one left standing.

"One night, the sky turned to day, and this got everyone's attention. A man with no name, he come down out of the light and stood there looking at all the People. They stop fighting because of the eyes of this man. When it was quiet, he say, 'I come because I hear your blood. It no longer sings from your hearts, it cries out from the ground. It is not meant that you should perish from Creation. It is not meant that you should spill one another's blood. It is meant that you should be known as the Adongohela.'

"Many hearts were filled with fear on that night," Tioco said as though he, himself, had been there to see what had filled their hearts, "but the women, they were happy that he had come. No more fighting. The women say he must have been walking with the sacred ones to have eyes that could bring peace. They say it was easier to turn night into day than it was to bring peace.

"Then a young warrior who was known for his bravery in killing many enemies," Tioco said, pausing for a moment, smiling, and then adding, "many,

many enemies—he walk up to the man and ask, 'Why do you call us Adongohela? We do not know this word.'"

"Man say, 'Come with me and you will learn your true identity. I will take you to a new land that is good. In this new land, you will become the Adongohela.'

"Not everyone want to go. Man knew this. He felt sorrow for the frightened ones. They stay.

"The others say, 'Okay. We will gather our belongings, and then we will go with you.'

"But Man With No Name, he raise his arms and tell them, 'Leave all that you have owned behind. You will need nothing in the new land. Throw your pots and your weapons down upon the ground, and walk away with me into the night. From this moment on, all generations will know that you were once here and that you vanished. They will have many questions about the ancient ones who disappeared.'

"Well," Tioco said, now lowering his voice into a whisper as though he were telling a secret rather than a story, "the People want to take something with them of the Old Land—just a little something to keep their hearts one with the spirits of the relatives they were leaving behind. Man look into the People's eyes and see what is in their hearts."

Joseph nodded and shifted the position of his cramped legs.

"Man was very wise. He say, 'Yes, it is good that you should keep something as a reminder. The reminder will also speak of your origin here in the Old Land.' And so he tell the last of the warriors to gather something sacred.

"Then Man With No Name say, 'Come with me now. Let the Grandmothers come first, and then the younger women, because the women will now have a voice. They will lead the Adongohela. Let the warriors follow in the women's footsteps.'

"The warrior who had killed the most, he who carried the sacred medicine bag which contained the reminders of the Old Land, he took his place behind everyone else. He was last.

"The sky opened and the great light appeared before the People. Man say, 'Do not be afraid,' and the Grandmothers led the People into the light. They walk through the light until they arrive here, in this land that we call the Land of the New Sky."

Joseph nodded in understanding. He had taken the same strange walk. He also understood why they had named this land the Land of the New Sky. It was the night sky alone that indicated they were far, far from home.

Tioco continued, "Man say, 'Let not one drop of blood be shed in anger in this new land. These are sacred grounds. Learn good lessons from one another. And walk in peace.'

"Man With No Name look at young warrior. 'Guard what you have carried from the Old Land. The generations of those left behind will awaken one day and search their skies for answers and teachers.'"

Tioco now stopped talking and studied Joseph for a moment.

Joseph took the silence as indication that the story was now concluded. "That was a wonderful story," he said.

"Story not over yet," Tioco answered.

"You will know when this time comes. A Stranger from the Old Land will come to you," Tioco said, pausing, "he will sit lost and confused before the oldest of the Adongohela, wondering how and why he came to be in this Land."

Joseph smiled with a little embarrassment. Tioco was honoring him by weaving Joseph's recent unexplained appearance into the legend.

"Give to this Stranger the objects that you carried from the Old Land. If he knows what he holds in his hand, then you will know that he is the one you have awaited. You will know that it is time for the Adongohela to return to Old Land."

Tioco reached to his neck and removed the ancient hide medicine bag that was suspended by a brown cord. Inside the pouch were the objects he had gathered and guarded so long ago.

"I am now the oldest of the Adongohela," Tioco said, offering the pouch to Joseph, "and the last of the warriors. This is the pouch that Man With No Name told me to guard. Open it, Joseph, and we will see what time it is. We will see if you are the confused stranger we have waited for."

Tioco placed the bag in Joseph's hands.

"Open," Tioco said.

The brilliant triangle of Orion had now risen out of the lake as the moon and other stars had. Joseph untied the pouch string and spilled its contents into his cupped hand.

The objects, golden, old, and withered, glistened in the light. They were still filled with the promise of life. Joseph's mouth fell open. Catching his breath, he touched what lay in his hand with fingers that dared not shake at a moment such as this. He had no words to speak.

Tioco was pleased to see that Joseph appeared to be stunned. It meant that he recognized the objects in his hand. It meant that he was the stranger. It meant that it was time for the Adongohela to return to the Land of the Old Sky.

Joseph closed his hand around the objects that had been born in that distant land, and carried by the Adongohela on their walk through the Universe. Carefully, he poured the corn that had been gathered by Tioco in his last moments on Earth, back into the pouch.

"And 'Adongohela,'" Joseph whispered, mouth dry, "what does Adongohela mean?"

Tioco smiled. "Adongohela," he said, "Tribe of All Nations. We are the Children of Peace."

Tioco stood up and offered Joseph a hand, pulling the younger man to his feet.

"Come on, Nephew," Tioco said, "we gonna

35

walk back to that place you call 'Earth' now and surprise a few people."

I was among the first to be surprised.

It was barely two, but I knew that my writing session for
the day was over and turned off the computer. For a long
moment, I sat as stunned as Joseph and stared out the window.

Clouds were gathering on the horizon, and the sound of
thunder could be heard in the distance. The green Earth grew
hushed as it awaited the cool rain that would come very soon
from the heavens.

Life in need of water sent a hazy message skyward, where
it touched the heavy clouds, reminding them of the need
below. Held within the clouds was a lake that would soon be
released, not as a lake, but gently, quenching the thirst of the
life below one drop at a time.

Green reflected upon green, thirst upon promise. A shaft
of light from the sun pierced the clouds and eerily lit the awaiting leaves of a nearby tree. The leaves shimmered lime and wil-
low green against the steel, pearly gray of the clouds.

Even now, before the first drops fell, the air would be filled
with the fragrance of a promise about to be kept. The thunder
sounded again, and for a moment, I allowed myself the thrill of
falling completely into the story of the Adongohela. Perhaps it
was not thunder that I was hearing. Perhaps it was the sound
of a thousand People from many nations, many tribes, walking
again through the Universe.

Perhaps it was the sound of the Adongohela returning to
Earth.

I went out the back door and stood on the steps. The hot
air was no longer still. It was restless as busy swirls of cooler air
wove their way through the heat. The summer blew its breath
through the Spanish moss that hung in long, Rip Van Winkle
beards from the oaks until the trees seemed transformed into
old men, swaying to the ancient voice of the wind song.

Other little breezes sent parched and brittle leaves scut-
tling out of their way like small creatures. Thunder sounded
again, approaching thunder.

I sat down on the steps, and as I did, something near my

hand—something small and dark in color—caught my eye. I leaned closer to look at it.

There, on the step were four more pieces of pottery. This time, they had been placed in such a way that they effectively dismissed the theory that they were the work of busy gophers. This time the shards were lying neatly stacked, one on top of another. I picked them up, feeling another thrill.

My attention was then drawn away from the pottery in my hands as a low eddy of whirling wind circled over the grass and leaves nearby, catching up enough of the dry fragments to make its swirling path visible. It settled upon a certain spot several feet from where I sat, and there it continued to swirl a moment before stopping abruptly, and dropping the leaves it had carried. They fell upon the earth forming a circle, a bull's-eye. The area inside the bull's-eye had been swept clean by the small wind.

This was a sign. There was something in that clearing that was meant to be seen, and so, as I had done on the Day of the Roses, I stood and took the necessary steps toward discovery.

Lying in the cleared center was a mound of knapping chips, fragments of amber agate that someone had chipped off a larger piece of stone during the process of making an arrowhead.

The small, shiny mound was lying in clear view, not more than five feet from the back steps. It appeared as though the native man fashioning the arrowheads had just stepped away for a moment to take a break. That the break could have only logically occurred approximately 450 years ago did not seem possible. Yet, that was the reality of the situation.

I gathered up the beautiful, sharp chips and added them to my collection of affirmation.

The tide continued to rise on that day.

By late afternoon, the water from the sky had made its way down to the earth, and the sound of thunder ceased. The rains then ended, leaving the earth replenished.

Thoughts of the Adongohela were reluctantly pushed aside by the demand of routine and domestic tasks. There was grocery shopping to do, followed by cooking. That would be followed by cleaning.

At approximately nine o'clock, the evening of July 9th, 1987, as I stood at the kitchen sink washing dishes, I glanced out the window in front of me, and saw that the northeast corner of the front yard was illuminated.

The ground was glowing in a warm, amber color similar to the hue of the agate knapping chips. I dried my hands and went outside to look at this.

As I approached the glowing area—which was clearly demarcated, measuring about twenty feet in diameter—I saw that the source of this glow was a beam of light streaming down from a strange-looking yellow cloud in the southern sky, just over the roof of my house.

The beam was coming from the south. The sun had already set in the west. This called for witnesses.

I shouted for the family to come outside and see our glowing yard, hoping that Craig would at last be convinced that something inexplicable was indeed happening here, but this was simply not meant to be.

"What do you think it is?" I asked, my personal awe apparent.

For a moment, a brief moment, it appeared that he had no ready answer, but it was understandably necessary for him to say something that would re-establish the normalcy that was now hanging by unraveling threads. Craig's previously normal household was now a place where the black and white Laws of Reality had taken on noticeable new colors.

As we stood staring at the illuminated front yard, I realized the humor of living within the world of black and white reality. It is that world that exists only as an illusion. The real world lies beyond. It can never be fully explained.

I stepped over the line that separated his world from mine that night, and stepped into the orange light. The kids "ooo'd" at my glowing appearance.

"Well?" I said, turning to face Craig.

He looked grimly at the light, and then at me. Half of my face and body were now glowing amber. He tested the area with one foot, as one might test unproven waters. Finding that this caused no ill effect, he stepped into the light—casting a shadow to the north as I was—and said, "It's nothing—it's just the sun."

"But the sun has already set," I said, pointing to the empty western horizon, "over there in that direction."

He looked toward the west to verify this fact, and said, "I don't know what it is, but I'm sure it's nothing."

The kids and I remained outside in the orange glow while it lasted—approximately twenty minutes—but Craig stepped out of the light and went back inside.

At about midnight on that evening, I was awakened by what appeared to be flashes of lightning. Since there was no accompanying thunder, I went out into the front yard to investigate.

Overhead, the sky was clear, but a light sprinkle of rain was falling like stardust. Low in the far southern horizon sat another strange, lone cloud. It was this cloud that was flashing brilliantly at one-second intervals. Although I stood in the sprinkle for several minutes, watching the distant flashing cloud, there was no sound other than that of the light rain falling from the clear, star-filled sky. Just as there were no clouds from which the rain could be falling, there was no thunder accompanying the lightning. It was the lack of the thunder that was the most curious.

In this eerie stillness, I wondered about the meaning of this strange display on this night when the heavens seemed to be producing a memorable show of unexplained signs in the southern sky.

The following morning, I returned to the area of ground that had been glowing amber and found a number of small white stones on the grass that I added to my collection. Several hours later, I returned to the area, and found more white stones lying where the first had been. I retrieved those as well. An hour later, when I returned to the same area, I found another handful of stones along with several pieces of pottery and now, clear quartz knapping chips.

I knew that I was in need of help interpreting this situation, and it seemed that as soon as I came to this understanding, help was immediately launched in my direction. Within forty-eight hours, a fellow lawyer told Craig that a bona-fide medicine man was passing through town visiting friends. She added, "Would you like to meet him?"

Craig found this to be an extremely fortunate opportunity to obtain something akin to professional help for me. He gratefully accepted the offer.

Never will I forget the day that I met Fred, the Medicine Man. He was not merely impressive in his carriage and self-assurance, but he seemed somehow larger than life. His easy humor and ability to understand the inexplicable, as well as his willingness to share his knowledge were comforting. After he assured me at least a half dozen times that nothing was happening here that I should fear (I never believed him, however), I asked him to review parts of my novel about Joseph, in the wild hope that he could make some sense of the language that I could not understand.

We had a lunch of shrimp and pasta salad—another Joseph Two Horse Recipe—and then Fred the Medicine Man put on a pair of half-rim granny glasses, and began reading. After reading only a couple of selected paragraphs, he began chuckling softly to himself. This slightly annoyed me. I had not intended for this work to be interpreted as a comedy. There was nothing funny about it but, I kept quiet. Fred turned the page, read one more paragraph, and then burst out in laughter so hard he had to put the manuscript down, remove his glasses, and actually wipe tears from his eyes. It was then that he noticed the frown on my face.

"What's so funny?" I asked.

"Nothing—really, nothing. I'm not laughing at what you've written," he said, still laughing, "I'm just—well, do you know what any of this means?"

"No. I can't understand what they're talking about. Does it mean anything?"

"Oh, yes. It certainly does."

My eyes widened. "You mean this is an actual language?"

"No, not exactly," he replied, replacing his glasses on his nose. He had regained his composure.

"Well, what then?"

"These are a number of different languages. There's some modern Apache, ancient Apache, Lakota, Uto-Aztecan, and Mayan to name a few."

"You're kidding aren't you?" My eyes were now wider.

"There's nothing to be afraid of," he said quietly, noting my eyes, " . . . nothing to be afraid of."

"Well, what are they saying?"

"'Greetings!'" he said, and this brought on another round of laughter. Squinting through tears again, he managed to say, "These are all greetings in different languages. They're saying, 'I give you greetings as the sun rises!'"

I do not remember anything more about that day other than at some point, Fred and I sat on the floor of the bathroom where I had found the scallop shell. There, as my knees shook uncontrollably, we shared the sacred pipe. I have never been more shocked in my life than on that day when affirmation of the unknown came by way of my new friend, Fred, as he interpreted for me the words of the Adongohela, the Tribe of All Nations.

After Fred returned to his home in the Okeefenokee Swamp that afternoon, I remained in a daze.

The following morning, as I stood again at the kitchen sink washing dishes, I glanced at the northeast corner of the yard— the area that had glowed amber on the night of July 9—and saw that a white cloud had settled upon the area. This odd haze was of such density that I could not see the white pickets of the fence through it.

I noticed that the haze was still there later in the afternoon. It was still there that night. It was still there the next morning.

For two days, this cloud remained where it had settled, growing in size.

On the morning of the third day when I looked out the window, what I saw stunned me. The cloud was no longer a cloud.

It was a gathering of Native Americans.

There were at least a thousand of them standing, milling about, talking to one another—except for one giant of a man. He alone, had ventured just inside the fence and was sitting in front of the others on the grass that had previously glowed orange. What appeared to be a long spear rested upon the palms of his outreaching hands.

In awe, I ran from window to window to see if what I thought I was seeing was actually there. It was. They were all there. Through each window, and from many different perspectives, they were all there.

When Craig arrived home that day, I immediately pointed the gathering mist out to him.

"Look!" I said, barely able to contain myself.

He looked.

"Well? Can you see anything there?" I asked.

To my great surprise, he answered, "Yes."

"You mean to tell me you can actually see this?" I said.

"Sure," he shrugged as though it were nothing at all out of the ordinary, "I can see it."

He turned away from the window and walked past me toward the kitchen table where the day's delivery of junk mail was stacked, and began leafing through the flyers. I followed him to the table.

"That's all you have to say about this?" I asked, amazed.

"What is there to say?"

"I don't know. I just thought that seeing all of them out there might bring a bigger response."

"Them?" he said, "What do you mean 'them'? What are you talking about?"

"The Indians," I answered.

He put the mail down, closed his eyes, and leaned heavily with both hands upon the kitchen table for a long moment. Still slightly stooped as though bearing a great weight upon his shoulders, he walked back to the window and looked out at the yard.

"Well?" I asked, "What do you see?"

He stared at the area in silence and then turned and walked out of the room. His answer trailed along behind him.

"Swamp gas," he answered.

I was somewhat offended by this interpretation, but I made a concerted effort to see things as Craig was seeing them.

Going out into the yard, I sat there for twenty minutes, watching. I attempted to disable my eyes' focusing abilities so that I would be blind to the faces of the people who were looking at me, but no matter how I tried, I was unable to reduce the enormous gathering of Indians into a puff of swamp gas.

As I sat there, their numbers grew. When the cloud of Native Americans had extended completely up the block, I went back inside and took the only logical course of action. I phoned Fred for help.

"You have to see this," I exclaimed, "there are thousands of them! They're lined up in the driveway, and completely filling the street all the way up to the end of the block."

"Can anyone else see them?" he asked.

"I think the kids have seen something. They've been talking about Indians non-stop, but I don't dare ask them about this. We've been telling them that they were imagining things, and Craig would be furious with me if I did anything that would suggest otherwise."

"What about Craig, is he seeing anything?"

"He can see a cloud of swamp gas."

"Interesting," Fred said.

"Well," I said, interrupting, my voice cracking slightly—I was not as accustomed as Fred was to situations such as this— "what do you think they want?"

Fred was already well aware of my tendency to react with fear. "I don't really know," he answered calmly, "but whatever it is—it's nothing to be afraid of. No one's going to hurt you."

"How do you know? What if this is a war party?"

"I'm sure it's not. If they're still there tomorrow, call and let me know. We'll drive back over and check them out."

I was not happy that the matter would have to wait until the following day. I was desperate for affirmation. I wanted to hear someone else confirm what I was seeing—that the glowing haze in the front yard, in the driveway, and now filling the street—was anything but swamp gas. I wanted reassurance that I was not alone in what I was witnessing. But it's a long drive from the Okeefenokee Swamp to my yard. So, it was understandable that Fred wanted to wait until morning.

Late into that day's night, I watched the People. Their presence provided illumination in the dark street. I hoped with something bordering on prayer that dawn would not find them faded, absorbed without a trace into the dawn and dew of tomorrow.

In the first light of morning, I rushed to the window to see if they were still present. They were.

As soon as the hour permitted, I phoned Fred. He and his wife, Eunice, left their home around lunchtime and arrived that evening at my home along with a mutual friend—the lawyer who had introduced us to each other. The kids were in bed.

The cloud of People was still present. The seated man was still seated upon the grass.

Placing five lawn chairs in the yard, we now sat facing what, to both lawyers, appeared to be a cloud of swamp gas, but to three of us was a great gathering of Native Americans.

"What do you think?" I leaned toward Fred and whispered.

"Stunning," he answered. He, too, was whispering.

"Can you see the large man sitting in front?" I asked.

"Yes, I see him."

"Why is he the only one sitting down?"

"I don't know."

"Well, what's that he's holding?" I asked.

"It looks like a planting stick—but maybe it's a talking-stick."

"What's a 'talking-stick'?"

"Whoever's holding it gets to talk."

"You don't think it's a weapon? It looks like a spear to me."

"No," Fred said, and I don't think he meant for me to see him roll his eyes, but I saw him do just that before he continued his sentence, "It's not a weapon. He's not threatening us—he's offering it to us. I think he wants to talk to someone."

"Good," I said. "Go ask him what they want and why they're here."

Fred considered this for perhaps two seconds before answering.

"No," he said, "I don't think it's me he wants to talk to."

"Well, he certainly isn't waiting to meet someone who thinks he's swamp gas?"

"No, no," Fred said, turning toward me and smiling. "I think it's you he wants to talk to," he said.

My blood immediately pooled in my feet. It's a strange sensation.

"I'm not going to talk to him," I said, "you're the medicine man, you go and talk to him."

"Nope. It's you he's waiting for."

"Well, tell him he can stop waiting right now, because I'm not going over there!"

"He's not going to hurt you!" Fred argued. The two lawyers were chatting pleasantly with one another about another situation and paying no attention to the argument Fred and I were conducting in loud whispers.

"I know he's not going to hurt me—because I am not going near him."

"Listen," Fred said, "you're being silly."

"No, I'm not. I'm being sensible."

"He's been waiting a long time to speak. It would be very disrespectful for you to deny him this opportunity."

The reasoning behind Fred's statement made sense to me. I looked away from Fred and back upon the solitary man sitting stoically alone on the grass. It was not my wish to appear disrespectful to any of these spirits, only to keep my distance. This did not seem overly self-indulgent, but Fred, too, had a point.

Fred must have sensed that I was weakening, because he moved right onto an unspoken assumption that all was settled.

"Go and listen to what he has to say," he said.

"Will you go with me?"

Incredibly, he answered, "No."

Before taking this short trip across my yard, Fred instructed me to first go into the house and obtain suitable gifts to give to the man with the talking stick. These items, Fred assured me, would indicate my social graces and deep respect. He sent me inside to obtain a little sage, cornmeal and some tobacco. I went inside and located gifts that were as close as possible to Fred the Medicine Man's instructions. I returned to the front yard carrying a half-empty, plastic bag containing instant grits and five Winstons that I raided from Fred's pack on the kitchen table. Unable to locate any sage in my cabinets, I was also carrying a handful of a popular Italian seasonings blend.

I stood in front of Fred for a moment, laden with gifts and contemplating an appropriate salutation and personal introduction for the large, seated Indian.

"Go ahead," Fred said.

"I'm going. Don't rush me."

I looked again at the seated man, and this time our eyes met. His gaze was not hollow and haunted as one might think the gaze of the long-dead might appear; it was filled with substance. It was filled with intelligence. As I looked at him, I felt my fear begin to leave, and I felt something unexpected take its place: compassion. I took a tentative step in his direction and noted that he made no move to stand up to meet me. It appeared that he intended to remain seated. I turned again to Fred.

"Why doesn't he stand up?" I whispered.

"I don't know," Fred replied.

I sensed that there was something odd behind the reasons why this man was not going to stand to greet me. I also felt that walking up to him and looking down upon him seemed inappropriate. With this in mind, I got down on my hands and knees and in front of an audience, approached him in this manner.

When I had advanced to within three feet of him, I decided that was close enough, and placed the gifts on the ground between us. He looked at the gifts.

He did not reach for them, but instead turned his head to exchange glances with those who stood behind him outside the fence. There appeared to be some confusion. I smiled, raised one hand in what I hoped was an authentic native greeting, and said, "Aho."

He didn't respond, so we simply sat and looked at each other. Etching his features into my memory, I noted first his impressive size. This was an extremely large man. He was, in fact, a giant. If he were to stand, he would have clearly towered over me in spite of my own height of five-foot-nine. It occurred to me that perhaps this was why he remained seated—perhaps he merely did not wish to intimidate me with his size. But I realized even as that thought occurred to me that I might never find the explanation regarding any of this.

After a long moment of silence, another thought occurred to me. There would surely be a great language barrier between us, a barrier that I would be incapable of bridging. If there was to be communication between us, the bridge builder would have to be the seated giant.

The man then closed his eyes. Everything was still as I watched a glistening, circular cloud forming over his head. It appeared to contain a static charge. When it reached a size of about four feet in diameter, it began slowly drifting in my direction through the night air. It was necessary for me to fight hard against the impulse to jump to my feet and run, but I managed to remain seated. The cloud touched me first on the shoulder, and then slowly settled all around me.

It was a dense cloud, and the static within it was clearly visible in the form of small, sparking veins. My skin tingled slightly but not uncomfortably from the cool charge, and I became aware of a fresh, salty fragrance. The small hairs on my arms were standing up, electrified, but I was not afraid and I remained seated.

It was difficult to see beyond the cloud's sparking perimeter, and so, isolated by its covering, my attention became focused on all that was within the cloud.

Images began to form like holograms within the electrical field, clear images, and, as I watched spellbound, the images began to tell a story without the use of any spoken language about the People now standing in the street.

It began as a good story, a remembrance of good times. There was happiness in their faces. But what I was to see next will haunt me forever.

An army of strange men with strange ideas came into their village one winter. Some of these men wore metal clothing and odd headgear; some wore tall black boots.

Although it was clear that the People had no idea who these men were, I was able to recognize them from what I'd seen in history books. Their images were frightening, indeed.

This was a story about the unexpected arrival of the Spanish Conquistadors in Florida.

Many of the villagers were killed outright as the conquerors took over the Indian village now buried under Tallahassee, and they claimed for themselves the entire stock of food and winter provisions set aside by the Indians. They also took the Natives' dwelling places. The people of this village, therefore, were left with no shelter or provisions in the middle of winter.

I watched as the native people tried to fight the army of soldiers; as they died from battle, exposure, and hunger.

As they disappeared, one individually conceived and worthy life at a time, there remained nothing within the sparkling cloud except reversed images—negatives of the memory of lives wrongfully taken. I saw each face. When I was surrounded by nothing but memories, the cloud lifted away from me and returned to the man in whose heart and consciousness it still lived.

We stared at each other a final time, and I wondered who this keeper of history was—what his name might be—and wondered how long he had been waiting to give another view of the taking of Tallahassee. I hoped he understood the anguish I felt upon witnessing his personal account. It pierced me more deeply than any spear.

He then spoke in clear English the only sentence I was to hear from him: "Let it be known that my people were not savages," he said.

"I will," I answered. Our meeting was over.

I turned to go back to my group in the same manner I had left it—on hands and knees. I noticed that my skin was glistening in the moonlight from the salty mist that had touched it. I took my seat next to Fred.

"What was in the cloud?" Fred asked immediately.

"You saw it?" I asked, thankful again for the knowledge that I was not the sole witness to the event.

"Yes," he said, "I saw it advance and settle on you. What was in it?"

"Tears, maybe, and a story." I told them what I had seen, but my words were hardly as moving as the images. It is possible that this story was never meant to be told by words alone—that it was meant to be told by the heart. A story told by the heart would be remembered long after words might be forgotten.

"I guess it's just kind of hard to describe," I said to Fred.

"Have you looked at the west side of the yard, yet?" Fred asked.

Looking to my left, I saw another enormous gathering of Native Americans.

"They arrived during your meeting up front," Fred whispered.

"Go over and meet them," Eunice said, nudging me with her elbow, grinning.

"No," I said. It would take a while for me to recover from what I had experienced meeting the giant. I could not bear to witness anything more on this night.

"Come on," she said, pulling my arm and grinning, "I'll go with you. You won't have to be afraid!"

"That's not the point," I explained. "I'm not afraid any longer, I just think I've seen enough."

She pulled my arm again, and so I stood up reluctantly and the two of us walked across the yard to take a closer look at the newest arrivals.

This group was dressed differently from those who were gathered in the north and east of the yard. Those standing in the west appeared to be People of the Plains, People of the Hills, and others. Some were on ponies. I looked through the crowd for the man from my dreams on the white horse, but did not see him. There did not seem to be a designated spokesperson in this group as there had been with the first group. However, a young man stepped forward from the crowd as we approached, and we stood facing him at a distance of approximately three feet.

He studied us wide-eyed, in what appeared to be utter amazement, as though we were the glowing apparitions. Perhaps we were. Perhaps time had crossed its own path on that night.

Slowly, very slowly, he advanced a step closer to us, and then, apparently testing to see if I was real, he leaned closer, looked at my face and then reached forward with his right hand. Very lightly, he touched my left upper arm.

The result of his hand coming into contact with my arm was a crackling explosion of light that knocked the young man to the ground, and nearly did the same to me.

"Run!" I shouted at Eunice, but there was no need for my warning because she was already several feet ahead of me, heading at a good speed for the safety of the lawn chairs.

As I ran toward Craig and my friends, a slowness settled around me and the distance between myself and them suddenly became very great. I seemed to be running in the air and not advancing. Again, the air seemed heavy and silent, and now it was filled with the fragrance of electricity. The warping of distance and time remained until I inexplicably found myself filled with a growing sense of love for the young man who had touched my arm. I understood without any doubt that he had meant no harm by his gesture, that he was simply in awe of what he was seeing, and had been as startled as I at the explosion. I stopped running, overwhelmed with love, and turned to look back at him.

He had regained his balance and was standing up again, brushing himself off. When he saw that I was looking at him, a hint of apprehension came over his face. I smiled and waved. He apparently understood, and raised his own hand returning the gesture.

Whatever it was that we witnessed on that night—and not even Fred the Medicine Man had a good explanation for it—there was a common element through it that served as the bridge for our communication, and that bridge was love.

The next morning as the sun was rising, I returned to the front yard to look at the grass where I had sat the night before and faced the seated giant. Lying on the grass, where I had left gifts for him, were sixty-three white stones.

I gathered the stones, walked to the western edge of the yard where the past had touched the present, and caught my breath. Lying on the spot where I had nearly been inadvertently knocked off my feet was a beautiful feather.

Holding gifts that I would have never thought to treasure in an earlier time, I returned to the area on the grass where the stones had been, and sat down to watch the sun rise, wondering about the meaning of the events, and why they were happening.

"One who stands alone and speaks into the wilderness can bring about little change," a male voice said softly, "but one who stands alone within a multitude and speaks, can bring about great change."

I turned around, but saw no one.

"Who's there?" I asked. Something brushed against my cheek, but there was no spoken reply.

"If someone just spoke to me," I said, "then give me a sign."

"You've already seen the signs," he said. "See with your eyes open. See with them closed. Then you will see them all."

Again I looked around me, but saw no one.

"Where are you from?" I asked.

"We are already here," he replied.

"No, I mean, what is your place or origin? What planet are you from?"

"If you do not know your own origin," he answered, "of what importance is mine?"

On the eastern horizon, a sudden commotion caught my attention, and I turned toward it. There, flying upward into a sky now flushed with the gold and pink hues of dawn was an endless flock of blue jays.

There are not enough blue jays in the entire state of Florida to have made a flock of this size, but there it was, making no sense whatsoever. There was no end to it, and I could not see any point from which they were originating. They were simply there, calling out loudly to the morning so that no one would miss this moment—their grandest of displays.

I watched this unending flock until the sun rose fully and climbed into the space that had been, a moment before, royal blue and roiling with the motion of uncountable wings.

It wasn't until that happened that an old fact, a biological detail, made its way into my thoughts. It was an old piece of information I'd picked up during my many years as a wildlife rehabilitator. The feathers of the blue jay only appear to be blue when light is shining upon them—not when light shines through them.

If the sun was rising behind them, what then was the source of great light shining upon them?

I got up and walked into the house to begin preparing breakfast for my family and guests.

"I don't understand any of this," I said out loud crossing the yard.

No one answered me.

After brunch, Fred and Eunice departed for home. Fred had answered any questions that could be answered with complete frankness. Those which could not be answered with words (by far the majority), he had answered with a smile and a shrug—let's wait and see—and with reassurance once again that whatever was happening was nothing to fear.

Possibly preoccupied with the events which had been occurring in my yard, I was unable to produce further messages from Joseph Two Horse, wherever he was, or from the Adongohela, who were now apparently just outside the front door.

Unable to write further, I decided to read. Specifically, I sought information that might describe the native inhabitants of the old village being excavated in my neighborhood. I was not expecting to find corroborating details of a ghost story, of course, nor was I expecting to find the name of the giant with the talking stick. But, in the vast building known as the State Library of Florida, that's exactly what I found.

The explorers kept diaries (English translations of the Garcilaso de la Vega narration are available).

Recorded history, written mostly by the victors of the Earth's wars and battles—by the conquering survivors cum heroes—is only as accurate as one-sided, sensational reporting can be expected to be. The logs and diaries of the conquistadors are no different.

Here, in such logs, one can find that the conquerors were filled, to the man, with the belief that they were supreme and civilized men on missions from God. Their purpose was to find new land to claim for their homeland; and, because each new land discovered was already populated by human beings, to obtain new converts for the Church of conquering choice. They also sought treasures to help finance their efforts of lordship and salvation.

New lands were vast and plentiful, and it was assumed that the converts would also be plentiful because the non-converted natives found inhabiting the various continents seemed simple-minded and innocent. Having no noticeable intelligence, as the diaries noted, it was assumed that these "savages" might be led as easily as children into church, into conformity, and into slavery. The conquerors never guessed that this group of not-quite-human People would sooner die first—a miscalculation that led to much confusion and bloodshed.

As the conquering parties landed on new shores proclaiming their ownership of the land to its inhabitants, it was this miscalculation of the People's will that sorely tested their patience. The indigenous did not seem to grasp the importance of baptism, nor did they appreciate the efforts of their new governors and mayors to save them from Hell. They, in fact, did not even know about Hell.

Such ignorance was horrifying to the ambassadors of salvation. It meant that there was important work to be done: Their first job would be the elimination of ignorance.

Dissidents refusing the baptismal waters of conversion were given a baptism by fire, and burned at slow-burning stakes. Some horrified non-converts saw their family members fed alive to dogs who had a fondness for the more tender flesh of children and old women. Stubborn heathens were horribly and permanently mutilated so that they might learn new lessons in obedience, shame, and humility, thereby serving as living examples for others who refused to conform.

In the name of God, the uncivilized natives were brought to their knees one way or another. Severing their feet from their legs was a guaranteed method.

The conquerors spoke of a God of vengeance and wrath, and no one seemed to notice when Christianity made an apparent departure from its purported tenets. The first lesson taught by civilized man to the innocents living on this and other continents was the concept of Hell.

With force, vast numbers, and self-made laws on their side, those in power were free to rule the Earth, and history was free to repeat itself. Parades are still held in honor of those who conquered, while the lives and identities of the conquered have passed unnoticed into unrecorded history.

That is not to say, however, that all of them passed into history unnoticed. The party of Hernando de Soto made note of at least one remarkable "wildman."

De Soto's long march through Florida and beyond began in Tampa Bay, in 1539. It was an exhausting journey, made difficult not only because of the swampy, insect-ridden terrain, but also because the indigenous people's memories here were fresh regarding the brutal treatment they received at the hands of previous explorers.

It was not easy for de Soto to befriend the surviving natives, but by practicing moderation and keeping torture to a minimum, eventually de Soto managed to form a few tentative friendships as he journeyed.

Once among the natives, he apparently did not notice that they displayed a cleverness and humor previously unsuspected of wildmen.

The indigenous people assured him that, yes, indeed, there was a land of great treasure exactly as he was seeking—more gold and pearls than he could imagine—but it was just to the north, south, east, or west of the spot upon which he was currently standing.

Following the suggested directions given to him by his new friends, de Soto and his party then went north, then northwest, then west, east, northeast, northwest, due west, south, southwest, due south, due north, and finally, due west again before de Soto perished on the Mississippi. He covered a lot of ground, passing through numerous future states, but died without ever finding anything of value here.

It was about midway through his adventure that de Soto arrived in Tallahassee—just in time for Christmas.

While the inhabitants of this village had fled from their homes in terror of the advancing soldiers, they made their presence in the surrounding woods known to the troops by bombarding them with volleys of arrows.

With arrows flying past them, and sometimes making direct hits through their chain mail; with smoke presumably still curling up under the clay pots of the village fires, one can only wonder at de Soto's rational basis for declaring—according to the log—that they had discovered an uninhabited village.

The village consisted of 250 homes, well-constructed of daub and wattle (intertwining wood with a plaster-like covering), and hundreds more such homes were located in the nearby clearings.

In addition to the homes, there were well-tended fields, bountiful in a harvest of ripe squashes, and there was a rich supply of fish, beans and corn which had been thoughtfully put away for winter provisions by the natives. Those provisions now belonged to the newly-arrived army.

With winter bearing down upon them—winters in the northern part of Florida frequently bring hard freezes, and sometimes even snow flurries—perhaps the de Soto troops were chilled to the bone the day they found the village upon which Tallahassee now rests.

Without hesitation, de Soto and his men moved in.

He personally occupied the comfortable living quarters of the leader of the village, a lodge that was located not far from my own front yard. The leader, the Cacique, in Spanish terms, was a strange man named Capalfi. Capalfi was a giant.

The remaining homes of Capalfi's people were assigned to de Soto's men as barracks, and the Indians to whom this village belonged suddenly found themselves without food or shelter.

The Indians then took reasonable steps to right such a wrong. With everything that any reasonable man values now stolen from them, they waged a war to regain what was rightfully theirs.

Day and night, according to the log, they waged a battle upon the Spanish. To the offended de Soto party, however, this uprising did not appear reasonable at all. It was simply another example of the baffling behavior of wildmen.

For reasons that escaped the Conquistadors, the natives seemed unable to take a hint: they simply would not go away.

They stubbornly tried to hang onto their land in spite of the fact that Spanish flags were now flying over it, and in spite of the fact that legal documents proclaiming new ownership of the land had been dutifully read aloud (in Spanish) to them.

Irritation was growing for the new landlords.

Adding to their irritation was the fact that Capalfi was proving himself to be a diligent strategist. The maneuvers of this wildman easily outfoxed the Spanish army, and left them not only smarting from wounds and exhausted, but also puzzled—puzzled because Capalfi was leading his men in battle through the woods and swamps while remaining completely unseen. The Spanish did not know how to fight such a creature.

Legends can grow quickly in the long, dark nights of winter, and even more quickly in the darkness of strange frontiers and swamplands where the eyes of the unknown glow at night like embers from Hell.

It is in that particular type of darkness, where the unknown looms just beyond sight and sleep cannot be dared, that it becomes difficult to distinguish the sound of a four-legged forager from that of an approaching warrior, or the shriek of a barred owl from that of a demon.

De Soto's men, pushed to their limits and deprived of sleep, now took a step over the edge. No longer merely mystified by Capalfi's ability to wage war while remaining unseen, they were now spooked.

During the long nights, talk in the encampment focused on the giant. Each passing hour seemed to confirm their growing fears of Capalfi. Tales had been told before about the strange abilities possessed by some of these wild natives: They had powers. They had secret powers.

It did not take long for the men to convince themselves that Capalfi's powers were great indeed. They did not know with whom—or with what—they were doing battle because they were now convinced that Capalfi was not merely hiding from their eyes. Capalfi was able to become invisible at will!

When dawn broke, it was decided by those who still had a grip on reason that there was but one way to obtain peace, quiet, and sleep. They would have to capture Capalfi himself. They knew from previous experience that capturing a village's

Cacique put them in a good bargaining position. The Natives could then be persuaded to calm down—or it would be their chief's head.

All efforts were then focused upon capturing the giant.

His capture did not come easily, but after great struggle, the army finally accomplished its goal. Capalfi was bound and held in his former village with the most sophisticated methods of imprisonment available, placed under twenty-four-hour armed guard.

Predictably, the natives were quiet on that first night of Capalfi's incarceration.

To the casual observer it might have appeared that the soldiers had won an important round, but Spanish victory was to be short lived. The first night of Capalfi's incarceration was also to be his last.

In the stark light of morning, the Spanish army discovered that everyone was present and accounted for in their new village—with the exception of their prisoner. While under armed guard, Capalfi had simply disappeared without a sound.

De Soto's men were bewitched and bewildered, but there was no shortage of explanations for this disaster. Capalfi's disappearance merely served as confirmation of his powers.

Witnesses came forward and gave statements that the giant had simply vanished, before their eyes! Still others came forward and swore that he had been carried off by spirits!

De Soto must have found these explanations plausible, because no one was punished following this embarrassing escape.

While the incident, as it stands, is indeed bewildering, the full extent of its unexplainable nature cannot be completely appreciated until one reads a small, but memorable, detail in the log about the man known as Capalfi.

Capalfi—the vanishing leader of the local wildmen, the strategist who could not be captured and held by an army of soldiers in chain mail, the giant who remained just out of sight and reach—was a paraplegic.

Unable to stand or walk, Capalfi conducted all of the duties expected of a great leader while sitting on the ground.

When he wished to relocate to a new area, he dragged himself on hands and knees, or allowed himself to be lifted and carried by several of his men—both options were difficult, considering his great size.

How he managed his escape remains a mystery. It also remains a fact. Capalfi vanished on that night without a trace, without a sound, and was never seen again by civilized man. At least, not for about 450 years.

—3—

Dreamwalking

I never saw Capalfi again after that night in the front yard.

However, as the weeks passed, when I visited the area where he told his story and where I left gifts of grits, cigarettes, and Italian spices, I found many objects lying on the grass. Colorful glass beads, carved bones, pretty stones, shells, pottery, and a bone whistle were left there—left where they were sure to be seen by someone who was growing increasingly delighted with objects more likely to delight a child than a grown woman. I drew great comfort from discovering and gathering the gifts of affirmation that were—in my mind, heart, and eyes—clearly coming from another world, or perhaps coming from a portion of this world to which we all, with the exception of children, have been blind for many generations.

Children can see this other world clearly, and they are then taught by us not to see it—causing great confusion in their pure minds. This fact was emphatically demonstrated to me a few months after the Capalfi incident.

I was invited to attend a pre-powwow supper to which a number of Lakota and Comanche People had also been invited. I agreed to bring some Italian dishes—lasagna and stuffed manicotti—and also decided to bring my children so that they might meet some of my new friends who had traveled here for this event, some from remote reservations.

When I arrived at the house, a young Comanche man who was sitting on the porch with several friends recognized me, and came down to the car to help carry the provisions inside. He was wearing two feathers in his long black hair, and a leather vest. A necklace of tine bones was around his neck.

Both large casserole dishes were on the front passenger seat, hot and steaming. My oven mitts were sitting on top of the foil coverings.

John and Emily were in their child seats in the back seat.

I opened the car door for the man, and he reached in for the large dishes, his long hair falling forward, across his bare upper arms.

"Be careful," I said, "I've just taken them out of the oven, and they're hot."

He picked up the orange and yellow oven mitts and put them on, smiling at the incongruous appearance, then he raised the mitts so the kids could see them, smiling at the children, as well. They did not respond with laughter or smiles.

John, who was still enjoying an occasional bottle now and then, pulled the bottle from his mouth, and stared, gaping at the man. A tiny rivulet of milk trickled slowly down his chin as he stared.

"Emily?" John raised his hand and pointed at the man, and then looked at his sister. "Indian?" he asked.

She nodded. She, too, was staring at the man in wonder as he now prepared to lift the lasagna and manicotti from the front seat.

"Yes, son," Emily answered solemnly and quietly, using one of her favorite names for her brother, "I see him, too."

Both children's eyes were wide with awe. Finally, Emily was unable to maintain further silence.

"Mom?" she leaned over and yelled out the window at

me—she, too was now pointing at the man who was wearing my oven mitts—"is this a real Indian, or are we seeing things again?"

My Comanche friend stood up with the casserole dishes and looked at me somewhat accusingly—just a quick glance, but it was a powerful quick glance. There was no doubt in my mind that he was wondering about the manner of teachings that I had been giving my children. There was no time, however, for me to explain the long story that was growing longer by the moment.

My face was as red as the marinara sauce that the manicotti were swimming in.

The friendships continued to grow, however, in spite of my many blunders, and I grew particularly close to several people from the Lakota nation.

It was the Lakota people who eventually sent a pipe to me from the Pine Ridge Rosebud area. It was sent by messenger, along with a message that I will never forget.

"If you accept the gift of this pipe, it joins forever your heart with the hearts of the Lakota People."

Unexpectedly, the Lakota People sent something else, as well.

One afternoon I received a package in the mail. It was wrapped in brown paper. I opened it to find that it contained an empty hide box with fringed tassels. The hide was tan, as were the soft tassels attached to it. A design was painted on the top and four sides of the box in colors of yellow, red and green. It was a beautiful design of circles that carefully overlapped each other in such a way that the circles formed almond-shaped crosses on each of the sides. It was perfectly balanced, and the crosses pointed in the direction of the four winds.

A note came with the box. It was from my friend, Kathleen, who lives on a remote reservation in North Dakota.

"The grandfather that I told you about made this box," she said in the note, referring to an elder she had written about in a previous letter. Stories of his life had caused me to stop and think with wonder on more than one occasion. He lived according to philosophies of his own choosing, some of which were difficult for me to fully understand. Among the most difficult to grasp was his choice to live without electricity in that distant portion of the world where he walked upon Mother Earth, in a place of harsh winters known as North Dakota.

"The box is for the white stones," the note went on to explain. "He asks that you please keep the white stones in it."

This seemed strange to me. I would have thought that, if anything, he would have wanted his box to house the old pottery—but it was for the plain white stones that he made this box, with its perfect circles and crosses. I didn't understand the reason behind the elderly man's request any more than I understood how he could live in North Dakota without electricity, but I honored it. I placed the stones I had already gathered into the box, and those that would be gathered in the future would be placed there as well.

From the Lakota People I received gifts of laughter, lessons, a pipe, and a sense of belonging—of kinship.

And from the Lakota People, the white stones received a carefully made home in which to be safely kept.

As much as my perception continued to change during those weeks and months, Craig's never faltered.

While I grew closer and closer to that other world, or as it grew closer and closer to me, a chasm continued to develop between Craig and myself. It grew quietly, yet steadily, almost unnoticed until one day it had somehow become too enormous to bridge. I no longer fit into the socially acceptable mold of an attorney's wife.

Craig and I eventually separated, not abruptly, but in stages. We lived for a long time—quite amicably, actually—in opposite wings of the house before actually divorcing.

As the partnership continued to unravel, the threads of our individual lives were rewoven into two separate and unmatched tapestries. The tapestry of Craig's life remained grounded, while mine appeared to take on characteristics that more closely resembled a magic carpet.

Even more unsettling and baffling than my very first

encounters with a spirit world were the next events that occurred. Without warning, I went to sleep one night and somehow became a dreamwalker.

At first, the dreamwalking consisted only of very brief excursions (lest I fall over dead from shock, no doubt). I would go to sleep, and suddenly awaken, while dreaming, to find myself fully conscious, intensely aware of my surroundings, and startled to find that I was no longer in my bedroom. On the first night this happened, I awoke to find myself standing calf-deep in a mountain stream, wearing a long, loose-fitting dress that I was holding bunched up around my knees. It was the cold water that jarred me into consciousness, and I looked around at the strange surroundings. It appeared to be late afternoon. I was in a deeply wooded area that I had never seen before. The babbling stream possibly kept me from hearing the two men on horseback approach me quietly from behind. Sensing that I was being observed, I turned around to find the two young American Indians sitting in silence on brown and white pintos.

"Wash day," one said.

"Wash sheets, too," the other said.

Then they reined the horses off onto a path and disappeared, walking unhurriedly into the woods.

The following morning—a Saturday—when Craig emerged from his wing of the house, I announced to him that it was necessary for me to wash every sheet in the house because I had received mystical instructions to do so. This project took several hours out of a day that already had a full agenda, because Fred and Eunice were going to drive to town and stop by around five P.M. for shrimp and beer.

When they finally arrived, Craig quietly mentioned my morning's laundering efforts to Fred, presumably hoping that Fred—a medicine man who now seemed to be quite normal by comparison to me—might be able to talk some sense into me, and to quell some of this increasingly disturbing behavior.

Fred took me aside and asked me about my mystical instructions. I explained exactly what had happened, and then waited the customary length of time it took for him to stop laughing.

"Those were Lakota Indians," he said.

"How do you know?"

"Because 'washtahey' is a Lakota word. It means 'good.'"

"Well, why did they tell me to wash the sheets?"

Fred was overcome again. I waited.

"They didn't tell you to wash the sheets," he said in gasps—he was now crying—"'Washeechu' means 'white person,'" he said. "They were observing you and commenting on you."

It was good to have Fred available to help interpret such events, but the time soon came when he and Eunice suddenly divorced, and he moved even further away than the Okeefenokee Swamp. I was left to more or less sort things out on my own, or to seek his help with an occasional long distance phone call.

Before moving away, Fred gave me two gifts. One was a small stone from his travels to Machu Picchu. The other was a flat rock from Bear Butte, the place where the great holy man we call Crazy Horse went to pray in solitude.

I placed both under my pillow, not knowing about the powerful, charged auras that stones possess, or what might transpire if one falls asleep with one's head in such close proximity to two stones of incredible energy.

As soon as my head hit the pillow, I was immediately launched into parts unknown.

I awoke to find myself suddenly standing near a camp fire, next to which a white-haired elder was sitting. It was a particularly dark night, and I did not see a moon in the sky. The area was illuminated only by the fire. When the man saw me, a look of disbelief came over his face, and he immediately jumped to his feet and faced me. The man began speaking to me—or, actually, he began shouting at me—not in English, but in his own language. I was unable to understand anything he said, so I merely stood staring at him. Frustrated, he took me by the arm, and motioned that I was to sit down next to his camp fire, and to stay there. He walked off into the darkness, and a long time passed before he returned. I stared into the flames while I waited, and wondered where, exactly, I was.

When he returned, he was accompanied by a younger man, who, I assumed, was something akin to his apprentice. The elder and the young man sat down, and the elder began speaking.

The apprentice then interpreted what he said in English.

"He is assigned to be one of your teachers," the apprentice said, referring to the elder.

"Oh, good!" I said, smiling broadly. "It's nice to meet you!"

The elder did not return the smile. He began talking again, this time animating with both hands, punctuating, and counting off with his fingers one, two, three, four—many, many instances of whatever it was he was apparently angry about. He talked and talked, and I looked at the apprentice for input, but he was staring at the elder and listening raptly to this lengthy account. When the elder finally finished his long dialogue, he stared at me, seemingly exhausted.

"He's not happy about the assignment," the apprentice said.

The elder began talking again, this time slightly less angry, and then paused for translation.

"He was assigned as your teacher a long time ago—many years ago," the younger man said, "but you only listened to him for a while. You stopped listening to him when you were a child."

The elder spoke again and paused, staring at me.

"He's been talking and talking to you—waving his hands in front of you—but you've been pretending that he doesn't even exist. He wants to know why you have treated him this way."

"Please tell him that I apologize," I said, hoping for the mercy awakening soon from this embarrassing nightmare, "but I didn't know about any of this. I couldn't see him! Maybe it's because I'm only part Indian."

The elder spoke again, and the other man began to laugh.

Still smiling, the apprentice said, "He has been trying to awaken you with pottery and shiny beads. It was a last resort." He began laughing again.

"Oh—of course," I said, "the pottery!" and I too laughed

in embarrassment due to the size of my treasured pottery collection.

The elder spoke again.

"He says that you are either Indian or not Indian," the
apprentice said, "it is a decision of the heart. You cannot be
'part' Indian any more than you can be 'part' alive or 'part'
dead."

"Then I'll choose living."

The apprentice spoke, the teacher shrugged, and uttered a
final message.

"Whichever you choose, remember one thing. We are all
related."

The dream ended. I had finally met one of my teachers.

The following morning, I awoke with a sense of satisfaction
in knowing at least a portion of the mystery about the pottery—but then I realized that my teacher had not mentioned
anything about the white stones.

I telephoned my mother to tell her about my dream, and
she confirmed that when I was a young child I spent many
hours alone, having long conversations with someone she and
my father could not see. When they asked me to whom I was
speaking, I told them, "George the Bear."

In the winter of 1987, I became quite sick with the flu—
too sick to move, too sick to sleep or dream—and it was my
teacher from dreamtime who intervened.

The deep ache of bronchitis reminded me with each
breath that all was not well. My body stoked itself up to 102
degrees, in an attempt to rid itself of the small enemies within.
It then further immobilized me with joint and muscle pain. I
made an appointment to see the doctor in the morning.

It was well after midnight when I finally drifted off into
another bizarre "sleep." Closing my eyes to this world, I opened
them in the other world. I found myself lying inside a dimly lit,
rectangular wooden structure. With me were two elders, one
of them my teacher, and the other a man whose face I could
not see.

Opening my eyes in this "dream," I found that the teacher
I had met beside that campfire, whom I had named George the

Bear as a child, was leaning over me and had apparently been watching me rather closely. He stood up. On this night, he would address me in English.

In a raspy whisper he said, "We have been waiting for a long time!" His irritation was clear—he was perhaps living up to his name. "Why did you not sleep earlier?"

"I couldn't," I said, "I'm in too much pain."

"Turn," he said, "lie on your stomach."

With great effort I did as instructed. The back of my shirt was lifted and I felt small grains, comfortably heated, poured in a circular pattern on my back.

"What is that?" I asked.

"Cornmeal. Now be silent."

A heated bowl was placed over the cornmeal, cupping it, and he sat down next to me and began a soft, heart-regulating drumming. The other healer, whose face I could never clearly see, began singing quietly and shaking a shell rattle. The vibrations seemed to be passing through everything, including my bones. The heat from the bowl and the cornmeal seemed tremendous, and I broke into a profuse sweat.

After several minutes, the bowl was removed from my back. As it was lifted away, it seemed to take the heat from my body. I no longer felt feverish—I felt cooled and comfortable. The teacher instructed me to sit up, and handed me another bowl, this one filled with steaming soup.

"What's this?" I asked ignoring his request for silence.

"Pumpkin soup," he answered. "Drink."

I did as he asked. (George the Bear's pumpkin soup was delicious—I tried to identify and remember the possible ingredients so that I could make it for my own family, but have never quite been able to duplicate it.)

I was thankful for this attention in spite of his gruffness, but I wondered if his medicine was going to work. I was still not fully convinced of the "realness" of the dreamworld. Then I fell asleep within the dream, and remember only a sensation of floating through empty space.

In the morning, as I stretched my limbs, expecting pain to set the limits of my motion, I found instead that I was no longer in pain. Breathing deeply, I found that my lungs were clear. I went into the bathroom and took my temperature. It was normal.

Turning my back to the mirror, I lifted my shirt, half expecting to see the circular mark of the bowl, but there were no marks left on me. No evidence remained to suggest that what I had dreamed had been real—except for the apparent one: at some time during the night, I had been healed by corn, pumpkin, two elders, and sweet medicine.

Experiences such as this led me to understand that the word "dream" is not really an adequate description for what was happening to me each night. I was startled to find that I was visiting places in my dreams the night before, and sometimes even weeks or months before physically visiting those areas while awake.

This was first discovered during one of the final vacations that Craig and I took as a separated, but still-married couple. As we drove toward the Carolina mountains in early 1988, the road up ahead suddenly looked too familiar. I had "dreamed" about this stretch of road the night before, and had seen what was on the other side of the hill we were approaching. I immediately gripped the dash with both hands.

"Oh no—slow down!" I shouted. "Something's happening."

Startled, Craig hit the brakes, "What do you mean something's happening?"

"I don't know—something's happening to me—something's wrong!" I said.

I felt dizzy and out of sorts, clammy. My heart was pounding, and I was overwhelmed with nausea and déjà vu.

"I think I'm about to die or something," I said.

He slowed down further. "Die? What's wrong?"

"I was here last night."

"What do you mean?"

"I mean that I dreamed about all of this that I'm now seeing—I was here. You have to be very careful when we get to the other side of the hill. There's going to be a big semi up ahead that's disabled—jackknifed partially into the road."

Perhaps my appearance of overwhelming distress was obvious and convincing, because he continued to slow the car and we approached the hill with great caution. When we reached the other side, we saw the disabled semi, exactly as I described, and exactly as I had seen it the night before. We did not discuss the matter. I had no explanations for any of it. The sensation of experiencing this was truly awful in the beginning, and for many months when these first affirming events of dreamwalking occurred, I was convinced that I was about to die on the spot.

Many of the dreams occurred in a way similar to the way I had received the story of the Adongohela. They unfolded before my closed, yet open eyes in languages that I could not understand. On some occasions, however, I was addressed in my own language.

Night after night, I was permitted to watch as the People cooked, planted vegetables, healed their sick, and celebrated. Once, as I watched from behind a stand of cottonwood trees, several men rode past me on painted ponies, without comment. They were aware of my presence, I knew this from the hint of smiles on their faces, but except for those smiles, they did not otherwise acknowledge my presence. This was not unusual. I was frequently ignored completely. It became undeniably clear that these people were not visiting me in these bizarre, lucid dreams. I was visiting them.

I visited many native people while I was sleeping and fully conscious—those of the bay, those of the plains, those of the mountains and the desert. On many occasions, I met with my teacher and was given numerous small tasks to do—most of which I failed to accomplish, sometimes because he refused to speak to me in English, and other times because he did not fully explain what he expected of me. Often, I was left to journey alone and he was not present.

While walking through the desert on one occasion, I found myself near an ancient village, and watched as a man worked in a small field of short corn. He was wearing a bright red shirt, and wore in his shoulder-length black hair a blue bandana that was knotted at the side. He stopped his work when he saw me, studied me for a moment, and then smiled and waved. I returned his greeting—and he returned to his work. As I continued walking through the village, I noted the details of the homes as well as individual gardens behind the homes. I wrote those details down in small, spiral-bound notebook where I had begun keeping a record of what I was seeing while dreaming. It would be that simple collection of spiral-bound paper that would eventually suggest to me that, while there might be a threshold between the spirit world of dreamwalking and the physical world—a threshold that one must cross over, there is no boundary. We are free to enjoy both worlds. We are welcome in both worlds.

The corn dreams came frequently, and as they did, my fascination with corn grew. One night, I found myself sitting on a sandy yellow hill, watching as an entire village worked together planting corn in the brilliant sun. They were not toiling, or begrudging the sun as it bore down on their backs; they were celebrating. The sun would be necessary to call the seeds to life. The seeds would then bear gifts; such is the destiny of a seed. I was watching a celebration of faith and of hope. Each person here was aware that no seed is ever planted in Heaven or Earth, in dreams or wakefulness, without the presence of hope. They were not planting corn, they were expressing hope. And their faith was clearly demonstrated by their manner of planting.

The people of my dream did not plant their corn in shallow furrows as modern man does. They planted it by dropping a dozen or so dried kernels at a depth of nearly a foot inside impressive mounds of earth. At the heart of each was buried a fish. I remained silent, never voicing my doubts that corn planted so deeply would ever see the light of day, but several times during this celebration when I smiled at the innocence of these people, they looked at me and returned my smile.

In good time, I would understand why they were smiling, because in good time, their corn came up—just as they knew it would.

It was borne on stalks that were thick and strong, and spoke well of the dense and deep root system within each fertile mound. There were no tall, spindly stalks here, and not a single sprout was discarded. Nothing was wasted in this continuing celebration.

The dreams of the corn continued, until one day in spring I realized that I could no longer look at a field of corn, or even a photograph of it, without feeling its sacredness. I made a second realization on that same day. It finally occurred to me that the brain stores dreams in the same manner that it stores any of life's experiences. Dreams are etched into the memory with the same precision as wakeful experiences—neither weighing less than the other.

In the late spring of 1988, the yellow roses began to bloom again—according to customary laws of nature.

I was unprepared for what happened next.

The bush abruptly stopped blooming.

I interpreted this as I interpreted all painful events, as an omnipotent punishment for some nameless transgression.

The nursery experts I telephoned, however, advised that rather than an "act of God," the bush was probably just passing into a dormant stage, and that this was customary.

For two weeks I clung tightly to that explanation and kept watch, waiting for further budding to signal that the gods of vengeance were at last appeased and my punishment was over.

At the end of that second week, however, those moody gods demonstrated that they were not yet close to being pacified. I opened the front door one morning and found that the entire bush had simply disappeared.

In the area that had once caught my eye and attention with its brilliant yellow blooms, there was now nothing but empty space. The space was as effective in catching my eye as the roses had been.

Quickly, I went to the areas where the white stones and pottery were usually found. On this particular day, I found only grass. There were no stones, no gifts of any kind left for me.

Later, in the afternoon of that same day, the feather that I cherished—the feather that I had found in the front yard after

71

the young man from the west had touched my arm—vanished as suddenly as the rose bush.

A phrase came to mind, "The Lord giveth, and the Lord taketh away." It seemed to sum the situation up, but it was hardly a comforting summary. I sat in the front yard mourning my losses, clutching the rock from Bear Butte for any strength that it might provide, and wondering what I had done to provoke such action.

"You are not being punished," a quiet, masculine voice said. It came from behind me. It was the same voice that had spoken to me on the Day of the Blue Jays. I turned, hoping to finally see who this curious person was, but again saw nothing.

"I'm not?" I answered, "If this isn't punishment, then what is it?"

"What you are mistaking for punishment is instead a lesson from the depths of all compassion," he said.

"Compassion?" I asked. "My gifts have been taken from me. This is not compassion. The roses are gone—the whole bush is gone! I'll never see them again."

"The roses are not gone," he answered quietly, "they are blooming elsewhere, and they are yours forever. Physical possession of a gift is not the heart of the treasure. The treasure lies in your awareness that a gift was given to you. This is awareness of the love from which the gift was given. While the physical object representing love might pass from this world, your awareness of its existence and of the existence of love is eternal. The petals of a flower may fade, but your awareness that a rose once bloomed here will not. The true gift is the act itself. It is yours for eternity."

"Then my gifts haven't been taken away?"

"No. It is only the physical objects representing the gifts that you are missing. The act of love in which they were given is yours forever."

I suddenly felt much better. Only the proof was gone. Knowledge that these gifts had been given to me was mine to keep. This was a strange new concept, a different way of looking at loss. The shift in perception was subtle, but it made me feel light-headed, and for some reason, I was also suddenly quite thirsty. Laying the Bear Butte rock down on the grass, I stood up, dizzy, and began walking toward the house. As I walked, I saw that I was casting two shadows, one from the sun, and the other from another source of light. I turned again, hoping to see the owner of this compassionate voice. I searched the sky behind me for another sun, another source of light, but there was no visible cause for the second shadow.

I made a glass of iced tea for myself in the kitchen, and repeated the soothing message to myself. A sense of awe filled me for a moment—it was apparent that the owner of this voice was a great teacher, and because he had arrived in my life at the same time as so many Native Americans, I wondered if he might be a holy man such as Crazy Horse, Chief Joseph, or Black Elk. My rational mind then spoke a rare warning: it is not considered normal to hear unexplained voices, and it is even worse to enter into conversations with them. Nevertheless, I heard what I heard, and held a conversation with another conscious being.

Carrying my tea outside, I felt weightless. With the slightest effort on that day, I felt that I might have found myself floating, no longer touching the Earth at all. I saw once again that I was casting two shadows. I walked with both of them to the grassy area where I had left my rock, and then stopped, staring in disbelief at what lay on the grass. Having only moments before given myself a rational warning, I was now faced with more evidence that the unexplained exists, regardless of my beliefs or the beliefs deemed acceptable by society.

Where there had previously been nothing but a single rock and grass, there were now forty-three white stones, four pieces of pottery, a carved bone, three shell fragments, two knapping chips, and in the center of it all was the Bear Butte stone. On top of it lay my missing feather.

I telephoned my mother.

"I don't know what's going on here—or why all of this is happening," I said to her.

She, of course, did not have any answers either. But we both had a sense of expectation on that day—"the heebie-geebies" as we called this inner feeling of waiting for the other shoe to drop. It was palpable. The return of my feather was something wonderful, but we both sensed that something else was about to happen. Nothing else happened until sometime around midnight.

I awoke in the dark to find myself standing in front of a mountain. It was a strange mountain, sharply peaked, and the shadow of its peak loomed against the backdrop of a black and star-filled sky. There were no trees on this mountain, no vegetation that I could see. Standing nearby were my teacher and his apprentice, both carrying torches that would illuminate our way. The night was clear and cool, and it was very still. I looked down and saw that I was dressed in something unusual. It was a long black dress with threads and ribbons of many bright colors hanging from it in long fringes. Poncho-like, there were no sleeves. It was simply a long circular garment that had been placed on me over my head.

"Why am I dressed like this?" I asked.

The teacher answered me in English.

"This is the Dress of the Midnight Rainbow. You will wear it one time only, to dance the Dance of the Midnight Rainbow. Come."

I followed the two men in a steep climb up a rocky path, wondering what this Dance was all about. When we were nearly to the top of the mountain, the path ended in a flat ledge that jutted about twelve feet out of the peak, like an outstretched hand. We walked into the palm of the hand. My teacher turned to me.

"Now, dance," he said.

"Dance? I don't know how to dance," I answered.

He looked at me for a moment—he appeared to be very concerned about something—and then he and the apprentice turned and, taking the torches with them, they walked back down the mountain without another word, leaving me alone in the palm of the dark ledge's hand.

"I don't know how to dance," I said again out loud, but there was no one to hear me. This was yet another of my teacher's instructions that would most likely result in my great humiliation. He seemed to think that I already knew what I was supposed to do and just needed a few reminders. He was wrong, wrong, wrong. No one had taught me the dance that was expected of me—and, besides, I was still new at this.

Overwhelmed with self-pity regarding another miserable situation that I found myself in because of this teacher—who apparently hated me to begin with—I sat down and cried for a while.

I don't know how much time passed. It might have been years for all I know. When I stopped crying, I noticed that it was getting chilly. A warm fire would have been nice, but there would be no wood to burn on this barren, lonely mountain, and that's when an idea occurred to me.

I could just go back down the mountain to my teacher's camp and tell my teacher that I had done as instructed—that I had danced the Dance of the Midnight Rainbow—and he would never be the wiser about my little white lie.

It was a tempting thought. But they had taken the torches with them when they left, and I would not be able to see the path or find my way down.

I shifted my position on the uncomfortable rock ledge, and noticed that one of the blue ribbons on the black dress sparkled with static light. It was beautiful.

I moved the dress again, and other threads sparkled as though the dress was somehow alive and was just waiting for someone to move it.

Standing up, I decided to at least try to dance. The long black dress hung on me in vertical folds from my collar to my feet as I surveyed my next problem. The ledge was not wide enough to allow much movement—in fact, it was only large enough to accommodate the full size of the circular dress if I were to turn around and around and around in the center of the palm—and like a bolt of lightning, the understanding came to me. That was the dance that I was to do; that was the Dance of the Midnight Rainbow.

I stood in the center of the ledge and began to turn, slowly at first. As I turned, the black dress began to flow outward with my motion, and the ribbons and threads began to arc and glow in many colors. Turning faster and faster, the dress continued to rise into a full circle until it was spinning around my neck. The sparks from the many fringes suddenly rose, swirling and swirling into the midnight sky. I looked upward and saw that overhead, the sparkling lights from a million threads had joined together to form a rainbow—not an ordinary half-rainbow, but a full-circle rainbow, a perfect circle that was now lighting the whole sky. It was lighting the mountain. It was lighting the path.

When the dance was completed, the black dress fell back down again in folds. The rainbow remained in the sky, and in its light, I walked down the mountain.

The teacher and his apprentice were waiting for me. They were both smiling. I had never seen my teacher smile before this moment.

We sat by the campfire, and the teacher brought out some food that he had packed away, in the hope that we would have something to celebrate on this evening. Other people who had seen the rainbow joined us, bringing more food but, I could not clearly see their faces. We enjoyed the food, and laughed as George the Bear told many funny stories about his difficult students—such as myself. I had no idea that he had a sense of humor.

Then he stopped laughing and motioned that I come and sit closer to him. I moved closer.

He was quiet for a moment, deep in thought, then he said quietly, "You are just a woman," and I felt certain that he was about to reprimand me again, or perhaps he was merely going to humiliate me in order to remind me that a woman's place is in the kitchen.

"And you only have the voice of a simple woman," he said, almost in pity.

I nodded, humiliated. Tears formed in my eyes as I realized that he was about reiterate the very old (and tired) concept that had been embraced by numerous groups, cultures, and nations for far too long. He was about to tell me that I could not ever amount to much of anything because I had had the misfortune of being born female.

"But one day," he said, " you will speak." He touched my

hand in a gesture of kindness and leaned even closer to whisper something, "And when you do, you—a woman—will speak like two men."

I looked at him, not sure that I had just heard him correctly. One tear escaped.

"What?"

"Like two men," he said holding up two fingers. "And so, that is your name now. You are 'Woman Two Man Speaks.' You are no longer just a woman, you are an equal."

This came as totally baffling news—I wondered what I was to speak about.

"Write this all down," he said, "so that it will not be forgotten."

On a summer's hazy afternoon, as I sat in the front yard during quiet time, I closed my eyes and I found myself immediately surrounded by my dreamwalking friends. They were working in a field of corn.

Startled, I opened my eyes. My friends were gone, and so was the corn.

I closed my eyes again, and they resumed their celebration. Eyes open, they disappeared and only grass lay where the corn had stood.

It took six more repetitions of this exercise before I understood the message. If I could not surround myself with my friends with eyes open, then I could at least surround myself with their celebration. All I needed was a field of corn where the sod now lay.

The cicadas began to sing loudly.

When Craig arrived home from work that afternoon, I approached him with what I personally felt was a very, very good idea.

"I'd like to dig up the front yard, and plant a field of corn," I said.

A look of horror came over his face.

"No," he said, "you're not digging up the front yard."

"But why not? The corn would be beautiful!"

He looked at me strangely, as though he had never thought of corn as a thing of beauty.

"No," he said, "I want the front yard to stay the way it is—grassy."

"But I want it to change."

"No, and that's final."

"Well, how about just a small plot?"

"No!"

"But the yard is big—it won't hurt anything to have a plot of corn!"

"The yard should remain the way it is—an uninterrupted lawn so that the kids can play volleyball on it someday."

"But I want to use it now."

"Please," he said, "I don't want you to dig up the front yard, and that is final. There's probably an ordinance against it, anyway."

I gave good thought to this difference of opinion for approximately sixteen hours before digging up the front yard. That was the day when Craig came home to find not only a woman who was becoming stranger by the day, but he found a complete stranger—a woman with a shovel, a purpose, and a new identity.

Horror appeared on his face yet again as he pulled into the driveway and emerged from his car.

"What are you doing?" he asked, probably not really expecting an answer, and then when the full impact of my afternoon's excavations hit him, he said, "Look at what you've done!"

I then responded.

"I'm planting a field of corn," I said, pausing for a moment. My hair was plastered to my forehead with the sweat from my labors, and my hands were black with earth. I was wearing a purple bathing suit (it was hot), cotton socks rolled down to my ankles, and combat boots. It was the last day I ever wore nail polish. It was the last time my hair would ever have been coiffed, permed and sprayed.

It was my first day as an individual, a real person—a Narraganset Indian.

In the ensuing conversation, we covered such topics as the man's place as household decision-maker, the woman's subordinate place in the household, why my actions might prompt social disapproval as well as a visit from the Lawn Police, and why one who is the mother of two children has no business trying to consider herself an individual.

But none of this truly applied or made sense to me any longer. I had been given a new name that elevated me to male status—and I was no longer a subordinate, I was an equal. And the children could only benefit from having a mother who is an individual.

It was an argument that could not possibly be settled.

I remember that my ears began to buzz, not with the sound of the cicadas, but with the dizzying white noise that I suspect is nature's way of faithfully protecting one from too many discouraging words. It was during that buzz that a new awareness slipped lightly and delicately into my thoughts of equality and protest: I had uprooted much, much more than the Bermuda sod that afternoon. I had uprooted myself and delivered the final coup to any remaining hopes of salvaging the marriage. My victory was bittersweet.

Craig turned and walked toward the house. I heard him call out, "It'll never grow. Corn doesn't grow in the middle of town."

When I didn't answer, he added, "You're making a big mistake."

Perhaps I was, but it was too late to turn back, too late to allow sod to cover my dreams, and too late to return to many things. I was no longer living in Craig's world. I was living in another world—a world of two shadows, of good teachers, and of dreamwalking.

I pushed the shovel down under another square of sod with my boot, lifted it up, and turned it over, exposing the earth that was now eager to grow corn instead of grass.

The corn was planted according to the practices of my dream friends. Large mounds were first formed, and a fish buried deep within each mound. The seeds were then also pushed deeply into the mounds—down where they would be close to the fish.

A week passed, followed by another, and each day the plot

of ground that I dug and formed into mounds lay seemingly barren, devoid of all greenery. It seemed to be a taunting reminder that my first act as a dissident had apparently been a failure. The bare patch seemed to be saying, "You have made a big mistake—corn does not grow in the middle of town!"

But on the fourteenth day after I planted it, the corn rose up strong from the ground.

I sat there alone, close to the corn, as often as possible during the days that it grew taller and the summer days grew shorter. I watched and listened.

It was there, close to the stalks that drew their strength from the Earth, the sun, the moon, the waters, and the fish, that I first understood that the corn's needs for its life were the same as my own.

If my needs were the same as the corn's, then we must be sisters. If my heart could understand the love song of the cicada, then he must be my brother.

The comfort I felt while sitting in the cornfield came because I realized I was not merely sitting alone amid a field of corn. I was sitting with relatives.

The man joined us there in the field of corn, the invisible man with the gentle voice who had spoken to me on the Day of the Blue Jays, and the Day of Compassion—the afternoon of the Midnight Rainbow.

For three days, when I sat there, I heard him singing a song. I still could not see him, nor could I hear the words of his song as they were carried off on the summer's breath to mingle with the cicadas' song.

On the late afternoon of the third day of his song, his singing stopped. I looked toward the west, the direction from which the sound of his voice had come. Amid the standing corn was the setting sun. Low and glimmering, it was illuminating the field of my sisters with brilliant, flickering beams and shafts of white light. It seemed not to be a far and distant star, it seemed instead to be here, descending to touch the Earth while held within the embrace of a corn field.

Just as surely as I knew that summer followed spring, I sensed what was next without knowing any of the spoken details. It was time for me to follow the sun and take a long, long journey alone—the longest I had ever taken.

When Craig arrived home that evening, I told him that it was now necessary for me to take a trip. In the autumn, I told him, I would go and stand alone in the middle of the desert as I had once done in a dream. I would face west and await whatever was to come, and if it came with thunder on a white horse, then I would try to be brave.

My bravery did not last long when put to the test of reality.

Craig agreed to stay home with the children while I traveled to the desert, thus removing all possible obstacles from my departure. Throughout the remaining weeks of that summer and into the early fall, however, I delayed the time of departure again and again—due to cold feet. The weeks were passing too quickly.

During that time, I made several final attempts to write a new chapter about Joseph and Tioco, but was unable to write anything more about them, about the Adongohela, or about Harvest Moon. I finally retired the bizarre manuscript to the floor in my bedroom closet.

By the first week of September, my anxiety over the still-indefinitely scheduled upcoming trip was increasing by the hour. I had never been away from the children before, had never been alone in the desert before—except in dreams—and had never planned anything quite as strange as this trip.

Craig, aware of my tendency to become lost in Tallahassee despite having lived here for nearly twenty years, purchased a topographical map of the desert for me should the inevitable occur out west. This added slightly to my angst.

By the first of September, I had worried myself into a state of near disability. Every part of my physical body seemed to bear afflictions that were actually the result of my mental state of mind—unending apprehension and anxiety. I had four impacted wisdom teeth from nightly anxiety-grinding, and a strep throat that my worn-down immune system couldn't correct. The strep then entered my esophagus, and I couldn't eat. A collection of unsightly styes formed on both eyes. Bronchitis settled heavily in my chest. I wondered what could possibly happen next, and in a fit of coughing, slipped a disc in my back. Immediately following this, a little sore that had been on the bridge of my nose for far too long erupted into something resembling a small meteor crater and could no longer be ignored. A biopsy revealed that I had cancer. The little sore was a cancerous tumor, a basal cell carcinoma.

Caught up in a whirlwind of horror, I went (stooped, hoarse, and blinking) from the first surgeon's office to that of the second surgeon, a plastic surgeon. As I marched between their waiting rooms, and then joined them in their strategic command posts, they drew up battle plans for a war they were going to wage on my face.

The first surgeon estimated he would need approximately four hours in order to remove the tumor and as much of the nose as necessary. The second surgeon felt that he, too, would need four hours to make whatever reconstructions were necessary in the wake of the first surgery. The entire procedure, from start to finish, would take an estimated block of eight hours.

It was the second portion of the surgery, the reconstruction, that my mind reviewed again and again, stuck with numb fascination on the doctor's graphic demonstration of the intended procedure. He was going to reconstruct me all right.

He handed me a mirror so that I might watch as he began to draw on my face with a black pen.

First, he drew a thick circle around the offending crater. Another large circle was drawn to the right of my nose, followed by two "X" marks on my forehead. Then he connected the circles and "X" marks with dots, dashes, and arrows. Within a moment, my face looked like the diagram of a football play.

"What we'll do is this," he said, his voice hushed and tense as he focused on his plans, "we'll use this area of your forehead, here"—he pointed to the large X marks—"between your eyebrows. We'll use it to grow a new nose flap. It'll remain attached to your forehead, but we'll fold it down and over, and attach it here," he said, drawing an arrow down my face. "The flap from your forehead will be attached to your cheek, right next to your nose. Then we'll wait for it to start growing."

My mind began to swirl as I followed his pen on its journey across my face, visualizing myself with two noses. That familiar white buzzing sound began to rise in my ears, ready to protect me should I require all other sounds to be obliterated.

"In a few weeks," he continued, "when it's big enough, we'll detach it from your cheek and move it to the area of the nose that's missing."

Almost as an afterthought, he added, "This will leave your eyebrows permanently sewn together, but that shouldn't be a problem. Next, we'll . . ."

That did it. I did not hear any portion of what came next.

It was not the image of having two noses temporarily abutting one another on my face (one large damaged nose and a junior blob with aspirations) that caused my hearing to be obliterated by the white buzz. It was the suggestion of joining two perfectly good eyebrows into one giant brow, spanning the full width of my forehead—thus leaving me with a slightly startled, hooded appearance—that brought on the buzzing.

"Wait a minute," I said, interrupting him, "what do you mean my eyebrows will be sewn together?"

"Well, we need that section of your forehead for the new nose flap."

"Can't you make a nose flap from some area less visible to the public—like my behind?"

"No," he said, chuckling at the suggested image, "it has to remain attached at its base as well as next to your nose so it can grow. Why? Is there a problem with this?"

"Well, yes, there's a problem with this! I don't want to have just one massive eyebrow!"

He chuckled again, this time as though I were being silly. "Don't worry about it. You can always shave a path through it—or pluck it."

But I did not find either of these recommendations appealing. He, however, did not seem to share my concern. As I sat helplessly, he continued planning to rearrange my face so that if he realized his vision, very soon I would resemble the mother of Cro-Magnon Man.

"Listen," he said, somewhat offended by my lack of enthusiasm, "this is a state-of-the-art procedure, and it needs to be done immediately."

"Well, I can't have it done immediately!" I said. The trip to the desert suddenly looked far more appealing than dealing with this situation. It was the least fearsome of the two. "I'm going on an important trip. My nose will have to wait until after I return."

"Can't you reschedule your trip?"

"No! Under no circumstances can it be rescheduled!"

"When are you leaving?"

"I'm not sure yet," I said, standing up as best I could.

He looked confused by my answer and then shrugged, slowly shaking his head in amazement at such a display of vanity and foolhardiness, "Well, you'd better call us immediately—as soon as you return."

"I will."

"Don't forget," he said, "we're not playing games here. You have cancer!"

I looked at him through a visual field that contained not only a very visible crater, but also the black bull's eye he had just drawn around it.

"I won't forget."

I drove home with the drawings still on my face, and stood in the bathroom crying as I tried to scrub the disfiguring plans away. I remember only broken pieces of the remainder of that day.

Unable to sleep that night, I opened a book that had been loaned to me by a friend. Its contents served as the proverbial final straw. It was a book about the end of the world, and about long overdue punishment to the world. When I finished reading the book, I threw it across the room in disgust, distancing myself from it, but unable to rid myself of its gloomy predictions.

My despair deepened that night into something so unfathomable that I knew I'd never experienced anything quite like it before. A sense of resignation came over me, perhaps not unlike that which comes over a rabbit when seized by a python. The prey simply surrenders and awaits the inevitable without further struggle.

I turned off the light and was aware of only pain and darkness for a long while that night of September 11th, 1988. Mercifully, sometime after midnight I fell asleep—a sleep that, befitting my condition, was without dream, light, or hope.

Not even my dreamwalking friends could find me in the darkness that claimed me. It was my darkest night.

I did not know that the victory of the darkness would be short-lived. I did not know that I was about to finally see the man who had spoken to me on the Day of the Blue Jays and the Day of Compassion—the man who had sung a love song in the corn field. I did not know that I was about to be reassured that nothing written by the pen of man is indelible.

I did not know that the darkness would end at four A.M., and the night would be turned into day.

—4—

The Awakening

 At approximately four A.M., on September 12, 1988 the darkest night of my life ended suddenly and abruptly.

I was not called to a campfire in a dream. I was not called to dream at all. I was called, in silence, out of my sleep.

I was awakened by a bright light shining in my face.

As my consciousness rose up out of sleep and into its first foggy thoughts of the day, I wondered vaguely if the sun had suddenly risen, and if so, why it had risen in the west on this particular morning. I then opened my eyes, and looked directly into the source of the light.

Floating approximately six feet from my bed was a perfect sphere of light.

It was large, perhaps seven feet in diameter, and it was slowly revolving from its left to right. As the light swirled around and around, waves of it radiated out from the sphere, passing over me first in quiet, cloudlike flashes, and then the light passed directly through me.

There was more to this light than mere illumination. It did far more than simply turn night into day.

I felt it touch the strep infection; I felt it touch the slipped disk; I felt it touch the impacted wisdom teeth, the stomach flu, and the styes as it corrected each of those situations. Then, as though it knew exactly where it was needed, the light found my despair and it touched that, as well. Only the bronchitis and the tumor on my nose remained waiting for their healings.

I suddenly felt exceptionally well in spite of this apparent oversight, and stared dumbstruck, at the sphere as questions began rising in my mind. How could a sphere of light be so beautiful that I couldn't turn my eyes away from it? How could light be passing through me? And why was I suddenly feeling a growing sense of happiness?

Then the sphere spoke in a voice that was barely louder than the softest whisper. It was the gentle voice of a man, and it was a familiar voice that I recognized right away. His first words to me on that night were, "You're not afraid, are you?"

The man who sang the love song in the corn had come and found me in the darkness. I smiled at the stunning sphere.

"No," I said, "I'm not afraid." In fact, I felt wonderful.

"Good," he said, "none of this is meant to frighten you."

"My pain is all gone," I said, grinning.

"Good," he answered again, "you are not meant to suffer."

"Well, we suffer a lot here on this planet," I said, assuming from his appearance that he was from elsewhere—possibly deep space.

"What is the cause of all this suffering?" he asked.

"I guess we're being punished."

"Oh?" he said. "And who is punishing you?"

"Most of us assume it's God. He's filled with vengeance."

"Perhaps what you are experiencing, and thinking of as punishment, is actually only cause and effect."

I thought about this for a moment before disagreeing with him.

"No, that's not possible," I answered, "that would mean we're causing our own suffering, and we would never do that. No, it's definitely coming from an outside source."

"This 'God,' of yours," he said, "who is he?"

"Well, first of all, he's not mine—I'm not into religion, and I try not to dwell on the possibility of his existence because I don't like his image. Most religions teach that he's omnipotent and filled with wrath. He's old and angry—kind of like the granddaddy of all loose cannons," I said smiling at my daring portrayal.

"And so he inflicts pain and suffering?" the voice from the sphere asked.

"Yes. People believe that he does all sorts of things," I said, "floods, earthquakes, famine, pestilence—sometimes he burns our houses down. We refer to these as 'acts of God,' and there's no telling what he's going to do next—or why."

He was quiet, possibly absorbed in my explanation, so I continued.

"If we disobey his laws, people believe that's a sin," I explained, "then comes the punishment. It's crime and punishment, here."

"Perhaps you are not punished by 'God' at all, but by yourselves," he said, "and, perhaps instead of being tormented by 'God,' you are, instead, unconditionally loved."

"Well, sometimes we carry out the punishments for him," I said in agreement, "but, other times, he punishes everyone, and no one knows why. We are not unconditionally loved—if we were, he wouldn't have invented Hell."

"Maybe he didn't."

The light continued swirling out from the sphere and through me, and after an extended moment of silence he said, "Will you come with me? There is someone I would like you to meet."

"Okay," I said. The light also dissolved any fears that I might have normally had about traveling with visitors from space, which was my guess about this being's origin, as he certainly did not appear to be familiar enough with life on Earth to be from these parts. Regardless, the decision was mine, and was not influenced by fear.

It was at this moment, when I agreed with my free will to go with him, that what I perceived as a "death" occurred. It was painless. In one breath I was residing in a body of physical matter, and in the next, I simply floated out of that body and found my consciousness residing, fully intact, in a perfect body of light. I looked around and saw that I had hair, fingers and toes—all made of light.

I floated for a moment near the ceiling, looking down at my physical body where it lay unmoving on the bed. Its mouth was agape, and the path of a tear glistened where it had fallen from the now unseeing eyes that were still wide with wonder. They had seen something not usually beheld in the middle of the night. They had seen the sun rise. A sense of overwhelming compassion flowed through me, and I wanted to tell the body, "Don't cry, everything is all right."

"What do you see?" the voice from the sphere whispered, aware of my awe.

"I don't know what I'm seeing—maybe that there is no death? I don't understand any of it—but I'm feeling incredible love for all of it."

"Good," he said, "it's not really important to understand everything. What is important is that you feel the love that you are feeling."

In the next instant, we were no longer in my bedroom but on the summit of a mountain. The wind howled around us, neither hot nor cold, and as we walked I looked closely at the terrain. The summit was dry, rocky, and devoid of trees or vegetation. The sand and rocks under my feet were a tawny, golden color as though we were walking through a scene that had been tinted sepia with age.

We walked without speaking until we came to the opening of a cave in the face of the mountain. The opening was framed by several ancient and gnarled pieces of wood that must have been carried to the cave from a great distance. Hanging from the wood was a brown blanket made from homespun cordage.

The voice in the sphere called out to someone, and in a moment, a woman with long white hair pulled the blanket aside and looked at us. She glanced only briefly at me before turning her focus to my companion, the sphere. She looked at the sphere with unmistakable love in her eyes, along with apparent relief as though she had been awaiting his return for a long while.

They talked briefly, exchanging words that I could not hear, and I wondered who she was. She was beautiful. Her garment was made of the same rough homespun as the blanket, and I assumed that she was the weaver of both.

Their conversation ended when the sphere said something so strange to the woman that she fell into silence. She turned to look at me again, this time in disbelief. Her mouth fell open slightly, and she raised a hand to cover it as she continued staring at me.

I felt somewhat self-conscious, but was completely mystified by her next action. She bent over, slapped both hands against her lap, and began laughing uncontrollably.

Whenever her laughter started to subside, all that was necessary to rekindle it was for her to straighten herself upright just enough to look at me again.

Within seconds her laughter became contagious, and my embarrassment vanished. I found myself first smiling broadly, and then, unable to resist any longer, I joined her, laughing wildly. I had no idea what we were laughing at, other than it had something to do with my appearance, but it was one of the heartiest laughs of my existence.

The sphere of light then led me—still laughing—away from the woman and back to the summit. I did not learn who the beautiful and ancient woman was that night, because neither of us could stop laughing long enough to speak to each other.

After walking for a moment on the rocky summit of the barren mountain, I immediately found myself back in my bedroom, and back in my body. It seemed heavy and awkward. I felt it gasp for breath as it filled its lungs with the night air. Because my consciousness was still overwhelmed with the laughter from the mountain, the physical body responded according to the spirit, and it awoke from its suspended state laughing until its sides ached and new tears streamed down its face. My breath was no longer raspy with bronchitis; the laughter had cleared my lungs.

I looked at the sphere. It was so beautiful, so perfectly compassionate, and I wondered again what form of life this was.

"Where are you from?" I asked through my laughter, hoping that this time, he'd tell me. I'd asked him this once before, in the front yard.

"We are already here," he answered for a second time.

"No, I mean, what is your place of origin?" I asked.

"If you do not know your own origin, of what importance is mine?" he answered, giving me the same answer he'd given me the first time I asked.

Assuming that he was shy about places of origin, I decided not to pursue this particular issue.

"You were correct to question the statements in the book you just read," he said.

I stopped laughing. "You mean the book that I threw across the room tonight?"

"Yes."

"It was an inaccurate prediction?" I asked with hope.

"Yes."

"Then, there is hope?"

"There is always hope," he said, "you are hope—but negative thoughts and predictions can damage hope."

"I don't understand."

"Thought is a form of energy," he said, "and belief is a form of thought. To place your beliefs in a prediction gives the prediction energy—it becomes empowered. Once empowered, it then gains an opportunity to occur."

"Thoughts are that powerful?"

"Thought is the tool of creation, but mankind sometimes shapes it into a tool of destruction."

"Yes," I agreed, "mankind is very powerful."

"Powerful and out of control," he added, "it is time for mankind to evolve. It is time for new thoughts to take the place of old concepts."

"No," I said, correcting him, "I don't think that'll ever happen—old ideas are hard to change. People worship tradition on this planet."

"If you would change the entire world," he said, "you may begin with a single thought—such is its power. You have seen with the book that you read how one person can be greatly influenced by the thoughts of another, regardless of the accuracy of those thoughts."

"Yes," I said, I had certainly been influenced by the book, "which part of the book was inaccurate?"

"The book contains partial truths," he said, "your heart already knows this, but you believed what was written by another rather than what was spoken by your own heart. Seek the truth yourself. When you find it, examine it closely and from different perspectives. Examine all of it, and leave no part uncovered. The truth is never weakened by close examination. It is made stronger."

"What should I have examined in the book?"

"The book named only one carrier of the plague."

He was correct. The predictor had mentioned only squirrels— an unlikely choice because I knew from my own experience in working with wild animals that squirrels are not usually flea-infested. "That's right," I said, "there would be other more likely carriers—mice and rats!"

"Again, this is only partly correct," he said.

"What have I left out?"

"The domestic cat."

"Cats?" I said, in disbelief. He had surely made an error. It would be too cruel an irony to think that something thought to control the rodent population could carry one of its worst diseases. I made a mental note to investigate his statement at a later time, although I was certain that he was in error—just as he was in error in thinking that we were causing our own problems and that we need to change.

"It is good to seek the truth with your own eyes," he said, perhaps perceiving my doubts. "Seek it, and examine it well— it will lead you out of your primitive state. It will show you the way to heal the Earth."

"Primitive?" He had made another mistake. "We're not primitive!" I laughed. "We evolved a long, long time ago."

"Evolution is not a process meant to be stopped. It is an ongoing process—a tool of perfection. It is not so much a journey of technical achievement as it is of spiritual achievement. When the journey is abandoned or interrupted, the whole of the land stagnates in primitive concepts. Sadness and turmoil prevail in this condition. Sadness and turmoil," he repeated, quietly, "they are the marks of suffering brought about by an interrupted or abandoned spiritual journey."

"But we're evolved," I insisted, "both spiritually and technologically. We've come a long way."

"No one prays anymore."

Another mistake within the short time frame of tonight's meeting. Although our previous conversations had been brief, I could not recall any other conversation in which he had made so many errors.

"People here pray!" I said. "Some people pray all the time."

"How do you pray?"

My mind floated back to a scene from my childhood. I viewed the scene as though reentering the consciousness of the child. I was in church. My back was pressed against the hard, wooden pew, my starched slip and dress were itchy and uncomfortable. The church was hot and stuffy, and I was very, very bored. A beam of amber light flowed down through a stained glass window, and I stared at the motes of dust moving through the stale air. Barely audible in the background, I heard the drone of voices as people chanted somber words of Latin to each other. I did not understand what they were saying, but I knew that this was the solemn ritual of prayer, and that the heat, the starch, and the hard pews were necessary tests of endurance. The scene then ended, never to be thought of again until its reenactment on this night over thirty years later. I returned to the present with my answer.

"We pray with words," I said, "we memorize words and repeat them, over and over again."

The sphere began glowing more brightly, as though something in the core had just ignited. The soft waves of light continued flowing outward for a moment, in spite of what appeared to be an internal fire of growing passion. The waves passed through me in their slow, steady, tidal pulse that had first restored order to chaos and was now going beyond a mere healing of body and mind. An awakening seemed to be occurring in me. Senses and emotions, long buried under heaviness were being awakened. With great clarity, I was experiencing the senses most humanly desired, yet most commonly elusive—joy, pleasure, and delight.

I felt that I was on the brink of something indescribable, and at that moment, the waves of illumination stopped abruptly. A strange, heralding silence filled the room.

The fire in the core of the sphere intensified until it was glowing with such a brilliance that its energy was beyond anything known to me. Floating in my room, not more than six feet away from where I lay, was a sphere of light that was brighter than the sun, brighter than any light I had ever seen. It was a fire that did not consume, and I could not look away. The world seemed to stand still as the swirling radiance within the sphere continued building until it became impossibly white—liquid and alive. My ears seemed to perceive a high humming in the stillness.

Suddenly, the sphere opened itself in an explosion of sound and light, and a beam of white light flashed from its core directly into my core. I heard myself gasp, because when it hit me, it ignited something within me I'd never felt before, something massive and passionate. This was followed quickly by a second and third explosion of light, each one passing through me, intensifying the fire already started within me. I was unable to move or speak, and seemed to be suspended in time by the flashing beams now connecting my core to that of the sphere. I had never before felt such complete love.

"Think of your worst enemy," the voice from the sphere said.

I thought that this was a strange request at such a moment. I was at the highest point of joy I'd ever experienced, but I did as he asked, and thought of that enemy. A clear mental image of her came into my mind.

"Now send all that you are filled with to her," he said.

As I did this, the light that was filling me erupted in a straight beam that streamed directly toward her image. As it flowed out of me, the light within me remained constant, not dimming in any way, and I remained connected by flashing beams of light to the sphere.

I watched as the beam I was sending moved out into darkness

like a searchlight through space, and then it touched her. When it did, it ignited another explosion. A corona of light surrounded her, and then, like the reflection of the sun in a mirror, all the light that I had sent to her flashed back to me, hitting me with overwhelming force. I was now beyond the summit of love that I had experienced before. I had been blown through the doors of consciousness, and my consciousness was scattered like stardust in the Universe. Each particle was separately aware of itself and its separateness, and yet also aware that there is no real separateness, that all portions are parts of one wholeness, and that there is no aloneness. This was a state of joy that was unspeakable and complete. My physical body did not know how to respond to such a state, and so it responded in every possible way. I was paralyzed, but shaking. I was laughing, but crying. I could not breathe, but I felt that I did not need air. All that I ever really needed was light.

The night was filled with light and an incredibly beautiful sound. It was the sound of a song being sung. As I listened, I wondered if I was hearing a Song of the Spheres, but knew that couldn't be possible because the song seemed to be coming from my physical body—which was also separated, particle by glowing particle—and I realized at last that I was hearing the sound of my own cells singing. I had never known until this moment that my body could sing a song unknown to me, or that the cells had a consciousness of their own. I felt overwhelmed with compassion, awareness and respect for each cell as it sang the most beautiful song I had ever heard.

The glowing brilliance of the sphere ebbed from its impossible state beyond all beauty into a lovely radiance that could be humanly endured.

My consciousness began to return from space, and took its place at the head of the body that was still paralyzed and trembling. The singing began to soften, and a stillness again filled the room. My cells stopped vibrating, and life as I knew it returned to as normal a state as it would ever be again in the aftermath of what I had just experienced.

He waited until the room was quiet enough that I could hear him whisper, and he whispered, "Now—you have just prayed for the first time in your life."

"That was a prayer?" I asked. My voice sounded weak, not clear and beautiful like the singing I had just heard.

"Yes," he said, still whispering as though anything louder than a whisper might intrude on this moment, on this experience.

"Prayer is a love song," he whispered, "you had forgotten how to sing."

As I looked at the sphere, I was suddenly able to perceive something moving within it. With hands that were still shaking, I wiped tears away from my face, and looked at it again, not believing what I was finally seeing.

There was a man standing inside the sphere of light.

The light radiating outward from him, and surrounding him, had been of such intensity that I had not previously been able to see the man from whom it radiated.

I sat forward in the bed, propping myself up on the elbow of my left arm, looking at him. He looked down at the floor while I stared at him, studying him. His face was perfect and beautiful. His hair was long—past his shoulders—and it shimmered with soft yellow light. A luminous white garment was draped over him, covering him from his shoulders to his feet. A moment ago I thought that the perfect sphere was the most beautiful thing I had ever seen, but now I knew that he—this man whom I was finally able to see—was even more beautiful than the sphere. He raised his eyes and looked directly at me. I felt my own eyes grow wide the moment that our eyes met. Deep inside, I felt a locked chamber being opened. He was unlocking it with his eyes.

I knew that I was in the presence of something—someone—with great capabilities.

While I might have considered myself to be a disciplined person—someone certainly reserved enough to address such a dignitary in an unselfish way—before I could ask for anything profound on behalf of others, my attention returned to the tumor growing upon my nose, and I blurted out, "Can you do something about this thing on my nose?"

He laughed out loud, looked down at the floor again, and then back at me.

Still smiling, he shook his head.

I mistook this as a refusal. "Please," I said.

His smile vanished, and a look of sadness came over him when he saw that I thought he was refusing to help me.

"When you return from your trip to the desert," he said, "you will no longer need the surgery that you are dreading."

"I won't?"

"No."

The trip to the desert suddenly took on new meaning and importance.

"However," he said, "it is not that which is upon your nose that should be the cause of your great concern."

"It's not?" I answered, now even more alarmed that he might have discovered another malignancy while looking through me.

"There is something else of greater importance in need of your attention," he said.

I sat upright now, facing him, no longer leaning on my elbow. I was very concerned.

"You've seen something else in me?" I asked.

"Yes," he said.

The color drained from my face. "What is it? How bad is it?"

He was quiet for a moment before responding. I would eventually come to understand that these long moments of silence were characteristic of this man. He gave matters great thought before speaking.

"There is an imbalance," he said. "We shall refer to it as a 'deficiency.'"

He smiled after saying this, and I had no idea why. Perhaps he did not grasp the seriousness of this situation.

"Well, can I be saved?" I asked.

He nodded, looking directly at me again with those eyes. "Yes," he said.

"Okay, then," I said, relieved, "tell me how. What do I need?"

"Fish," he answered.

"Fish? What kind of a deficiency is this?" Before he could

answer my question, however, I answered it myself. "Oh! I must have an iodine imbalance!"

He laughed.

"Seaweed might also be useful for an iodine deficiency," he said.

"Okay," I said, willing to take whatever steps were necessary. "I'll start eating fish and seaweed immediately."

He smiled but didn't answer, and the light coming from him began swirling around him, partially obscuring him from my sight again. I knew that he was about to leave.

"Wait!" I shouted, not ready for him to depart—we had barely met face to face. "What's your name?"

"You would not be able to understand my name."

"That's okay," I pleaded.

"And you would not be able to repeat it."

"That's okay," I said again.

There was no reply, and I could no longer see the man, only the sphere of light, so I shouted, "Please! Just tell me!"

He returned and spoke his name. It was a beautiful sound made of many sounds, similar to the singing I had heard.

He was correct. I would not have been capable of repeating it, not because it was a secret name, but because I had only one voice and could not create the many sounds that formed his name.

The light again surrounded him, swirling. As it swirled, a great area similar to an iris rotated to the front of the sphere, giving it the rather eerie appearance of being a large eye looking at me. As the swirling winds of light within the sphere continued to move, the sphere suddenly took on the appearance of the planet Jupiter.

"I know what you look like!" I shouted through the winds, wondering if he could still hear me, "You look like the planet Jupiter! Is that where you're from?"

"Something wonderful is going to happen," he said from a distance, a line that I believe is from a Hollywood movie about space.

"Find out all that you can about the tenth moon of Jupiter," he said.

"Okay," I answered, puzzled.

Mary Sparrowdancer

"Remember, the tenth moon—not the ninth, but the tenth."

"I'll remember."

"And remember how to pray."

"Don't worry, I will." I thought of my old enemy, but was startled to find that I no longer considered her an enemy. We now seemed to be connected.

"Wait!" I shouted at him again. "What if I run out of enemies?"

"Then pray for those you already love!" he said, laughing, "And tell others how to pray."

"Okay."

"Now, lie down," he said.

But I couldn't lie down. I was super-charged and wanted to sit forward and watch him for as long as possible. My mind began racing through the events of the previous years, the events that must have been leading up to this strange encounter. I saw flashes of days, flashes of color, flashes of time, flashes of dialogues and dreams. Words from the past echoed into the present, one after another, in an unending stream.

While I was in the middle of this spectacular flashback, the sphere vanished instantly, the room fell silent, and I fell back onto the bed, unconscious.

I do not know how long I was unconscious after the radiant sphere and the man disappeared.

The sun rose in the east, as expected, later that morning, and when it did, I awoke with a sense of wonder, looking for him. Light has had this effect on me from that day forth. I am reminded with each sunrise, of that day when I saw the dawn come twice.

I put my feet onto the familiar rug in my familiar room. No longer suffering from the variety of ailments that had kept me bent over and shuffling, I stood up straight for the first time in weeks. The rug and the room might have been familiar, but nothing else in my life would ever be the same again.

I ambushed Craig as soon as he emerged from his wing of the house.

99

"Something happened to me last night," I told him.

"What do you mean?" he said.

"I saw something incredible," I said, eyes wide for dramatic effect, "there was a bright light in my room, and it woke me up and changed me."

He was, of course, weary of witnessing nothing at all odd or out of the ordinary, except for myself and my obsession with pottery, shells, lights, and Indians.

"It changed you? How?"

"I died."

This might have come as good news to him except that I was standing there, personally relaying this report, thereby indicating that I had apparently not stayed put.

"Well, you've felt dizzy before—you've thought that you were going to die before," he reminded me, referring to the physical effects that I described on our car trip to the mountains.

"No, this was different. There wasn't any fear this time. The light was there, the man was there, and there wasn't any fear. I walked into the light. There is no death!" I said. "We are really made of light! And the man inside the light," I continued, trying to explain everything I'd seen as quickly as possible, "he showed me how to pray—we're supposed to pray with light!"

Craig closed his eyes for a moment.

"He showed me what it means to love my enemies! I finally understand what that means—if we just let go of anger and fear, we can love! But we can't . . . !"

"Who was this guy?" he asked, interrupting me.

"I don't really know—he told me his name, but I can't pronounce it. I think he's from space."

He quietly asked me to accompany him into the dining room, where we would be out of hearing range of the children, who were in the living room watching TV.

"Look, you need to get a grip on reality. This thing is going to take over your life."

"Well, I have a grip! I'm telling you that I died last night—I walked into the light. And this man—well, he hit me with beams of light, and then he told me to tell other people how to pray."

"Oh, God," he said quietly, under his breath. "Do you realize how you sound? You are beginning to sound like Aimee Semple McPherson."

I would have to look her up in an encyclopedia for a full account of her life, but that did not sound like encouragement.

"Who's she?" I asked.

"A preacher—an evangelist."

"Well, I'm not either one!"

"No? Well, you just said you're supposed to start preaching about this. Look," he said, "I'm not sure what's going on here—maybe you had some sort of religious experience—but no one wants to hear about this kind of stuff."

"It was not a religious experience!" I said, deeply offended. "It had nothing to do with religion!" And that, along with everything else I was saying, was God's honest truth.

"I only hope that you are not planning to start shouting from the rooftops," he said, clearly very distressed. "Don't you understand that you are becoming an embarrassment?"

"I'm not going to shout from the rooftops, and it's is not taking over my life."

"Then, keep it to yourself, all right? I don't want you upsetting the children with this type of talk, and I don't want to hear any more about it, myself."

He walked out of the room, perhaps already knowing that he was going to hear a lot more about it.

"And it was not religious," I called after him, reaffirming my stance.

After Craig left for work, I contacted Fred the Medicine Man.

"I'm not sure what happened," I explained to Fred, "but I left my body and walked into a light, and the next thing I knew, I was on a mountain." I expected the usual laughter, but he did not respond as I expected.

"Wow," Fred said, "and you're sure that this wasn't another dream?"

"Positive. That's what's so odd about it. I was awakened from my sleep, and then it all happened. And it wasn't a hazy apparition—he was as clear as day."

"He who?"

"The man who was in the light."

"Do you know who he was?"

"No, but I'm assuming he was from space—he had some ideas and concepts that were definitely not from Earth."

"Like what?"

"Like 'cause and effect' versus 'crime and punishment.'"

"Did he have anything else to say?"

"Yes, he told me to eat fish and seaweed, love my enemies, that rodents aren't the only animals that can carry plague fleas, and to find out all I can about the tenth moon of Jupiter."

This brought on the laughter.

"That's quite a range of topics," he said, still laughing.

The laughter dampened my enthusiasm in a way, and so I changed the subject. We talked about more mundane topics briefly, and then we hung up.

I busied myself with the kids for a while, fixing their breakfasts, dressing them, and then giving them crayons, paper, and coloring books to work with at the kitchen table. They loved this time for morning creativity, and as they worked, they watched in fascination as the crayons of their choice created colorful magic on previously blank pages. It was a bright, clear fall day, and the morning sun poured through the kitchen windows bathing their drawings in its light.

John drew pointy splashes of purple, added other colors, and then worked with two crayons at once, until his page was filled with many colors.

Emily began her own work. Her drawings always seemed to tell happy stories.

I made the beds and stood for a moment in my room which was still and offered no trace of evidence for the pre-dawn events that I alone had witnessed that day. Confirmation had always been important to me, but now, following the most spectacular encounter of my life, there was none.

I completed my chores, and went back into the kitchen to admire the kids' artwork. They had finished their morning's production moments earlier, and were now in the den, playing.

I saw that John had beautified four more sheets of blank

paper, and then worked on a coloring book, superimposing his own brilliant designs over the page's plain ink drawing of Geppetto.

Emily drew and colored a family portrait that contained the house, the picket fence, all four of us standing in the yard as stick figures—waving and smiling—and a bright blue sun overhead. I gathered their efforts up and carried them off to place them in the dresser drawer where I saved most of their early works. Opening the drawer, I noticed a sheet of paper with something I hadn't seen in a while. I removed the paper.

On a creased and dog-eared piece of paper was a drawing that Emily had done one year earlier. I know the approximate date of this drawing, because I made note of it in one of the diaries that I kept—noting it because it was unusual and eye-catching.

It was a crayon drawing of a blue sphere with a darker circle within it that appeared to be an eye. Two swirling lines rotated outward from the inner "eye." What appeared to be a beam of light extended outward from the sphere. Not yet four at the time when she made this picture, she had somehow managed to draw a nearly perfect circle.

She was not able to explain the meaning of this drawing to me when she first drew it, but now, as I looked at it on September 12th, a year later, I knew exactly what it was.

It appeared to be nothing other than the planet Jupiter.

I immediately suspected that I was reading too much into what was possibly nothing more than a gifted child's simple drawing, so I went, drawing in hand, to find Emily and ask her about it for a second time.

She and John were were in the kitchen again, and Emily was pouring small cups of punch for her brother and herself.

"Emily," I said, "do you remember this?" I handed the drawing to her.

She looked at it for a moment, and recognized it immediately.

"Oh, yes," she replied. It was another solemn answer.

"What is it?" I asked.

"Well, Mom," she said, taking a deep breath, "this is the biggest one."

"What do you mean? It's the biggest what?"

"It's the biggest of all big things."

She began trying to explain this to me, using every word and phrase that she possessed in her young vocabulary—a vocabulary that had grown a year's worth since her last attempt to explain it.

It was a round thing, a marble, a ball—all items familiar to a child, all implied a sphere—except that this one, she repeated, with her arms opened wide, and her eyes widened as well, this one was the biggest one of all.

"It was too big, and too beautiful," she said.

And she had seen it long before I ever did.

We stared at it for a moment.

"And, it is blue," she said, finishing her punch.

Something that looked like Jupiter seemed to be playing an unexpected role in our lives.

The year-old drawing was certainly a small piece of confirmation about the mysterious nature of my own encounter, but I felt as though I needed more—more than a child's drawing.

I decided to begin checking the validity of the messages I had received from the man whose sphere of light resembled Jupiter. I began a search for accuracy or hidden meanings, hoping to find something that might provide the full dose of confirmation I craved, the assurance that would remove all doubt that I had met a messenger.

The first of his statements that I checked was his comment about the other possible carriers of the plague. I located my old veterinary manual, and began to read.

There were only a few paragraphs devoted to "the plague" and its potential carriers. Almost immediately, I discovered the sentence referring to the cat. I read the sentence in slow motion as a vague sense of awe set in, and then I read it again. The man had been correct. According to this old manual, the cat is another of the potential carriers.

I had been unaware of this until meeting the man in the light. As a longtime wildlife rehabilitator, I should have already known about this, but it had somehow escaped my attention.

While the information was new and startling to me, I still needed more corroboration of this man's messages.

I put that book down, and sat thinking for a moment about where and how I could locate information regarding a potential tenth moon of Jupiter—if there was a tenth moon—I thought Jupiter only had four. Looking through the phone book, I found the long listings for Florida State University, and among them was one for their astronomy lab. I placed an anonymous phone call.

A weary sounding gentleman answered the phone. I pictured him in my mind, wearing the trademark rumpled lab coat worn by gifted scientists, half-rimmed glasses, and his hair mop-like and disarrayed in a cobweb of white tangles.

"May I speak to an astrophysicist, please?" I asked.

"Speaking. What can I do for you?"

"Yes—I'd like to find out something about the tenth moon of Jupiter?" I said as casually as possible.

"Excuse me?"

"Jupiter's tenth moon," I repeated. "Jupiter does have ten moons, doesn't it?"

"Well, yeah, it has more than ten."

"Oh?" I said. "Well, good—I'm glad to hear that. Could you possibly tell me a little about number ten?"

"Is this a joke or something?"

"No—it's an assignment. From a teacher." I hoped he wouldn't ask the teacher's name.

He sighed, presumably looked around the lab, and said, "Okay, maybe I can find something here. When do you need it?"

"Um, right now?" I didn't want to give him a full description of my homework, because I suspected he might hang up the phone.

"Okay," he said, "hold on."

He put down the phone, clomped away, then clomped back.

"Jupiter, Jupiter, Jupiter, here it is." He read to himself for a moment, before asking, "Okay, by the 'tenth moon' do you mean tenth in distance from the planet Jupiter, or the tenth moon in order of its discovery?"

"I don't know. He just said 'the tenth moon.'"

"He who?"

"You know—the teacher."

He sighed, and began reading about the moons. Several minutes went by, and I was about to tell him never mind when he shouted, "Here! Here it is! This must be what your teacher wanted you to find!"

"You mean there actually is something written about the tenth moon?"

"Yes," he said, with a hint of wonder in his voice, and although I couldn't see him, I knew by his voice that he was smiling, "there is something written about it, and there is also something unusual about it, but you have to examine the information closely and think about it."

"Okay."

"Jupiter's tenth moon is a very small orbiting satellite—it's only about ten kilometers in diameter."

"Uh-huh," I said, "how big is that?"

"Roughly, a little over six miles."

"Oh."

"Usually satellites this small are just oddly shaped rocks, or chunks of ice. But this one is different."

"It is?"

"Yep," he said, concluding his findings and slamming shut the book, but I didn't know enough about astronomy to draw a conclusion at this point.

"Well, what do you mean?" I asked. "How is it different?"

"The tenth moon of Jupiter," he said, "is no chunk of rock or ice."

"What is it then?"

"It's a perfect sphere."

"Oh, God . . ." I said under my breath, "that is unusual, isn't it?"

"Yes, it is unusual," he answered, "and that teacher of yours—he's sort of unusual, too."

"He is?" I asked, my eyes widening. "How do you know? What do you mean 'he's unusual'?"

"He knows how to teach."

I hung up the telephone and called for the children.

"Come on, kids, we have to go to the store."

I put them into their car seats, and we drove immediately to the fish market so that I might obtain fish and seaweed to correct the deficiency that had been detected by my teacher, a messenger from space worthy of an audience.

Arriving at the market, I lifted John from his car seat and a flash of light caught my eye. Looking up, I saw a strange gleaming object floating slowly and soundlessly overhead in the cloudless autumn sky. Its surface was highly polished, and as it made its way through the blue heavens, its shape changed like mercury. Glimmering, quivering as though it were something alive, yet created from water, it sparkled as it caught the reflection of the sun in its mirrored finish. This was surely a sign. It was an indication that I was on the right track.

"Look, children," I said, pointing overhead.

We watched the object for a moment and then, following my lead, all three of us waved at it.

—5—

Butterfly Lessons
and Storm Warnings

I entered the fish store, and was pleased to find that they also had a supply of dried seaweed. I was not certain which type of fish I needed because the messenger—my new teacher from the light—had not specified which type of fish my deficiency called for, so I purchased a little cod, some grouper, and several cans of sardines in mustard sauce. I also purchased some clams, in case they, too, might be of help. Then I selected a bag of dried seaweed. It did not look very appetizing.

After lunch that day, during nap time, I called the bus station and obtained several bus schedules that would take me to Arizona and back. While the spiritual reasons for me to take the desert trip remained unknown to me, a very promising physical reason was clear and present each time I opened my eyes.

Although Craig had made plans around several tentative dates for my departure only to have me cancel them, now the plans were finally going to be made because the man in the light's veracity had been substantiated by what I had learned about the tenth moon of Jupiter.

That evening, when I phoned my parents to see how their day had gone, I told my mother that now I, too, had seen a light in my room, and that there was a man standing in it. He was not, however, dressed as an Indian. We talked for a while about who he might be, but I told her that I really didn't think he was anyone of note other than a very nice space traveler. Then we wondered why he seemed to be associated with the Indians.

I also mentioned that there was a possibility that my cancer might be healed without the surgical disfigurement, carefully using the word "possibility," because I didn't want to appear to be too great a fool if this particular portion of my new teacher's messages did not pan out.

That night, I went to bed with a sense of great anticipation in the hope that I might meet with the man again. I awoke the following morning with an equally great sense of disappointment. Nothing happened during the night—other than comfortable rest. I did not realize at the time that this was an important and carefully observed portion of the plan. Rest was as important as exhilaration.

On the afternoon of the next day—or perhaps it was even the day after that—as I stood in the kitchen looking into the refrigerator, I became aware of an exotic fragrance. I wondered for a moment which food had suddenly taken on this subtle scent of myrrh and spices, and then after finding the fresh bread dough I was in search of, I closed the fridge and walked to the stove. The fragrance was still present.

Maybe I had left a jar of spices uncovered, I reasoned, and turning around to begin a search for the source of the fragrance, I found myself looking directly into the eyes of the man from the light. He smiled, and so did I. I was thrilled to see him, and was immediately filled with a massive sense of love, and of happiness.

As I stood in front of him, I noted that he was about six feet in height. I also noticed that his white garment appeared to be a sort of sun-bleached linen with glowing threads. Along with the fragrance of myrrh and spices, he smelled like the faint ozone of a thunderstorm, and like clean sheets dried by the sun. He smelled wonderful. I breathed it in, deeply.

"It's a good day to take a trip," he said, "would you like to go for a ride?"

"Oh, yes!" I replied immediately, wondering what sort of vehicle we would be using.

"We'll take your car," he said.

"Where are we going?"

"To the beach—St. Marks."

Reality hit me. "Well, actually, I can't," I said. "My children are taking their naps right now, and I have no one to stay with them."

"Their father will take care of them," he said. He was still smiling.

"No, he's at work."

The man glanced over at the kitchen telephone.

Somewhat reluctantly, I phoned Craig.

"Hi," I said, "can you come home and mind the kids for a few hours?"

"Why?" he asked.

"I have to go to the beach," I answered.

"What do you mean you 'have to go to the beach'?"

"I just do. I have to go."

"Have you been seeing things again?"

"No."

Actually I was answering truthfully, because "things" suggested plural sightings, and I was merely seeing one singular "thing"—the man who was standing next to me as I made the phone call.

I was somewhat surprised when Craig immediately agreed to come home. He arrived shortly.

During our wait for him, the man and I sat in silence in the living room. He appeared to be deep in thought. This was not an uncomfortable block of time to sit in silence, and I did not feel compelled to fill it with meaningless dialog. It was a peaceful silence. He graciously pretended not to notice as I took this opportunity to once again stare shamelessly at him.

When Craig arrived, the man and I walked from the living

room to the kitchen and I studied Craig's face for any sign that he was able to see the man standing next to me. There were no signs that he could see anyone other than myself as I left for the beach.

The drive to the beach took approximately forty-five minutes, and as we neared the coast, I became aware of the many butterflies that were lying as casualties in the road. September is the month of their great migration, and they always seem to prefer the openness offered by the roads and highways, innocently oblivious to the fact that those highways had been constructed not for butterflies who weighed hardly more than a breath, but for vehicles whose weight was measured in hard tons.

Entering the St. Marks Refuge area, the man spoke.

"Go slowly, very slowly," he said. "If you are going too fast, you will not hear the answers to your own questions."

I slowed the car down, thankful that we seemed to be the only ones—other than the butterflies—bound for the beach that afternoon, but the man insisted that I slow down even further until we were barely moving at all.

The road was bordered by the large trees of the National Forest. The grey asphalt stretched out in front of us, dotted the whole way with a rainbow of colors formed by the tattered wings of those whose journeys had come to an abrupt end.

"Stop and gather each butterfly," he said.

I did as he asked, traveling only a few feet at a time, stopping the car, jumping out and retrieving handfuls of bodies and wings. Soon, the console between our two front seats was filled with a mound of yellow, orange, blue, and iridescent black butterflies, some still quivering as they clung to their small, but individually treasured threads of life. When we reached the beach, I stopped the car near the lighthouse, and sat for a moment looking at the dead and dying butterflies.

"They are beautiful creations. Gentle. They have harmed no one. Yet they have all been killed," he said.

"Wait a minute," I protested, "they weren't killed on purpose! No one deliberately killed them!"

"Nevertheless, the outcome is the same. They have been killed."

"But it was by accident!"

"Intent does not necessarily alter the law of cause and effect," he said.

"The butterfly does not die because he is being punished for trying to use a road that he does not own. The butterfly is loved unconditionally. He dies because he cannot survive the impact of a car—cause and effect. Should the deaths of the butterflies result in a decrease in pollination, the crop loss would not be upon you as a punishment from God for having killed the butterflies. You are loved unconditionally. The crop loss would be upon you because of cause and effect. Come with me," he said, his voice gentle and inviting.

We walked down along the beach. The tide was low, and the beach was fragrant with the tidal scents of salt, seaweed, and an occasional horseshoe crab drying in the sun. Small waves barely larger than ripples splashed in quiet laps onto the sand. Sandpipers waited for the shallow waves to retreat, and then ran down quickly on stick legs to probe the wet sand for morsels. As each small wave approached, they ran quickly back up to the dry sand again to wait—piping tiny sounds the whole way. It was as though the object of the afternoon's game was to run as fast as legs would carry them, back and forth along the shoreline, all while keeping their feet dry.

We walked in silence for a while, watching them, as they sometimes ran ahead of us on the beach, piping, stick legs barely visible with speed. Seven pelicans glided by just over the waters, sailing motionless on low air currents in a soundless V formation.

"It is time," he said.

"Time for what?"

"Time for man to evolve."

"But I told you, we are not a primitive society, we are evolved."

"Then give me an example of a primitive society," he said.

Without hesitation, I answered, "The ancient Aztecs."

He stopped walking and looked at me, puzzled, "The Aztecs?"

"Yes. Primitive societies like to live in jungles. They can still be found there."

"How, then, does a primitive society differ from your own society?"

"Their concepts are tribal and unsophisticated," I began. He nodded, listening. "Their religious concepts are bizarre, and based on folklore and myths—they believe they can appease their gods by carrying out strange rituals. They even kill children. They wipe out other villages. They . . ."

I talked uninterrupted for several minutes listing many points that set a "primitive" society apart from my own. He did not once interrupt me, nor did he comment in any way.

When I finished talking I realized that in naming all of the differences between a primitive society and my society, I had named all of the similarities between the two. I had, in fact, given a strong argument favoring the Aztecs' moral and spiritual sophistication over that of my own society.

Walking once more in silence, I wondered how he had tricked me into concluding out loud that I was a member of a tribal society that was not only primitive, but was also powerful, warlike, ritualistic, and out of control. Then I realized that he knew how to use silence as a tool for teaching.

"It is time for you to evolve," he said, "and to heal the Earth."

"Heal the Earth?" I asked.

"The Earth is in need of healing," he said, "are you not the caretakers?"

"Well, yes. I guess we are, but this is too much of a mess to expect us to do anything about it at this point. We can't possibly heal it ourselves. We need some outside help."

"Yours is a society that over-consumes," he said in a quiet tone that had no judgmental sting, and therefore did not cause me to rise up defensively. "The byproduct of over-consumption is waste. The Earth is suffering from the effects of waste."

"But how can we do anything about this?"

"Stop wasting."

We turned back now. He was looking down at the sand, his hands clasped behind his back as we walked.

"When you return from the desert, gather together a small group of people," he said, "tell them to select one day of each week, and to select a time on that day to sit quietly and consume nothing but the air they breathe—use no water, burn no candles, consume nothing. They do not need to meet as a group in order to do this. They can do it in their own homes, and select their own times. It does not have to be a long time; any time will do. Tell them to use this time to think. Think about the good things that bring them joy and happiness. Think of ways that they might fill their lives with joy, and ways to help heal the Earth. Tell them that if they will do this, a healing of the Earth will begin."

This struck me as being quite humorous—overly simple— and a short laugh escaped.

"First of all," I said, "I don't mean to be disrespectful, but I don't do public speaking. I'm not into that. Plus, I wouldn't have a clue about how to gather a group together—I wouldn't know who to gather. Second, there's no way I can tell anyone that a handful of people can begin a healing of the Earth! It would be—well, it would be misleading."

He stopped walking and looked at me.

"If you suffer a wound—an injury," he said quietly, "is it not the effort of a few tiny cells that brings about the healing of the wound? What would happen without the effort of those few cells?"

I had never thought about it that way, but he was correct. His sudden focus on something extremely small doing a job so very large and important caused another shift in my perception.

"Well, yes," I said, "that's right—just a few tiny cells." The job was not merely large and important. At a basic level, life itself depended upon a few tiny cells coming forward to do it.

"Do you not have capabilities at least as great as a tiny cell?" he asked.

"Yes," I answered, barely audible.

He nodded.

We stood for a while and looked out into the Gulf at the sparkling water, or, at least I looked out into the Gulf at the sparkling water. When I glanced at my teacher, I saw that he was standing there with his eyes closed. He was looking at something else entirely.

Opening his eyes, he began walking again in an unhurried pace, and I followed.

"When you return from the desert," he said, "a small gathering of people will be waiting to hear what you have to say. Tell them this," he said.

With that, he vanished, and I was left on the beach alone with the pipers, the low tide, and sunlight glimmering in jeweled flashes on a quietly moving sea. A laughing gull cried in the distance.

I walked back to the car, and then drove home accompanied by the butterflies that filled the console.

As the miles passed, their silent presence filled my mind with thoughts about unconditional love, cause and effect, and the importance of small efforts.

When I arrived at home that afternoon, Craig prepared to leave for work again, but paused on his way out the door long enough to tell me that a colleague of his might be phoning me later in the afternoon.

He explained that he had forwarded my potential schedules around his company the previous day so that a consensus could be taken about the least disruptive time frame for him to be absent. A short time later, he said, a colleague from down the hall, Ellis, phoned him to inquire briefly about the reason for the upcoming absence.

Craig told him that I was going to the desert for a short time, and he needed to stay home with the kids. Their discussion ended. He didn't give it another thought, because it was a perfectly valid question.

While I was at the beach, however, Craig said that something rather unusual had occurred. Ellis phoned him again, this time at home.

"I have to admit," Craig said, "it was sort of a strange phone call."

He had my full attention.

When Craig answered the phone, Ellis seemed so lost in his thoughts that he didn't even identify himself or say "Hello." He simply fast-forwarded directly into the heart of the conversation.

"Okay," he said to Craig, "let's have it."

"Have what?" Craig answered, recognizing the other man's voice.

"Why's your wife going out to the desert? It keeps coming into my mind, and I have a strange feeling that something really unusual's happening here."

"Oh," Craig said. "Well, it's hard for me to explain. I'm not really sure what's happening or why she's going. Why don't you phone her later and ask her yourself. She's been at the beach, but she's probably on her way back right now. She should be here shortly."

"Are you sure she'll talk to me about this?" Ellis asked. It was a valid question, because Ellis and I had never met before.

"Oh yes," Craig said, "I know she'll talk to you about it—you won't have any trouble at all getting her to talk about it."

After relaying this to me, Craig left for work, and I waited nervously for the call.

At about five P.M., Ellis finally phoned and introduced himself. The introduction was brief.

"You don't know me," he said. "I work with your husband."

"Yes, I know, he told me that you were going to call."

"I understand that you're going by yourself to the desert?"

"Yes."

"I'm not trying to pry, but I can't stop wondering about this. Why, exactly, are you going to the desert?"

"Well, something unusual has happened here," I said, not knowing how much to reveal—how much might embarrass Craig at work—and also feeling a jumble of emotions in disclosing what I'd seen. "I'm feeling compelled to go to the desert as a result of what's happened."

"Have you seen something unusual?"

"Yes."

"Can you tell me what you've seen?"

"It's a long story," I answered, "but maybe I can tell you about it when I return."

"Listen," he said, sighing as though he, too, had something hidden and personal—but something that he felt suddenly compelled to reveal. "I know this might sound strange, but please just hear me out for a second."

I could tell by his voice that he was having difficulty saying what he wanted to say. He was hesitant, clearly not accustomed to revealing personal aspects of himself to strangers.

"I'm a member of a small group of people. We have been meeting somewhat quietly and privately in the evenings to discuss man's philosophies and religions from different perspectives. Would you be willing to come and be the speaker at one of the meetings?"

Stunned, I agreed to speak to his group upon my return from the desert.

Two white stones bounced onto the floor of the living room. My son, John, witnessed this, as he had before. Picking the stones up, he handed them to me and said—as he had before—"Here Mom, these must be for you."

I placed them in the Lakota box with the other white stones.

Then, sensing that I should collect everything, I went out to the car, gathered up the remains of the butterflies, and placed them in a clear container. I brought the container into the house, and put it on a shelf in the kitchen where I could look at it, and be reminded of a day that was a good day to take a trip, and a good day to learn the butterfly lesson of unconditional love.

Another day or two passed without event.

No pottery or stones fell to the floor, and the man paid me no visits.

It was in this hushed atmosphere that a large storm began to brood and bulk itself coolly in the Gulf waters. An abnormal stillness filled the house during the hours that the tropical depression brewed, and all focus was on the storm. Another high tide was on its way.

On this day, a dark afternoon, I turned on the television to track the storm—now upgraded to an enormous depression in the Gulf of Mexico. The storm was sitting still upon the waters with what appeared to be nothing other than malignant intent. It had paused on its turbulent and changing course, and now squatted in a fixed latitude while it grew in size, amassing power.

Citizens along the gulf shores began making sensible preparation for disaster as meteorologists at a safe distance speculated as to where this storm might make landfall. Coastal residents boarded their windows with plywood and purchased bottled water and canned goods from grocery stores until the shelves were bare. The storm added to the overall anxiety by simply hanging there, suspended, harnessing its gales with a calculated awareness. It had not decided yet where to unleash its fury and count bloody coup.

Rain pelted the earth in a flow so steady that it signaled this was just the beginning of a storm to be remembered. Standing in the living room, I watched from one of the windows as gusts of wind howled through the giant oaks in the front yard and whipped the spanish moss into a swaying rag-tag dance. It soon appeared that it was trees that were howling on that afternoon. My image, reflected in the glass, was superimposed over the yard's dark scene as though the winds were wearing my likeness and staring back at me in an odd mockery.

"Mankind creates much in his own image," the man said. I turned and was startled to find him standing behind me.

"Well, that was just an illusion," I explained, referring to my reflection, "we do not create storms. And they are certainly not in our image."

"There is something for you to see," he said.

"Where?"

"St. Marks," he answered. He wanted to go to the beach again.

"Today?" I asked in disbelief, "in this weather?"

He smiled, but did not answer verbally. It was necessary for me to call Craig yet again, and ask him to come home and babysit the kids. This was not an easy phone call.

"What do you mean you have to go to the beach?" he asked.

"I just have to go," I said.

He didn't ask me if I had been seeing things this time. He seemed resigned to the thought that, because he expected no further rational explanations from me, he would ask no further questions.

While I waited for Craig to come home, the man sat in silence once again in the living room. I decided to feed the enormous black and white weaver spider that had somehow made her way into the interspace between the screen and window over the kitchen sink. This was the same window through which I had seen wonders in the past, the window through which I had first seen the gathering of the Indians and Capalfi, and the one through which I saw the yard glow amber one night. The spider had arrived about a week earlier, and since she had chosen this window I assumed that she must be very, very special.

She was quite beautiful, and was fascinating to watch. She sat in the center of her white web each day, hopeful that something might come her way, and each night she rewove her web with renewed hope, never acknowledging her seemingly hopeless situation. Nothing ever came her way, of course, except me.

I offered her parts of thawed insects that I kept on hand to feed the goldfish and the wild baby birds that I sometimes raised. Placing the morsels on a piece of broom straw, I touched them lightly against her web and shook the straw to mimic the movements of a live bug caught in her web. Although she was a bit hesitant to accept my offerings at first, she had, in the course of a week, come to understand what I was doing and seemed to look forward to my luncheon visits.

I was standing in the kitchen sink holding the broom straw with the bug on the end of it when Craig arrived home and walked through the kitchen door.

Had he asked why I was standing in the sink, or why I was shaking a soggy bug on a stick, I could have given him a simple, logical explanation for at least this portion of my day's activities. But he pretended to see nothing out of the ordinary, and did not inquire.

The spider graciously seized her prey and I climbed down, out of the sink.

Once again, Craig did not offer any objections about my afternoon's beach plans, and so I left with my friend.

The roads were devoid of traffic, as most of the area's residents were indoors, out of the storm. But even with the highway to ourselves, it took nearly an hour to drive to St. Marks.

During this entire journey, the man did not speak at all. His eyes were closed, and his head was bowed slightly, but I knew that he was not sleeping. He was thinking. From time to time, he sighed deeply, and I turned my eyes away from the watery road to look at his beautiful profile. I wondered about the cause for his intense thought—was he remembering private moments from his own past, a past that he did not speak of—or was he contemplating the future, which he spoke of only with great care. I wondered what might have called him to journey so deeply within, and in such solitude.

When we arrived at St. Marks, he opened his eyes. The rain had stopped, but the rage in the wind had increased. I parked the car, noting that we were not the only ones visiting the beach on this day. Next to us in a late model, white Pontiac were three white-haired ladies.

The man got out of my car and began walking toward the beach. I followed him, my sweater billowing like a sail as it caught gusts of briny wind.

The huge depression could be seen sitting on the Gulf waters, churning the sea and the air as it grew. Massive cloud arms reached out like tentacles from the nucleus of the storm, and they probed the sky, savoring their own power and pointing accusingly toward their possible land targets.

The beach was strewn with dirty foam and brown seaweed that had been purged from the salt waters. They lay upon the sand, tumbling according to the will of the wind. The beach was also dotted with sticky wads of thick, black petroleum—a common finding—evidence that a craft in some distant place had spilled a portion of its tarry innards into the ocean in yet another accident. Perhaps this accident had not been significant enough to reach the evening news, but the congealed flotsam had been buoyant enough to reach this distant beach. A discarded tire lay on some seaweed, having been disgorged from the sea and sent back to the land. Next to it lay a dead cormorant wearing a plastic six-pack holder around his neck. As it had attempted to free itself, it had placed its foot through another of the plastic rings, and in the struggle, garroted itself.

The man stopped for a moment and looked at the body of

the dead bird, and then walked to the shoreline, facing the winds.

Slowly, with what appeared to be great consciousness and intent, he raised his arms upward then outward. The wind's rage increased, and whipped at his garment as he stood with his arms outstretched.

In a voice that was clear, and could be heard well above the howling, he said, "Behold the work of mankind."

Then he lowered his arms, turned around and looked at me.

The wind was now at his back, its lashing gales tearing at his linen garment and blowing his hair into his face. He did not move to pull his clothing closer to him as I was doing, nor did he attempt to brush the hair from his eyes. He simply stood there looking at me, wind-beaten.

"We didn't create this storm," I shouted, approaching him, "we would never create something like this."

"It is powerful, deadly, and out of control," he said, "and it is created in the image of its maker."

"God?" I asked.

"No—mankind."

"But, no—we don't create storms!" I argued.

I heard the voices of the three white-haired ladies, and turned to see that they were nearby, on the beach. They, too, had come to view the depression. They, too, stopped to look at the dead cormorant. Talking among themselves, they began walking eastward and as they passed us, the third lady slowed until she was several steps behind her two friends.

Separated now from her small party, she looked first at me and then directly at my companion. She smiled, and nodded a silent greeting toward him, looked again at me, and then quickly followed after her two friends.

We began walking through the foam, westward.

"Mankind has become an entity that over-consumes," he said, quietly, "and the byproduct of over-consumption is waste. The waste has created pollution. The pollution has raised the temperatures of the oceans. When the oceans are heated, they in turn create powerful atmospheric reactions."

I had never heard this theory before. It would, in fact, be several years before I would read this identical explanation in a local newspaper, as scientists debated the cause of El Niño. I searched for something to say in defense.

"You understand that the storm is not a punishment for having created too much waste," he said, seemingly aware that I was about to offer another defensive explanation—another why, why, why.

"It is the end result of it—cause and effect."

I felt another shift in perception—this time a big one—as I began finally grasping the meaning of his words. I stopped walking and felt the full effect of the sensation. It was something akin to a dawning of awareness. He was rearranging my perception so that I could finally catch a glimpse of something apparently quite important to him: cause and effect.

"Damn," I said, "look at this mess we've made."

"Tell others," he said.

This time, I made the trip home from St. Marks alone. There were no butterflies in the car with me this time. I turned on the heater and then the windshield wipers as the rain began pouring again, and drove the distance trying to shelter myself from the furious work of mankind.

That night I was awakened by the sounds of rattles and low singing. I opened my eyes to find the room filled with strange, carved figures.

For several minutes I was terrified—I had never seen anything like this crowd of wooden entities before. Then I realized that they were kachinas—beings that the Hopi Indians believe represent essences of energy present and swirling around us in the spirit world.

Thunder spirits, lightning and mountain spirits, water spirits, spirits of living creatures—living essences held sacred by the Hopi, and depicted as kachina dolls were standing in my room.

Some of the costumes were painted in wild and bold sun colors, some in blues and turquoise bearing intricate designs. Some of the figures were holding corn, others were holding objects that I could not identify. Some had square boxes for heads, others oval shapes, and others perfect circles—one appeared to have a squash gourd head, another an eagle's, and one was painted with black and white designs reminiscent of the spider in my kitchen window.

Then I noticed that these kachinas could not be called "dolls." They were all over six feet in height, and they were moving. They were alive. I watched in awe as they moved to the rhythm of a haunting song, the words of which I could not understand, but the energy of which I understood well. This was a song of peace.

In the morning I looked "kachina" up in an encyclopedia to determine if this was, indeed, what I had seen. I found immediate confirmation. I also saw a map of the Hopi homelands, and discovered that my own Arizona destination, Winslow, was a relatively short drive from the Hopi mesas—one of which held their ancient village of Oraibi, in which they had lived continuously for over 1000 years.

Because my Lakota friends, and other friends, were helping me try to understand various aspects of what was happening to me, I reasoned that perhaps the mystical, gifted Hopi could explain why I was now seeing kachinas.

Having placed a very fruitful anonymous phone call only a short while ago to an astronomy department, I now dialed long distance information, and obtained the number of the Hopi Tribe in Arizona. I wrote down a list of questions to ask them, before dialing their phone number.

A gentleman answered the phone.

"Hello," I began, "Last night I woke up and saw that my room was filled with kachinas?" I spoke it as a question rather than a statement.

"Yes," he answered.

"Well, I'm wondering what this means."

"Oh. And you are in the San Francisco area?"

"No, I'm in Florida."

"Florida? Hmm. Well, we've had four calls this week from the San Francisco area."

"Really? About kachinas?"

"Yes," he said, pleasantly, "every year when the kachinas

visit Earth, we get calls from people wanting to know what they are. Were yours the 'big ones' or the 'little ones?'"

"I'm not sure—I've never heard of this before. Mine were over six feet tall—I guess about seven feet tall."

"Oh!" he laughed, "those were the really big ones."

"Well, why were they here?"

"No particular reason. They were just visiting."

"What does this mean, then?"

"Nothing," he said.

The Hopi way of looking at the Universe was clearly different from the way I had previously considered normal, and in spite of my new perceptual abilities, it was beyond my abilities to assume that the visit of the kachinas meant nothing.

"How can this mean nothing?" I said.

"They just like to visit people. Sometimes, when they visit off the reservation, people are startled and they call here."

Perhaps it was the fact that this all seemed so commonplace—that this man was so comfortable with ethereal visitors who just visited because they enjoyed visiting—that I decided to tell him more about my situation.

He listened patiently while I told him about lights, shells, pottery, rocks, the Adongohela, and my nose.

"I'm going to travel out there to the desert in a few days," I said, finally. "Do you think it might be possible for someone from the Hopi tribe to meet briefly with me and at least look at some of these stones?"

"Why are you coming to the desert?" he asked.

"I don't know exactly, but I'm going to stand there, alone."

"And—I mean no disrespect, I'm merely curious—you're a white woman?"

"Sort of—I used to be. I'm not sure what I am anymore, or what is going on here, but the way I see it, if anyone can figure this all out, it's the Hopis."

He laughed, "Well, I'm not sure about the explanations, but I guess I can meet with you briefly when you get here."

I thanked him profusely.

He gave me his work number, and the number for his home, where he lived with his wife and children on one of the mesas.

—6—

Facing West

 The spider wove a new web each day, and from time to time, she shed her skin, simply stepping out of her old skin and letting it fall, empty, to the window sill. I thought that it would be necessary for me to take the screen off and send her out into wild freedom before I left for the desert because there would be no one to feed her. But, on the morning of my departure, when I looked for her, I discovered that she had vanished. I placed the last of her beautiful discarded skins in with the butterflies.

This marked the beginning of a somber day.

I had tried to prepare my children for my departure, but because I had never before been away from them for any length of time, they were unable to comprehend the meaning of my "leaving for a while."

My previous times away from them had merely been small blocks of time—occasional afternoon lunches with my mother, and lately, my trips to St. Marks.

They were completely comfortable with my leaving until

the four of us arrived at the bus depot. Carrying a flight bag that contained a change or two of clothing, I stood in front of the bus and fought back tears. I told them I loved them, and that they should be good little children until I returned in a few days. A hint of apprehension came over their faces, but they agreed to be good, and we hugged and kissed.

Then I climbed the steps and entered the very large, older vintage bus, and took a window seat where I could see them. I could see that they were still staring at the door that I had just walked through, and Craig pointed their attention up to the window from which I was waving.

John's eyes grew wide as he saw me on the other side of the window, and suddenly he screamed in terror and anguish as the full impact of my leaving set in. From his perspective, his universe was unraveling before him. His tears were profuse. Craig tried to restrain him, and glanced at me briefly. I think I heard his thoughts that day. I think he was thinking, are you sure all of this is necessary?

Emily, seeing John's distress, also became distressed, and stood holding her father's hand, crying.

It was this sight—of my two children pointing at the bus and crying hysterically—that burned itself forever into my mind as the near-empty bus pulled away from the depot.

The seat that I selected was lumpy and the space between it and the seat in front could not accommodate the length of my legs. After a moment, I walked across the aisle, and selected a less-lumpy window seat, this time on the driver's side of the bus.

There was still not enough space between the seats, and so I had a choice of pressing my knees firmly against the metal back of the seat in front of me, or turning to the side and stretching my legs out. Turning to the side was preferable, and I sat sideways and comfortable for a moment before a woman from the back of the bus also decided to change seats. Inexplicably, she came forward and selected the unoccupied seat next to me. She was carrying a large purse, a tabloid newspaper, and a throw pillow. I was forced to pull my legs in, and sit up straight and jammed so that she could sit down.

Trying to ignore her, I looked out the window. Holding a Polaroid of the kids in my lap, I cried silently. I wondered, as the scenery flew past and the sun eventually grew low on the horizon opposite my view, what the kids were doing now, and now, and now.

"Oh, honey," the woman finally said, putting her tabloid newspaper down, "you must be the mom of those children, right?"

Pulled out of my thoughts, I looked at her and saw that she was not reading my mind, but was pointing at the photograph in my lap.

"Yes," I answered.

"Is this your first time away from them?"

"Yes," I answered again.

"Don't you worry," she said, whispering as though she were telling me a secret, "everything will be okay, and you'll be back home sooner than you think."

She opened her oversized brocade purse, and removed a large bundle of tinfoil wrapped in paper towels. She pulled the wrappings apart, and offered me a piece of the fried chicken that she had been carrying.

I thanked her for her kindness, and for offering to share supper with me, but declined the chicken. I explained that I had a serious deficiency requiring strict adherence to a diet of fish and seaweed—although the seaweed wasn't agreeing with me.

She nodded as though she had heard of this diet before; as though she were familiar with this particular type of deficiency, and started in on the chicken.

Also in her purse were soft drinks for two, a bag of chips, and fudge brownies—all of which she offered to share with me, but I just wasn't in the mood to dine that night. I rested my head back and closed my eyes for a while, listening to an occasional crunch of a chip, as she ate in solitude.

A short while later, she wrapped the uneaten portions of the meal up, returned everything to her purse and settled back into her chair, folding her arms over the purse.

"Enjoy the peace and quiet now," she said, "because we'll start picking up passengers at the next stop. By about midnight, the bus'll be full. Won't be a vacant seat anywhere," she said.

"Do you make this trip often?" I asked. She seemed to know the finer details of its schedules.

"No," she said, closing her eyes. Then, suddenly, she fell asleep.

Evening approached, giving the promise of full closure to this day at last. I tried to read a book as we made numerous stops until the bus was filled to capacity. I put the book down when I realized that I had read twenty-three pages without any recollection of what I'd read. My seatmate slept through everything, including stops in which all the overhead bus lights, with the blinding wattage, were unmercifully turned on.

I don't know how long it had been present on the far horizon before I noticed it, but long after the bus began rolling westward again, I looked once more out the dark window to my left and was stunned by what I saw. Rising slowly up from the glimmering black waters of a nameless harbor was Orion, his straight belt of three stars readily identifying him.

Nearby was a huge amber planet, and I wondered briefly if it was Jupiter.

The water above which Orion rose was glowing with a promise of something else that would soon rise from the bay and take its place next to Orion. I wondered what it might be.

When I looked again through the window into the night, I saw the cause of the glow and the promise fulfilled.

There, rising with slow and majestic patience just west of Orion, was the largest harvest moon of the century. An eerie sense of déjà vu came over me, and I realized that I had dreamed about the scene I was now viewing, as well as about Joseph Two Horse and Tioco, the night before.

I watched the moon until it was high in the black space of the night, and tried to remember the details of the dream. I remembered only that Joseph was traveling again, traveling in search of something that he must find, but I could not remember what it was.

That night I was awakened by the sound of an old woman

singing. She was singing a strange song consisting of ten notes, the first seven identical, the last three lowered and deep. I looked around at my traveling companions to see who was singing, but everyone else was asleep.

Shifting positions in my cramped seat, I realized with horror that the sound was coming from me. I shifted again. It was coming from my chest. I hoped, first, that I had not somehow sprung an inner leak due to the cramped seat, but I did not feel the presence of an injury. I took several deep breaths, but breathing did not alter the sound of the woman singing.

She continued to sing, her song flowing from my chest.

I had placed several stones in my bra prior to leaving: the sandstone carving from the desert, a strange triangular stone with carved designs on it, and several of the white stones that had fallen out of the air. I wondered if the sounds of this song might be coming from the stones. Maybe stones do strange things when it is dark and everyone is sleeping, I thought. It was as good an explanation as any.

The woman continued singing, and my next hope was that the sound would not awaken the lady sitting next to me—or the other passengers.

The song was repeated three times, and then the old woman was, thankfully, quiet again. At some point, I fell asleep.

In the morning, the lady with the fried chicken awoke refreshed, and clearly ready to begin a new day.

"Are you feeling a little better this morning?" she asked.

"Yes, ma'am," I said. I was feeling better emotionally, but my knees were badly bruised.

"Well, you just remember what I told you," she said, reaching into her bag for her lipstick. She put the lipstick on, reclosed her purse, and in a moment, the bus made another stop.

"Everything will be all right," she said with a smile. Then she stood up, and walked off the bus.

With the seat next to me finally empty again, I was able to stretch out a little.

My stretch would only last a few hours.

The scenery outside changed to the flat and short-brushed shrub look of desert territory. We were still far from Arizona, but hints of the awaiting desert were visible even now. For one long stretch of road, the bus seemed to be suspended in midair, making sounds as though miles were passing but the flat and blurred scenery made it seem as though we were standing still.

Up ahead, to the right of the highway, I could see a very small village that consisted of a few modest houses. The bus began to slow, and we pulled onto the village road and stopped in front of a one-room adobe depot.

A native man wearing a blanket was sitting on the front stoop, sleeping. Hearing the bus, he awoke and stood up. When the bus doors opened, he climbed up the steps. He was conventionally dressed with the exception of that blanket, which now hung over one shoulder.

He was a young man—a sun-worshiper no doubt, or perhaps a man whose job kept him in the field. His skin was deeply tanned. He was quite tall and fit, his hair long and black, and his face was handsomely chiseled.

He did not chose a seat for himself immediately, but stood in the doorway of the bus for a moment looking carefully at the passengers. He bent over and spoke briefly to the bus driver, listened to his answer, and then stood up and looked again at the passengers. Our eyes met for a second, and then he selected a seat five rows in front of mine, directly behind the driver.

When the bus started moving again, the man with the blanket stood up. He left his seat, and began slowly making his way down the aisle, smiling.

Our eyes met again briefly, and an irrational warning sounded its bells in my head. A premonition that something of a very extraordinary nature was about to occur leapt into my mind.

I quickly looked away from the man's eyes, and out the window next to me. He continued his slow walk down the aisle—I could see him with my peripheral vision—and he paused for a moment behind each seat as he passed it.

A paradox of feelings washed through me. I was filled with great anticipation and stark terror. I also felt trapped.

I fixed my eyes on the passing lack of scenery, hoping that if I avoided this man's eyes, which I could feel boring into me, perhaps he would keep walking past my seat. Perhaps he was merely heading toward the restroom facilities in the back of the bus.

He walked past seat three, and paused, still staring. I felt my heart begin to pound.

The bus rumbled on and my eyes remained locked on the yellow sands outside.

He walked past seat four and paused, and then he stood next to the seat in front of mine, pausing as he had done at all the others. A second passed, and then another. He wasn't pausing. He was stopping.

I glanced over quickly, and saw that he was looking down at me.

I looked back out the window.

He stood there without speaking for a moment, watching me, waiting for me to acknowledge his presence. When I did not do so, he spoke.

"Greetings," he said, grinning, pronouncing the word slowly as though he had chosen it carefully for this moment. It was an odd thing to say. "Hello," would have been better, certainly more normal. I pretended not to hear him.

"Would you mind if I sat down and talked to you for a moment?" he asked, pointing at the empty seat next to me.

I continued to stare out the window.

"I think you're the one I've been looking for," he said. "There's something I'm supposed to tell you. Can we talk?" he said.

I was grateful for the white buzzing sound that was once again protecting me from words. With any luck, it would grow even louder so that I would be unable to hear anything this stranger said. I continued my fixed gaze out the window, my face suddenly hot and flushed.

"It will only take a moment," he said.

I remained staring. The man bent over, leaned on the empty seat with his hand until his head was only inches from mine, and then he whispered, "I'm Joseph."

I felt my eyes widen in disbelief, and turned to look at him with what must have been a bizarre expression, because he laughed. He took this as an invitation to sit down, and seated himself next to me, offering me his hand. Reluctantly, I shook it.

"I'm Mary," I said.

He nodded, smiling.

"And Mary has seen something that she can't explain, hasn't she?" he said, skipping over anything that might have been normally expected as an introduction, and referring to me oddly in the third person.

"What do I look like, some sort of a nut?" I asked, nervous and offended, "You just walk back here and ask me if I've been seeing things?"

"No, no," he answered, completely serious for a moment as he mulled this over, and then in a slight accent he said, "no nut, no nut! You look like . . . how do they call it? Miss America."

Still serious, he looked at me to see if this was an adequate apology.

I could not keep a straight face, and tried to hide my laughter from him. He laughed as well, seemingly happy to see me enjoying his humor, and then he stopped laughing.

"But you have seen something, haven't you?" he said, dark eyes serious once again, "And now you're going to the desert. You think you will find something there—answers."

I quickly reviewed the list of people who knew which bus I would be boarding and at what time of the day. No one except my parents, husband, and kids knew of my actual departure time. Not Fred, not my Hopi friend, and not even Craig's colleagues knew. And not one of us, including myself, knew that I would be passing through a small, nameless desert village where someone named Joseph would be sitting on a porch step, waiting for a certain bus carrying a certain passenger.

No one except Joseph, that is.

He was not at all put off that I had once again become mute, and was ignoring his questions while running through my list of impossibilities about this situation.

"May I see your right hand?" he asked.

In the palm of my right hand there is a small, white triangle that I awakened with one morning when I was fifteen years old. He looked closely at my hand, and then pointed out the triangle, tapping it as though he had made an important evidential discovery. "Yes, you're the one. I knew you were the one as soon as I saw you."

"The one what?"

"The one I was sent here to find. I've traveled a long way to find you."

"What are you talking about?"

"I was in Germany when I received the message that you would be leaving soon for the desert. We weren't sure at first who it was going to be. I was hoping that I would be selected, but it was you."

"I don't understand what you are saying," I said, and then repeated, "what are you talking about?"

"You were selected for this. I was sent here to see that you arrive in the desert safely." Then he grinned as though he was enjoying the entire situation, "It's an honor to be here."

He noticed the photograph of the kids that was still in my lap, lying on top of the book I wasn't really interested in reading.

"May I?" he asked.

I handed the picture to him. He looked at it briefly, nodded, and handed it back.

"You are the mother of a high priest."

"I am?"

"Yes."

"My son is a high priest?"

"Your daughter is a high priest. Why did you not bring her with you?"

"Well, my God, she's not even five years old yet!"

"Age. What is age. Counting days is meaningless. She sees as you see, and you are to teach her everything that is taught to you. This is important. Do not think that she is merely a child, and do not leave her behind again."

"And my son?" I asked, because he, too, was clearly able to "see."

"Both chose to be a part of this."

"A part of what, exactly? What is all of this about?"

Perhaps I had finally reached a well-deserved and overdue state of sensory overload, because I do not recall anything more of my very, very long conversation with Joseph that day and night, except that he spoke about space and light, the stars, the sun—and he recited in eerie detail excerpts from *Harvest Moon.*

The following morning at eight forty-five, the bus pulled into a McDonald's just outside of Phoenix. As the people climbed out of the bus, I appeared to be the only one who noticed that we were disembarking in total darkness. The sun had not yet risen, and stars were still glimmering in the black, black sky.

I followed Joseph into the fluorescent-lit restaurant where we bought some coffee. He was quiet this morning, pensive. Everyone seemed pensive. And yet, no one seemed to be wondering about the state of darkness surrounding us.

"Joseph," I said, finally, "don't you notice anything unusual going on here this morning?"

"Like what?" he asked.

"Look at your watch."

He looked at it and nodded.

"Well, where is the sun this morning?"

He smiled and pointed toward the bus driver who was still standing in the middle of the parking lot in what appeared to be a daze. He was no longer wearing his hat.

"Why don't you go and ask him," Joseph suggested, "go ahead—go ask the driver where the sun is."

I walked outside to the driver. He was a tall, slender man with gray hair. He looked slightly disheveled and perplexed. I wondered why he was simply standing in the parking lot, by himself.

"Excuse me, sir, but do you notice anything strange happening here?"

He rubbed his forehead—my question appeared to have troubled him—and he replied, "No, everything is all right—fine," he said, now rubbing his chin, "just fine."

"But, it's almost nine A.M.," I said, "and the sun hasn't risen yet."

He looked at his watch, rubbed his forehead again leaving a shock of gray hair standing on end, and then looked up and stared at the stars in the dark sky for a long moment.

"Well," he said, "it has been unseasonably cold lately."

I turned to walk away from the driver and find Joseph, feeling as though I had just entered, passed through, or become a new permanent resident of the Twilight Zone, but as I turned around I saw that Joseph was now standing behind me, smiling. He raised his coffee cup in a gesture of cheers.

He took my arm and escorted me back to the bus. We were the first ones to re-board. We took our seats.

"Well, what did he say?" he asked, still smiling.

"He said they've been having unusual weather here."

Joseph laughed. "Well, don't worry about it."

"But where's the sun?"

"Mary," he said, taking my hand, his smile seemed almost perpetual, "the sun is fine. There is nothing to worry about. So stop worrying, will you? Everything will be okay, and the sun will be here very soon."

Just before we reached Phoenix, the lost sun rose.

Joseph accompanied me to the rental car dealership where the car I had reserved awaited me. He did not like the car that had been pre-selected for me, however, so he canceled that particular rental and, carrying my bag, directed me to a rental company of his own choosing up the street. When he found what he felt was a more suitable car—a more durable and sturdy vehicle—he placed my bags in the back seat.

He had completed his mission.

"Well, where are you going?" I asked.

"I don't know. Wherever I'm sent." he said.

He looked at me for a moment, and then he hugged me.

"I love you," he said, this man whom I met only yesterday, and there were tears in his eyes that seemed to confirm his emotional claim. "I wish I could go with you."

"Really? Do you really want to come?" I asked, suddenly grateful to have someone—even a stranger—accompany me on this increasingly odd trip.

"No, I'd best not. You are supposed to go alone."

"How do you know?" I asked.

"I'm not supposed to accompany you beyond this point."

I knew that there would be nothing I could say to change Joseph's mind.

"All right," I said, "but as far as I'm concerned, you're welcome to come with me. If you change your mind," I said, "I'll be staying somewhere in Winslow."

"If I need to find you, I will," he replied.

He began to walk away from me, but then stopped and came back. He took my right hand in both of his. "Mary?" he said.

"Yes?"

"You are going to be given an invitation to do something."

"Like what?"

"Something very unusual—something that will help provide answers to some unanswered questions."

"Well, I'm not going to do anything dangerous or scary," I warned.

Joseph laughed. "You don't have anything to be afraid of— try not to be afraid, okay?"

"Okay."

"I'd like to ask you to do something for me."

"Okay."

"When you see them," he said, looking down at his hands, which were still holding my own hand, "will you give them a message for me?"

"Yes," I said, not knowing to whom or what he was referring, but I did not wish to reveal my ignorance.

"Tell them that Joseph is still here. Tell them that Joseph is still waiting."

He then said good-bye and left.

I have never seen or heard from him since, and am still pondering the meaning of his message.

I drove to Winslow, stopping first to see the great meteor crater, which I walked around, marveling at the unbelievable hole it punched into the Earth. Then I purchased several meteor chips from the Meteor Crater Gift Shop for the purpose of placing them under my pillow to see where that might take me.

After renting a room, and freshening up a bit from my long

ride, drive, and hike around the meteor, I went to a restaurant, famished. There, I discovered that it is not easy to find fish and seaweed in the desert.

Luckily, the menu offered a shrimp cocktail, which I then ordered.

After nearly an hour passed, I was served a large soup bowl filled to the brim with ketchup.

Strategically arranged in such a way to remind me that I was now in the Four Corners region, were four tiny, pale shrimp that were possible remnants from the time when the desert just outdoors had once been a sea.

They had waited many, many years to be thawed for this occasion—thawed so that they might be served to someone who would one day travel west to a desert and then order seafood.

"Enjoy," the waiter said.

"Thank you," I replied.

When I returned to my room, I called home to speak to my children. They had calmed down, of course, but were greatly relieved to hear my voice, and to receive another reassurance that I would be back home with them "soon."

Then I called my parents, told my father about the meteor crater, and told my mother about Joseph of the Bus. Although I was now quickly approaching my fortieth birthday, she told me that I should be more careful about speaking to strangers.

I explained to her that traveling on a bus is like no other type of travel—there are no strangers. Everyone somehow becomes related, until it is time, one by one, stop by stop, for each person to climb back down the steps and disembark.

I wrote about my meeting with Joseph in the same spiral-bound notebook that I wrote in about the stones, the roses, the detailed dreams, and the man in the sphere—the being of light.

I looked forward to my tomorrow, my first day alone in the desert. That night I dreamed of some of the places that I would visit.

The following morning, I awoke just after dawn, famished again. Looking out my sliding glass doors, I saw that, conveniently, on the opposite side of the parking lot, there was a McDonald's—a place where I could order fish! Fish wasn't served until lunchtime, however, so I ordered an Egg McMuffin, instructing them not to put the meat on it, and a coffee, instructing them to put a few ice cubes in it. Then I drove off into the desert.

Not far from the main highway, I passed a man standing on the right side of the road thumbing a ride, and wondered if it was desert etiquette to pick up hitchhikers. After a few moments, I stopped the car, turned around, and drove back. He had crossed the road and was once again on my right, now thumbing a ride in the opposite direction. I drove past him, listening to a cautionary note within. All was not right here.

After I was out of his range of sight, I stopped and sipped the lukewarm coffee, thinking about this. First he was thumbing a ride into the desert. Then he was thumbing a ride into Winslow. I did not wish to appear rude to the people of this area, but there was something spooky about him.

I waited a few minutes and then headed again toward the desert on the same road.

The man had crossed the road again, and was on my right, thumbing a ride out into the desert—but there was something different about him, something strange about his face.

I slowed the car slightly so that I could see his face, and as I looked at it, it grew very, very dark. It grew impossibly dark, as though he had been slowly over-baked in a harsh and hellish oven. Then, to my utter horror, it changed its shape. My eyes grew wide as I saw this, and the man broke out into laughter, his smile framed by jagged coyote teeth. He lowered his thumb. He knew that I was not going to pick him up after witnessing this. He knew that I had seen him change.

I stepped on the gas and roared down the road, dry-mouthed. In the rearview mirror, I could see that the man was still laughing, and was waving at me. I needed a glass of water.

A mile passed, and then another, and I was irrationally afraid to look in the rearview mirror again, afraid that I would see the man with the strange face still behind me, still following. A gas station appeared up ahead on the left of the road. I pulled into it, heart still pounding. A Navajo man walked over to my car.

"Fill it, please," I said.

I must have looked rattled, because he asked me if I was okay.

"Yes," I said, "I'm okay, it's just that I saw something terrible. There was a man back there a few miles, and he was hitching a ride. I was going to pick him up, but—this is weird—well, something horrible happened to his face."

The attendant stared at me.

"What happened to his face?"

"It baked and cracked, and his nose got real big—and then his whole face changed into something else—with big teeth!"

"Well, why didn't you pick him up?"

"I . . . it frightened me!"

"Scared, scared, scared." he smiled, "Always frightened. You white people come out here, looking for adventures and mystical experiences, and you all wind up getting scared. You got this nice car, and that poor guy is standing out in the sun baking. And you just leave him there because he got a big nose."

I was offended by this. I was much, much more than just a "white person."

He began washing the windshield, and I got out of the car and went into the dusty convenience store. Inside, I bought a small styrofoam cooler, a little ice, a bottle of water, and a few soft drinks—in case my mouth went dry again in the desert. I put everything in the cooler, and returned to the car. After I got in with the goods, the man started in on me again.

"So I bet you're heading out to visit the Hopi, right?"

"Well, not today, maybe tomorrow, but yes, that's part of my plan."

"You got mystical stuff to discuss, right?"

"Well, something strange has been happening in my life—how'd you know?"

"The Hopi—everyone comes to visit the Hopi when they start seeing things, 'cause everyone knows the Hopi are mystical. No one ever comes to visit us, though."

I gave him the money for the gasoline. He took the money and leaned on the car's open window. He wasn't finished yet.

"Why don't you go back there and pick that man up?" he said. "I bet he's still standing there, waiting for you."

"Really? Do you think I should do that?" I asked, feeling a little guilty about having been so easily and thoroughly spooked.

"Sure. Go back and let him into your car."

"Okay," I said, grasping the steering wheel, and starting the engine.

The man reached into the car and put his hand on my left hand.

"Look, lady, I'm just joking. You stay away from him."

"Do you know him? Who is he?"

"No, I don't know him. But I know what you saw."

I looked blankly at him, waiting for him to finish—to explain.

"You don't even know, do you?" he asked, and then shook his head. Something bordering on alarm washing over his face for a short moment.

"No," I said, "know what?"

"What you saw was a shapeshifter. That's how come I knew were probably on your way to talk things over with the Hopi. If you got shapeshifters on your trail, lady, you'd better be careful."

"Okay," I said. The hairs were standing up on the back of my neck. I had never heard of "shapeshifters" before this day when I saw one.

"Be careful who you talk to. Be careful who you let in your car."

I nodded, wondering how much trouble I was close to getting myself into.

"There is an old woman who lives by herself in a hogan," he said, "she is my auntie—you should go and talk to her. She doesn't speak English, but that's okay."

He began to give me directions to the old woman's house—desert directions.

"Go that way for a while," he said, pointing to the horizon on the other side of the highway, "till you come to a big hill.

Then go around the hill, and there's a dirt road that hooks over to the right. On the right hand side of the road, there's a wire fence with some corn and sunflowers behind it. After you pass the corn and sunflowers, a ditch runs through the road. You'll see some sheep—and her hogan. You go talk to her. She'll help you."

I thanked the man for his help, and drove away with no intention whatsoever of visiting the old woman who spoke no English. It would be, obviously, impossible for me to communicate with anyone who spoke no English.

As I drove along the empty highway, I noticed from time to time that there were tire tracks occasionally crisscrossing the sand beyond the asphalt, and as the afternoon wore on, I took this as an invitation to leave the roads behind and explore the area more thoroughly in my sturdy rental vehicle.

I drove many miles into the sandy wilderness, stopping the car from time to time so that I might get out, stand still and face (hopefully) west, wondering if I was satisfactorily fulfilling my call to come here and "stand alone." Then, after standing in numerous spots, I got back in the car and took off again.

About a half hour after my last stop, something in the distance caught my eye, and I wondered what it was. I decided to drive closer and investigate. Without bothersome roads to redirect me into one direction after another, I headed directly across the sand, and approached the object rather quickly.

As I got closer and closer, I saw that the object appeared to be a human being. Closer still, and the human being raised his right arm out level with his body, thumb upward.

It was a human being thumbing a ride. In the middle of the desert.

A wave of horror hit me, but I was also very curious. I wanted to know if this was the shapeshifter.

With clouds of yellow dust marking my trail behind me, as I approached the lone figure, I saw that it was not the same man I had previously encountered. This was an elderly Navajo gentleman. He stared straight ahead with his arm extended, as though desert rules suggest that it is impolite to make eye contact with a prospective driver while they are deciding whether to stop or not. He stood there absolutely motionless. I wondered how long the poor man had been wandering around out here, and pulled the car up next to him.

I pressed the button that rolled the window down on the passenger side, and he stepped toward the car.

"Winslow?" he asked through the open window.

"Yes," I answered. It was time to be getting back, anyway. "Winslow," I said.

He got into the back seat of the car. I offered him one of my cold soft drinks, but he declined.

As we drove along, I began a solitary dialogue about who I was and where I was going, and after several moments passed, I saw that the man was looking out his window, not listening to me.

It took several more miles of conversation before I discovered that he did not speak English.

"Winslow?" he asked again.

"Yes," I answered, reassuring him, "Winslow."

He tapped me on the shoulder and pointed to the horizon on the left.

"Winslow," he said.

We had taken a nice ride, but I was heading in the wrong direction.

I turned the car around and began driving through the sand toward town, and he tapped me on the shoulder again. I looked at him—it's okay to look at passengers in the back seat while driving across the desert.

"Tioco," he said, "me Tioco."

There was no adequate response for me to give to this statement, so I just stared at him for a moment with my mouth open. It suddenly seemed to make some sort of absurd sense. I should have known that wherever Joseph was, Tioco was sure to be close by.

I finally located a paved road again, and then the highway that would take us into town.

When we arrived in Winslow, the man repeated again and again the only words in English he seemed to be able to speak, "Me Tioco. Me Tioco. Me Tioco."

Several times I responded, "Yes, I know. You're Tioco, and I'm Mary," but he did not appear satisfied with this response from me, and continued to repeat even louder, "Me Tioco!"

I stopped the car a few times, and said, "Winslow," not knowing where in Winslow he wanted to get out, but he remained seated at each of my stops.

He began pointing out streets for me to take, and I followed his suggested path, winding through several blocks of the small town until we approached an intersection where a gas station was located.

He pointed at the gas station, and shouted in my right ear, "ME TIOCO!"—which caused me to put my foot on the brake.

Stopping, I looked at the large star on the sign, and the letters next to it spelling out the name of the proprietor. The sign read, "Mike's Texaco."

I read this out loud, and the elderly gentleman patted me on the shoulder and flashed a smile.

"Mike's Texaco?" I asked again.

The old man nodded, happy to have arrived at his destination, "yeh, Me Tioco."

I pulled into the Me Tioco gas station and the elder got out of the car, greeting several of his very delighted grandchildren. Mike himself came to my window.

"Oh! I see you gave Grandpa a lift! Thanks for stopping for him," he said.

"You're welcome," I answered, somewhat dazed by the day's various events, "but you should know that he was out all by himself in the middle of the desert!"

"Yes," Mike laughed, "that's where Grandpa catches his rides into town."

"No," I said, "there were no roads where he was standing—he was out in the middle of nowhere, just standing in the sand!"

Mike laughed again.

"When Grandpa wants to come into town, he waits there for lost tourists."

Thus ended what I perceived to be a very good encounter with Joseph and Tioco.

That night, after I fell asleep, I followed the desert directions given to me by the Navajo man at the first gas station that I visited, and I visited Auntie.

I found her hogan exactly as he had described it. Entering it, I found her sitting quietly at the kitchen table. She stood up when she saw me, and walked to a wooden shelf against the wall that held numerous mason jars of various sizes. I did not see which jars she opened, but in a moment, she returned to the table in the dimly lit room. In a stone bowl, she began to burn the leaves and trimmings of several dried plants. A strange fragrance—new to me, and beautiful—wafted up from the red sparks. We had a very pleasant visit, although we never spoke a word. When the powder of the burned trimmings was long cold, I left.

The next day, I drove again into the desert and decided to pay a visit to the area known as the Little Painted Desert.

Following a map, as well as signs on the road, I rambled along for a while before finally reaching my destination. "X" marked the spot on the map, and a large sign in front of the car indicated that this was, indeed, the Little Painted Desert.

The problem was, from where I sat in my car, there was nothing to indicate anything new in the surroundings. The horizon in all directions around me remained the same—flat.

I sat there for a few minutes, wondering why one portion of the desert that looked exactly like the rest of the desert should have received a name distinguishing it. Finally got out of the car in order to read the finer print on the sign.

That was when I saw it—the Little Painted Desert. It was not jutting up from the horizon. It was down, below the horizon.

One must stand on the edge of the desert surrounding the Little Painted Desert and look down in order to see this wonder.

It is a strange and ancient place. I stood alone on the rim and looked into the canyons and archways of stone that had been carved by water and wind.

The corridors and caverns that once held a sea, held fish, and held water's promise of life were now waterless canals, haunted by the wind with its moans and whispers. There was much to whisper about here. This was a long-dead sea, a place of secrets. This was a desert within a desert.

It was there, while I stood alone looking down into the home where the wind now lived, that a shadow fell upon the rainbow hues of the canyons below me. At first I thought it was the shadow of a cloud.

The canyons turned orange, and then dark, as the shadow increased in size until it covered the entire desert below, painting it now with phantom hues. When it had finished with the Little Painted Desert, the shadow continued to grow, climbing with slow ease up the steep and jagged canyon walls.

Rising, it began to spread outward, claiming for itself the desert on which I was standing, as well as the desert down below. It spread like liquid over the sands.

Suddenly, as I stood there in the semi-darkness, my eyes fixed on the shadow at my feet, I became aware of the object that was causing this massive shadow.

Something was descending slowly and without a sound downward from the sky overhead, and it was now hovering, still silent, above me.

It was impossibly large, filling the sky, and I was afraid to look up, to look directly at it. Even though my eyes were looking down at the now-shaded sand, I could discern that the object was an enormous sphere, and at the core of this sphere was a black lens—an eye. I dared not even glance at this eye.

It was the eye of something that was larger than the desert and larger than the Earth itself. It was dwarfing and cupping my horizons within its own massive horizons. I knew instinctively that I must not look up—that some things are better left unseen—that if I looked up, I would see too much.

I would see Jupiter.

I had never seen anything this large before in my life. Emily's own attempt to describe something that she too had seen, came to my mind, and her words helped me for a moment as I stood there alone, in the presence of something too big to look at.

This was the biggest of all big things.

And it was blue.

It seemed to be offering an unspoken invitation. It seemed to be saying, "Look!"

Some of my instincts were very strong on that day, however. I knew that if I did as it wished—if I looked at Jupiter descending to touch the Earth—that I would fall upward, into it.

Terrified, I took a small, hesitant step toward my car—a mouse step, hoping that Jupiter would not notice—hoping that it would not read my mind and pluck me up off the desert sands in the midst of my planned escape. I took another small step, and it made no moves to grab me.

Realizing this, I burst into full speed, and ran to my car, jumped in and locked the doors.

If this was the invitation that Joseph of the Bus had told me I would receive, then it was being extended to the wrong person. I did not wish to fall into the eye of Jupiter on this day. I did not want to go for a ride through space. I wanted to return home to Emily and John, and make pies and cakes and peanut-butter sandwiches. I wanted to do just about anything but fall upward.

With certain mercy, the object acknowledged my terror and honored it.

It rose slowly back into the heavens, and the strange eclipse ended. The sun returned, first filling the horizons with its light, then the surrounding desert. I watched as the light took the place of shadow on the ground, and then my car. Then it flowed, presumably, into the canyons which were just up ahead, and below. I was not about to get out and check.

Still shaking, still careful not to look up, but to keep my eyes fixed down and on the desert in front of me, I started the car and drove as quickly as possible back to Winslow and the safety of my motel room.

I did not bother to eat that night, I couldn't. Nor did I bother to change into my night clothes. I would keep my jeans on in case I needed to make another fast getaway—in case Jupiter came visiting again. I bolted the doors, pulled the drapes tightly closed, and with every light in my room on, I kept watch from my post in an old ochre Naugahyde chair, watched TV, and drank a half a bottle of wine.

Morning came without further incident.

I felt an odd and unique sensation on this new day, the day after my encounter with Jupiter.

It was a sensation bordering on fearlessness. So far on this trip, I had managed to survive an encounter with a shapeshifter. Lost in the desert, I had received directions back to town from a man who spoke no English. And just the day before, I had lived through an encounter with the biggest of the big—without a hint of permanent scarring. I reasoned that I might quite possibly be capable of experiencing all sorts of events, and I felt wonderful and full of a new desire for adventure.

I decided to phone the Hopi man who was, no doubt, waiting for my call.

Telephoning him that morning from my motel room, he invited me to come to the Hopi reservation mid-afternoon where we would rendezvous in front of a coffeehouse.

The Hopi reservation, located on mesas out in the middle of the desert, is about a hundred miles from Winslow, so I allowed myself an additional forty-five minutes traveling time for getting lost.

I would need every minute.

Although I had made a weak promise to myself to stay on the roads this time, as I drove along the desert road an odd structure caught my eye. I immediately drove off the road to investigate.

Driving slowly across the sand, I pulled up in front of the structure.

It was a large abandoned building, ancient and strange, and it had been constructed of what appeared to be sandstone bricks. The windows and doorways, gaping and black, were T-shaped, much wider at the top than at the bottom, as though something had lived there once which needed special accommodations while passing from room to room.

I emerged from the car and photographed the structure.

Then, knowing that I'd soon be in Hopiland where photographs are not permitted, I put the camera back in the car, and zipped it into my flight bag. Then I approached the ancient structure. There were no footprints in the sand but my own, and I wondered how long the place had stood barren and unvisited. My stomach churned as I debated whether to advance closer—to step through this peculiar door—or to, more sensibly, return to my car and leave. I stepped closer.

A palpable sense of an age long gone suddenly filled the air, and I realized that I was standing in front of an Anasazi home. Even more phenomenal, I realized that I was standing on a threshold. It was a strange threshold where I might step forward and enter the past, or I could chose to step backward and reenter the present.

Suddenly, before I could make a decision, there was a loud commotion inside the building, and something large and black darted out of the doorway and flew directly toward my head. It was a crow, the strangest crow I had ever seen. While it's ebony body glistened Moroccan blue—as black sometimes does when caught in the light of the sun—the crow's head was feathered in pure white.

He called out loudly eight times, seeming intent to land upon my head, or perhaps just dance on it. I ducked and retreated to the car where I found myself completely disoriented. I was unable to remember how to get back to the road. So thorough was the disorientation that it took me several moments to realize that all I had to do was follow my own car tracks, which I then did.

It took me three hours to make the hundred mile trip to the Hopi reservation.

As I approached the reservation, the feelings of déjà vu became increasingly powerful. I was recognizing everything around me.

The Hopi gentleman, Allan, met me in front of the cafe where we then had a cup of coffee. He listened and I talked. He was, once again, a patient listener as I described the strange things I had been seeing: the déjà vu, the man in the sphere of light, and my unexplained encounters.

"And you know that abandoned stone building that's about forty miles outside of Winslow?" I asked, talking non-stop, jumping from subject to subject.

He looked puzzled.

"You must know it—it's spectacular. It's an old Anasazi structure that can be seen from the road."

He still looked puzzled.

"Well, anyway," I said, "I don't understand the meaning of that crow that lives there—the crow with the white head. Is it someone's pet or something? Or is it a guardian?"

"I don't know anything about such a crow," he said, and then added, "and I don't know anything about the building you're referring to."

After the coffee break, we drove around the reservation in his truck. As we did I, saw a vegetable garden that I recognized. Then I saw a house that I recognized.

"I've seen all this," I said, still amazed.

He did not appear to be amazed.

"That house there, can you describe what's inside?" he asked.

I described the contents, including the placement of furniture.

He nodded his head. "Yeah, that's correct. It's my brother's house."

We came upon a man and woman working in a field of short corn—a scene that I remembered very well. The man was wearing a bright red shirt, and a blue bandana around his shoulder-length hair. The bandana was knotted at the side. He looked up, said something to the woman standing nearby, and they both waved. I returned their greeting and they laughed. This was the scene that I had recorded in the spiral notebook several months earlier.

"See," my friend said, "they recognize you."

"How?"

"Oh, you been coming here in your dreams," he said, "we've been seeing you for a while, and we've been careful not to disturb you."

"But how can this be?" I asked. I had no idea that I could be seen when I dreamwalked.

He shrugged. "It's normal."

"Normal? How can it be normal? How can any of this be normal," I said, tears forming because the confirmation that I had for so long sought and desired was now overwhelming me. The new feelings of fearlessness were already evaporating like mist in the desert sun.

He looked puzzled by the tears, and it took him a moment to remember that he was having this conversation with someone not accustomed to all that he was accustomed to. He thought quietly for a moment, and gave me the one real and simple answer that I truly needed to hear.

"I guess that's the difference between your society and ours. Your society always asks why, why, why. We don't. We just accept things. If it happens, then it must be normal."

The proverbial light went on. He was making perfect sense.

He paused, and then continued.

"You people think you have to have a rational explanation for everything." Then, smiling, he said, "That's what'll drive you crazy!"

I had traveled many miles in order to hear this, and as he said it, I was reminded of someone else's words—words of the teacher from the light:

"It's not important that you understand everything you see—what is important is that you feel love."

I felt that I could now go home. I had faced west, and discovered all that awaited me there. It was not a warrior on a white horse that was waiting to thunder toward me, seemingly to overpower me, overwhelm me. It was confirmation that awaited me. I could go home now and bake cookies for John and Emily.

But first, there was one message that I still needed to deliver.

"Do you know a Native American fellow named Joseph?" I asked Allan.

"No, why?"

"I'm supposed to tell someone that he's still waiting."

The Hopi man nodded his head. "Okay," he answered.

I left the reservation that afternoon determined to find the Anasazi structure where the crow lived. I was unable to find it, however. In the weeks to come, when I had that roll of film developed, the picture presented to me was that of a starburst—a supernova marking another moment in which time seemed to have crossed its own path.

It became very clear to me during my travel to and from the desert that time was rippling and warping all around me, as though there were small openings in the Universe through which one might travel if so inclined.

Following my strong longing to return to my home, I left Winslow, returned the rental car that Joseph selected for me a week earlier, and boarded a bus back to Tallahassee.

I hoped that I might see Joseph again—I would have a lot to tell him—but he did not come looking for me.

The bus trip back was reasonably normal, with the exception that we arrived before dawn, approximately twelve hours early, in Tallahassee.

At first I was unable to recognize the town as we entered it, because there was not a single light on anywhere along the busy street that buffers the University. I did not know with certainty that we were in Tallahassee until the bus pulled into the bus station, and the driver stood up and said, "Tallahassee."

Once again, as we made an arrival in total darkness, I was the only one who seemed to notice that something out of the ordinary was happening. I decided to ask the two ladies sitting across the aisle from me if they noticed that we had arrived 12 hours early.

"We're a little early," I said, in a sweeping understatement.

They smiled. One said, "Well, isn't that nice! We made it here in good time."

"In good time?" I wanted to say, "Lady, we must have skipped over the entire state of Texas," but I kept quiet.

It was necessary for me to phone Craig and ask for a ride home. The phone rang several times before he awoke and answered it.

"What are you doing here at this hour of the morning?" he asked.

"I'm not sure," I answered. It was all the answer that was necessary, because I'd learned a valuable lesson from my Hopi friend. Not all questions have rational answers. "But can you please come and get me?"

He wasn't thrilled about being awakened before dawn with such a request, but he came and picked me up.

My surgery was scheduled for eight the following morning.

It had been a difficult ordeal for me to stick to my fish diet throughout this time, a situation worsened by the fact that the man in the light had apparently abandoned me now. It seemed like I hadn't seen him in ages.

The time for his prediction of a healing to prove accurate was running out. The tumor was still sitting on my nose.

As Craig drove me to the surgeon's office, I vowed with bitter resentment that if the surgery went according to plan, leaving me permanently disfigured, I would abandon the fish diet, and we would have steak for supper. Medium rare.

The surgeon came into the room where I sat waiting for the first portion of the disfigurement to begin, and he greeted my tumor.

"That's interesting," he said, "it appears to have shrunk."

He then measured it.

"Nope," he said, "it's still the same size. But it sure looks like it's smaller."

He approached me with a needle and syringe filled with some sort of numbing agent. As he moved the needle slowly toward my nose, I turned my head equally as slowly away in a senseless act of self-preservation. He tried several times without success to deliver the injection and finally said, "You're going to have to stop turning away."

"I can't seem to help it."

"Try closing your eyes."

That suggestion didn't seem to offer any comfort, so I compromised and squinted, gritting my teeth as he numbed my face with several injections. Following this, he removed a small sample of the tumor as a starter.

"I'll be right back," he said, taking the sample into the next room for the purpose of examining it with a microscope.

Within minutes he returned, smiling.

"That's it." he said.

"What do you mean, 'that's it'?"

"We're finished. I just got the whole thing!" He was now laughing.

"You're kidding?"

"Nope. It's all over."

He told his nurse to call the plastic surgeon and notify him that his services would not be required. The procedure that had been so carefully mapped out with a pen on my face some time earlier was no longer necessary.

Within fifteen minutes of my arrival at the doctor's office, my nose and I went home without needing a single suture, without shedding a drop of blood. I sported a simple Band-Aid on the tiny scraping.

We had fish for supper.

—7—

Journey through Space

I would have prayed that night—sent a "thank you" out—but the fact remained that I still hadn't found God. I had seen the impossible, witnessed synchronicity, had met a man of light who could prophesy rather well. But I still hadn't found the God who had been eluding me for my entire life.

Quite simply, although I now knew how to pray, and knew beyond any shadow of a doubt that it's a much, much bigger and more mystical world that we are a part of than I ever before dreamed—I was still not in any way inspired to pray to a vengeful overlord.

Additionally, I did not know where I should send prayers. In all my travels, I'd never found a trace of him.

I concluded that his identity and hiding place would remain a peculiar, unapproachable mystery.

The evening following my nose peel, I spoke to the group of people who were meeting secretly in their search for new philosophies. This was the group to which Ellis would later invite me—when I was at the beach arguing with my teacher that I didn't know how to find such a group.

I was, of course, a nervous wreck.

Each of the people in the room was introduced to me, and each one was either a Ph.D. or a Ph.D. candidate. I was clearly out of my league. I was merely in possession of a high school diploma. While it was true that I had received training in clinical laboratory medicine, and was probably the only one in the room who could read an electroencephalogram or do a full blood count the old fashioned way—with a microscope—I still only had one lowly diploma to my name.

To make matters worse, I was the only person in this room full of adults wearing a band aid on their nose.

It was to this group of scholars, philosophers, and theologians that I was going to speak, and tell them that while they had been reading, I had been seeing things.

I stood in front of the group and waited for everyone to finish pouring their coffee and tea, wondering what in the world I was going to say. I had deliberately not rehearsed anything.

A very lovely young Oriental woman, Ariel, walked into the kitchen with her partner to get a glass of ice water. She returned and took her seat, and several minutes ticked away as I stood silently in front of the group, waiting for her partner to come and take his seat, as well. The gathering began to fidget, nervously.

Finally, someone cleared their throat and spoke up.

"Ahem. You can go ahead and start anytime now."

"Well, I was waiting for that man in the kitchen," I explained.

"What man in the kitchen?"

"The Oriental man—Ariel's partner."

She looked around at her friends, and then said to me, "I don't have a partner. I came here alone."

(I would eventually meet the man I saw standing next to her. It was her younger brother, Gabriel, and he was not in the kitchen, he was in Aruba at the time. Unknown to all of us, Gabriel was about to valiantly fight the battle of his life against cancer.)

I began to speak, focusing not on myself or how foolish I must have appeared that night. I focused instead on the words of the man who had traveled through the Light in order to deliver his messages of compassion and love, of cause and effect, and his call to come forward and begin a healing of the Earth. When I finished, the floor was opened for questions and discussion.

Their reactions varied.

One gentleman held a crucifix strategically placed so that it might protect him from me as I spoke about my strange encounters. This was a new experience for me. I had never been identified as an evil or dangerous person before, at least not to my face. He was not the only one in whom fear rose that evening. Some were equating the Light—filled only with compassion—not with love at all, but with the sulfurous flames of Hell.

Ellis raised his hand. "I have a question," he said. He looked troubled.

"Okay," I said.

"This 'man' you have been talking to," Ellis proceeded, "you say he is extremely attractive?"

"Yes," I said, smiling, not knowing of the trap that I was walking into, "he's stunningly beautiful."

"Mm hmm," Ellis pondered this a moment longer, "then, just exactly how do you know that it isn't Lucifer you're entertaining?"

"Lucifer?" I said, weakly.

"Yes, Lucifer. The angel of light. The most beautiful of all angels."

I wasn't prepared for this question.

"Lucifer is very sneaky," Ellis went on. "He wins people over to evil with his beauty."

Ellis sounded very convincing, and I did not know how to respond. I stood in front of a crowd of people who now thought that I was entertaining beings from Hell. I was very embarrassed.

Ariel saw my embarrassment, and spoke.

"It doesn't sound like Lucifer to me," she said, and Ellis fell silent. "It sounds like Jesus."

If the words of Ellis came like a slap to my face, the words of Ariel slapped the other cheek. I knew that she was only trying to help me out in this very difficult moment, but to equate the most beautiful and loving encounter of my life with a figure I'd left behind ages ago was more than offensive to me, it was belittling. My visitor was from space. For these people to assume otherwise was an embarrassment. This crowd was getting out of hand.

"How do you know he is not Lucifer!" Ellis broke in.

"Because he doesn't have wings or a tail," I said.

"How do you know he is not Jesus," Ariel said.

"Because he doesn't have a beard."

This seemed to satisfy both questions, and the discussion soon went in other directions. A few bibles were brought out and passages studied, dissected, and quoted. My opinions were asked, but all I could say was that my encounter did not seem to have anything in common with biblical teachings. They agreed. While whatever had happened to me sounded vaguely "religious" or spiritual, it did not conform to scriptural guidelines.

After I staunchly maintained that the man I was now referring to as my teacher was neither Lucifer nor Jesus, another question was asked.

"Well, who do you think he is, then?"

"Personally," I said, hoping that I could soon go home, and vowing to never, ever put myself in this sort of situation again—my speaking days were now over—"I think he's from space."

"From space?"

"Yes, I think he's some sort of spaceman, and he's beamed down to help."

This seemed much more comfortable—if not fashionable—to consider. Several people nodded. It was as good a guess as any.

Although I pledged to never again be a speaker after that night, I was soon invited to speak to another small gathering of people and reluctantly acquiesced. There were a few familiar faces in this group. Some of the people who had attended my debut came to listen to my second presentation, following which I was roasted again.

Ariel was present, as was Ellis.

Ellis did not bring up the question about Lucifer this time, but two women in the small audience asked if the man was Jesus.

I carefully explained that I was sure he was not. I explained that I was not a Christian, nor was I in any way religious, and that my last religious affiliation had been with Judaism.

I reassured the people in the audience that, while I was having some sort of an encounter, I was certainly not so far gone as to be having one with Jesus. They seemed to enjoy this response, and whenever I gave this explanation in the future, it usually drew a few knowing chuckles.

In the course of the next few weeks, I spoke to several more small groups of people, and it seemed that no matter how small the crowd, there were certain patterns ingrained into the collective mind of the audience.

Regarding the teacher's appeal that we set aside one day of the week, sit quietly filled with joy, consume nothing and think, I was asked on nearly every occasion, "Where should we meet to do this?"

I explained again and again that he did not want us to meet as a group to do this—that using gasoline and driving to a specified location was contrary to the reasoning behind it. He wanted us to act as individuals. But the need to meet as a group seemed to be almost instinctive. Perhaps it has its roots in the ancient tradition of meeting as a group in temples or churches on a specific day of the week, whenever spiritual matters were to be addressed.

One woman listened carefully and then told me that she was incapable of "going without" for more than fifteen minutes. She asked if I thought this would be okay with him.

I reviewed his words carefully in my mind. He had said that each person was to decide when, and for how long, to fast and consume nothing. It was to be kept simple.

"Yes," I said to her, "that would be perfectly fine. He wants it kept simple so that everyone can participate according to their own schedules and capabilities. You can participate however you wish. He did not ever say that this was to be a marathon, or to cause suffering, just the opposite. We are to fill ourselves with joy as we heal the Earth."

The idea that we were being asked to "heal the Earth" also met with unexpected opposition on several occasions when this request was somehow interpreted as a suggestion calling for pagan ritual. This led some to ask if I was a witch. I was also asked if I was an angel, a saint, a holy person, a shaman, a medicine woman, a demon from Hell, and if I was delusional or mentally ill.

When I replied, "No, I'm just me," I was asked, "Then, why you? If there's nothing special about you, why were you picked for this?"

I had to respond that I had no idea, and had been asking myself this same question.

"It's possible," I explained to one audience, "that if someone with as many flaws as I have could be experiencing this, it's a good indication that everyone is invited. If the invitations had been extended only to saintly types, none of this would have happened to me."

Bible reading, and bible quoting, occupied at least a small block of time during nearly all of these gatherings as people repeatedly tried without success to locate in the scripture something—anything—backing what I was reporting.

On a cool October afternoon several days after the last gathering, I was walking by myself from my bedroom through the hallway, when something very strange, very unsettling happened.

There, in a hallway with no windows, in a dark corridor where no visitor venturing into my living room might ever see it, hung a very old, black and once-white image of Raphael's Sistine Madonna, its white parts turned shades of olive tan with age.

My mother had given it to me some time in the distant and forgotten past, presumably at a time in my life when it might have held some meaning for me. I kept it in the hallway because I had never gotten around to throwing it in the trash, and didn't want anyone to see it or assume that it meant anything to me. It had hung there unobserved for so long that I, for one, never even noticed it any longer.

On this October day as I walked out of my bedroom, I felt a subtle wind blow like a breath into my face and hair. I stood there for a moment, wondering what could have caused the air to stir in such a way.

"Go and find a Catholic priest," I heard a woman say.

I wasn't sure who had spoken these words, and I answered, "What the hell do I need with a Catholic priest?"

Then, as I looked around in the dimly lit hall for the owner of this voice, I found myself staring directly into the old picture of the Madonna.

I was not the only one who felt the breeze in the hallway.

The picture was moving. The veil around the Madonna and the child was being lifted by the strange wind. Clouds were swirling within the painting.

"Go and find a Catholic priest," she repeated.

And then the picture became very still again, frozen on an old piece of yellowed paper.

I pondered this strange and troubling instruction for much of the afternoon. I assumed that when I left Catholicism and Christianity that I had been excommunicated—which was fine with me. Now I was being asked to more or less re-establish communications. This was not fine with me.

Nevertheless, I went through the phone book, wondering if some name might magically jump out at me. None did.

I then telephoned my parents' parish priest, whom I'd never met. (They still attended mass once in a while.)

"Hi, Father," I said when he answered the phone, "you don't know me—I'm Mary and Charlie's daughter."

"Oh, yes," he said with a pleasant Irish brogue, "I've been missing them in mass lately—how are they doing?"

"They're fine."

"Good, good."

"I'm calling because I have something to say to a Catholic priest, Father."

"Oh? All right."

"But I'm not sure which Catholic priest I'm supposed to say it to."

"I see," he said somewhat cautiously.

"So, you'll have to think about this yourself, and decide whether you are the right priest to hear what I have to say, or not."

"Mm hmm."

"I've been seeing something very unusual."

Dead silence.

"If you want to know what I've been seeing, and if you decide that you are the priest meant to hear about this," I continued, "please phone me back."

I gave him my phone number and waited for about an hour for his call, but he never called me back.

That night, while I was cooking supper, Craig walked into the kitchen and mentioned that there was an American Indian activist scheduled to speak at Florida State University in about fifteen minutes. Knowing that every waking—and sleeping—moment of my life was now completely occupied with Indians, he suggested that if I hurried, I might be able to get there in time to listen to the activist's talk.

Because I was unfamiliar with the campus, we all jumped in the car and he drove me to FSU while I gave him instructions on how to finish dinner. He dropped me off in front of the auditorium, and I hurried in, just in time. Looking around the room, I saw a friend of my mother's in one of the rows, and waved to her. She returned the greeting and motioned for me to come and sit with her.

She was sitting with a young Native American fellow with long black hair. He was wearing a red cotton shirt and blue jeans. She introduced him to me as her friend, Yosef.

The speaker talked for over an hour and then asked if there were any questions or comments. Yosef raised his hand.

"Yes," the speaker said.

Yosef stood up. "Hi," he said, "my name is Yosef. I'm a Native American, and a Roman Catholic priest. I do a lot of traveling—missionary work—and have found that many native teachings combine well with some of the church teachings . . . "

I turned to my mother's friend, and said, "He's gotta be kidding, right? This guy's really a priest?"

She confirmed that he was.

"Bingo," I replied.

When the discussions ended and the people began dispersing, I asked the priest if I might talk to him for a moment.

"I think you're the one I'm looking for—I was told to come and find you," I said, not realizing that I was now perfectly at ease in greeting someone with the same opening statement that Joseph of the Bus had used with me.

"Oh, really?" the priest said, not appearing to find it out of the ordinary, "Okay, then, you can come to the office I'm using tomorrow."

"But I'm not a Catholic."

"That's okay."

"And I don't want to be one, either."

"That's okay, too."

"Well, I'm not a Christian, either."

He shrugged, "All right."

I sensed that it was going to be difficult to un-invite myself, so I accepted the piece of paper on which the man wrote his temporary address and phone number. We agreed to meet at three the following afternoon.

When I got home, I immediately typed out a long letter to him, explaining why he might not want to be in my company, that my latest religious affiliation before I became an atheist was with Judaism, that I no longer liked Christianity—or God—and that I would understand if he wanted to cancel our appointment. And, in case he did wish to cancel, I included my phone number.

"Call me if you want to cancel," I wrote.

First thing in the morning, I hand-delivered the letter to a receptionist in the building where his office was located, and went home to await his call. He never called. At a few minutes before three, I called him.

"Did you receive my letter?"

"Yes," he said, "I read it this morning."

"Well, you didn't call."

"You said to call if I wanted to cancel."

"Then you still want me to come?"

"Yes."

He met me out in the building's foyer.

"What can I help you with?" he asked.

"Well, I've been seeing someone."

"Oh, I see. And you're a married woman?"

"Yes—well, no—well, I mean I've been seeing someone, as in 'seeing' him. I think he's from outer space."

This was the grand test. I watched him carefully, but the priest never flinched.

"I'm probably from outer space myself," he replied. "Come on in and tell me all about it."

"Well, just a minute," I said. He paused and looked at me. "I'm not going to convert back to being a Catholic, or back into Christianity."

"Okay," he said.

"So promise that you won't try to convert me."

"I promise."

An hour later, I had had the longest confession of my life. The priest never said anything judgmental, and did not try to convert me. I told him everything.

"Who do you think he is?" I asked.

"I don't know," the priest said, deep in thought.

"Do you think he's Lucifer?" I asked, because even though I felt I had distanced myself from the Roman Church, some of its teachings still lingered in my mind, conjuring their residual fear; and this fear was perhaps the most unexplainable of all, because it encompassed everything. This was a fear of both darkness and of light.

"Has he asked you to do anything?"

"Yes."

"Like what?"

"He asked me to eat fish."

"Fish?"

"Yes, I'm supposed to eat fish and seaweed."

"Explain this to me," he said, so I told him in great detail the conversation that the man in the sphere of light and I had about fish. The priest listened and nodded.

"But has he asked you to do anything that would violate your honor, or your personal principles?"

"Oh, no," I said.

"So, basically, you are saying that he says good things—words of love and healing?"

"Yes."

"Then 'by their fruits you will know them.'"

"What does that mean?"

"He's not the devil."

"Am I having a close encounter, then?"

"It appears so."

Father Yosef requested that we meet again soon to discuss everything more thoroughly, and he asked me to keep him apprised of further developments. I went home feeling greatly relieved to have heard from an authority on such matters that I had not, after all, been entertaining the devil.

It would be several years, however, before I would learn that the object of that fear, Lucifer, was the creation of someone's pen. "Lucifer," I learned in time, did not even exist until the Hebrew bible was translated into Latin. Lucifer then appeared once in Isaiah 14:12, where it took the place of the morning star, and grew into an enormous new demon for humanity to fear. While most translations of the bible have since been corrected, and Lucifer is no longer to be found within the pages where he first appeared, the common knowledge of a demon from hell named Lucifer—the lingering, residual knowledge of something taught and something learned—lives on. The information that I would one day discover was not really important at the time. My sense of relief on that afternoon in October was real.

The profound relief boosted my feelings of respect for the man in the light. My next action was born of that new respect.

While talking with Fred the Medicine Man on the telephone, in a moment of benign submission on my part, I decided to refer to the man in the light as "my master."

Fred was stunned.

"What do you mean, 'master'?" he said, saying it as though he were spewing poison into his end of the telephone.

"That's what I'm going to call him. My master."

"Well, I have no 'masters.'"

"There's nothing wrong with having a master," I argued. "It indicates respect—submissive respect."

"Bullshit! It indicates you are limiting yourself. It's a cop-out."

"It is not!"

"Well, don't ever expect me to refer to him as 'master'! And furthermore, if he wants you to call him 'master' then he's got problems, too!"

I slammed the phone down in Fred's ear. He was not going to talk that way about my master.

That night, I was awakened by a bright light shining in my eyes. When I opened them, I was overjoyed to see my master standing there. He did not appear to be particularly happy, however. He was not smiling on this occasion. In fact, he appeared to be angry.

"Hi," I said, smiling.

"You are now referring to me as 'master'?" he asked.

"Yes," I said, still grinning.

"Please explain the reason for this."

"Well, you are beautiful, and you're not from Hell. You're good—and I am feeling great love for you, and great respect!"

He stared at me in complete silence for a moment and said, "Then shall I also start referring to you as my 'master'?"

"Well, no! Of course not!" I said—the thought was ludicrous.

He departed, leaving me to sort matters out for myself. It took at least a half hour before I concluded that, no matter how I reviewed our exchange of words, he had not only been very upset with me, but he had actually chastised me. This meant that, whatever he was, he had a full range of what appeared to be human emotions. He was capable of being displeased, and he was capable of expressing his displeasure. I finally went to sleep thinking that I would have to come up with another name for him—anything but master. "Perhaps I'd better just stick with 'teacher,'" I thought, "or 'being of light.'"

The following morning, as I was brushing my hair in front of the bathroom mirror, the being's image appeared in the mirror, blending with my own so that his features were in my features, and mine were in his. Then he was no longer in the mirror, but was standing next to me, and we were both looking into the mirror. He was smiling, and no longer angry.

"You understand that if you call me 'master' you place a division between yourself and myself," he said, "and in doing so you view me as unapproachable. If you presume that you cannot achieve my station of love, then you will be bound by your thoughts. Let there be no division, no separation, no distancing. Be exactly as I am."

There was no denying it. His beauty, his humility, his sincerity, his fragrance, his smile, his eyes, his intelligence, his compassion, and those wonderful beams of light he was capable of creating—there was nothing about him that was not lovable. I was falling in love with a being of light.

It would be wonderful to be exactly like him. In fact, I could not think of anyone else I would prefer to be "exactly" like. It would, however, be a supreme and unending challenge.

That night, I slept on my right side, facing the wall with my back to the open room. I was not awakened by his light because I did not see it. I was awakened when he whispered a greeting into my left ear. I was so startled to awaken and find him leaning over me with his head next to mine that I screamed before immediately realizing that it was only my teacher—my very gentle, quiet teacher—who had come to visit again.

When I looked up at him, I saw that the look on his face was one of utter anguish, and he quickly backed away from me, receding into an increasingly smaller point of light that seemed to be far off in the distance.

I waited for a while for him to return, and when he didn't come back, I fell asleep again, careful this time to lie on my left side so that I would be facing the room and would be awakened by his light if he returned.

He returned in a while, and he awakened me in the way with which I had grown most comfortable, by the soft beams of his light surrounding him.

He apologized profusely—seemingly far too much so for

having merely startled me. He was nearly in a state of anguish over this, as though he had done something unspeakable.

"You were not meant to be frightened by any of this," he said, "not by any portion of it whatsoever."

"But, I wasn't frightened," I explained, hoping that I could say something that would make him less troubled over something so utterly minor, "I was just startled to find you so close to me."

He whispered something under his breath that sounded like, "Dictus a deamos presidio proximo—anomi contestae didymous non sequitor arani tu quoum segundo a mundo . . ." I later wrote these strange words down as best I could although I couldn't remember their exact sequence and didn't know what they meant. They sounded as though they were a blend of several languages.

"Take my hand," he said, "and we'll go for a walk. I'll tell you a love story."

I took his hand and we walked into the light.

In an instant we were standing upon the rocky shores of a great body of water. The sea caught the light of the moon on its surface, and low clouds of warm fog surrounded us. I had never seen this beach before.

The being stepped down and led me across the rocks to the shoreline, positioning himself between me and the water's edge. Although I was unfamiliar with the area, he seemed quite familiar with it. I held his hand as we walked up the beach.

He talked about the complexity involved in passing judgment on others—that all of the facts must be uncovered before judgment can be passed, and that this is nearly impossible for mankind to do. The love story that he told to me was about Judas. When he was finished, I was moved to tears and I said, "This is the most beautiful story I've ever heard. I can't wait to tell people about this."

"No," he said, "this is not to be told to others. In the morning, you will not be able to remember the story I have just told you."

We continued walking down the beach, sometimes in comfortable silence, which I would predictably interrupt with questions, but he never seemed to grow weary of them. He seemed, instead, to invite them, and treated each question with patience and with dignity. I did not ever feel awkward or stupid because of my questions. On the rare occasions that I did not question him about his teachings, he would quietly ask, "Do you understand?"

On this particular night, he remained focused primarily on the subject of non-judgment, and the importance of seeking the truth.

In the morning, when I awoke, I was unable to recall the details of the story about Judas. I was able only to recall that it was a beautiful story of love, that we only have fragments of the truth regarding the alleged betrayal, and that passing judgment based on fragmented truth—or even creating rumors and talking about fragmented truth—is never appropriate.

In short, he seemed to be painlessly, quietly showing me ways in which I might become a more decent human being. At its core, each lesson had awareness or consciousness of actions, and the motivation of that consciousness was love. He was showing me how to love myself.

Thanksgiving was a memorable affair that year. Father Yosef was back in town, visiting again, and so we invited him and my parents over for the afternoon.

Since I was still eating fish and seaweed, and the priest did not eat red meat, I prepared seafood for the two of us, and turkey for everyone else. Father Yosef said a non-denominational blessing, careful not to insult my status as a heathen rebel. I followed it with a Hebrew prayer I'd memorized many years earlier. To the best of my recollection it was a prayer for the dead, but since none of us knew what any of the words meant, no one was offended, and I was sure that God, wherever he was, was not listening anyway.

It was a pleasant afternoon that led into a pleasant evening.

After everyone left and the kids were in bed, I retired early that night, read for a while, and then fell asleep.

At approximately midnight, I was awakened by a bright

light shining in my eyes. I opened them to see a different sphere of light floating just above my bedroom door.

It was small, a little over a foot in diameter. It alternated its appearance between a gold sphere with black spots, and a black sphere with gold spots. It took several moments for me to determine this, however, because I was only able to see it clearly with my peripheral vision. If I looked directly at it, I could not see anything at all.

My mind was filled with utter confusion. I was in the presence of something that could only be seen if I did not look at it.

A voice spoke from the sphere. Although I was unable to understand its words, I sensed immediately that this was the voice of a figure of authority, and I was in the presence of a very powerful teacher who was radiating strength and knowledge.

I was not filled with the serenity and calmness that the sweet, soft-spoken being of light filled me with. He radiated human goodness. This, I sensed, was not human. It did not radiate familiar emotions. It radiated knowledge so profound that I was filled with a sense of terrified respect. As I perceived small glimmers of this knowledge, I felt a dawning sense of personal ignorance. I perceived flaws in my core beliefs and my accumulated knowledge.

This sphere was causing me to feel the same emotions of expectation and captive terror that Joseph had first caused me to feel on the bus. Something was about to be revealed to me, and there was no place for me to hide. I was about to be taken on the bus ride to end all bus rides.

In the flickering and flashing of the gold and black lights, I viewed my imperfections. I was not seeing them in the kind of stark and open view that might cause me to be filled with shame. I was seeing them only in small doses, in compassionate glimmers that allowed me to continue viewing them with as open a mind as possible. The result of this was a sudden desire for knowledge, a sudden urge to seek knowledge and the truth; because, in reality, I had so little of it within.

The voice spoke from the sphere again. This time I understood it.

"I have come to show you where God is hiding," he said. "Step within me."

This confused me even further. "I can't," I said, careful not to look directly at it. "I'm larger than you. I'm down here, and you're up there near the ceiling."

"Enter," he said.

Suddenly, the laws of gravity gave way and I felt myself being drawn toward the small flashing sphere. I briefly resisted, clutching desperately at the sheets as though they might anchor me, but this proved to be a useless act. It was not my physical body after all that was being pulled toward it, it was my consciousness. Nearing the ceiling, I looked down and saw that my physical body—unconscious once again, yet still frantically clutching the sheets—was right where I left it. Without another second's delay, I was pulled into the tiny sphere head-first.

Inside was a universe.

The voice had taken on a new identity as well—one which I could not see at all—but I knew that he was floating next to me. I looked at the distant galaxies, slowly moving through endless space, swirling as though held within an awareness.

"What do you see?" the voice asked.

"I see the order of the Universe."

"What else?"

"Nothing. I do not see God hiding anywhere."

"Choose a galaxy," he said.

I selected a tiny distant galaxy, and the voice said, "Come with me—we will move through space to that galaxy."

We began approaching the cluster of stars, and as we approached it, the galaxy grew in size until it became so enormous that I could only see the stars of this galaxy, and could no longer see the other distant galaxies.

"Choose a star," the voice said.

I chose the smallest star in sight.

"Come, we will move through space to that star."

As we approached the star, it grew in size until it became enormous and brilliant—brighter now than any other stars that were flickering dimly in the distance. Caught in the embrace of this sun were planets hurtling through space on their own orderly paths.

There were large planets in this solar system, and there were small planets. As they moved through space around their sun, small moons moved through space around the planets.

"What do you see?"

"I see the incredible beauty and order of the galaxies, the stars, and now the planets and their moons."

"Anything else?"

"No."

"Choose a planet."

I did not chose the largest or the smallest of these bodies. I selected a planet that was nondescript.

"Come," he said.

We flew through space toward the modest planet, and as we did, it grew in size. It became larger and larger in our perspective until it was larger than the sun, larger than the largest neighboring planets, and larger than the entire galaxy. The sun grew smaller in the distance, but remained brilliant. Close enough to see the planet clearly, I saw that it had an atmosphere, clouds, land mass, and glistening seas.

"What do you see?"

"The incredible beauty of everything—the details."

"Come and we'll go closer."

We flew downward and entered the atmosphere, flew over an ocean, and then over a body of land.

Below me, I saw yellow grasses as they moved under the warm breath of a prairie wind, and then I saw the foothills of a mountain range. We passed over the foothills, and approached a mountain. On the side of this mountain, there was a ledge, and I detected something small moving on the ledge.

"There is life everywhere on this planet!" I said.

"Come, and we'll go closer."

We flew toward the ledge, and I saw a man. It was an American Indian. He had been sitting alone in deep thought. When we flew over him, our shadows touched the ground in front of him. I saw that we were casting the shadows of two winged beings. When the man saw the shadows, he looked up at us with unmistakable awe and slowly stood up. He raised his arms outward, baring his chest.

"Was he expecting us?"

"He has been waiting for a very long time. Come, and we will go closer."

We flew downward, closer.

"Come, we will go even closer," the other winged being said.

We were flying at a great speed, and as we grew closer to the man, he grew larger and larger—larger than the mountain which I could no longer see and larger than the planet itself. All I could see was the man.

We were now perilously close to him, close enough for me to look into his eyes, and there I saw our reflections. One was an eagle. One was a sparrow.

"Come!" the eagle said and he pulled me toward the man's bared chest.

His chest was heaving. The man's heart was pounding in anticipation of what was going to happen next, but he did not turn away from us. He stood perfectly still and offered himself to us and to the unknown.

I cried out, afraid that we were about to strike the man dead.

The eagle screamed a command, "Come! We will go closer!"

Going closer, and able to see only the man's heaving chest, I suddenly could no longer discern that it was a man's chest I was seeing. I was seeing the details of his flesh—flesh that had cells. Between the cells was space. Flying through that space, we entered the man's chest without harming him. Continuing onward, we passed between the cells of a small vein and entered the man's river of blood.

Here, the eagle allowed me to rest for a moment, and to calm down. When I was calm enough to look around, I saw the blood cells tumbling along. Each one was separate and distinct, each one carefully created to perform a task to sustain the man's life, although the man was probably unaware of their individual existences.

"What do you see?"

I was still shaking. "I see the incredible details of creation. I see that the Creator must have been here to put such order into every cell. But I do not see the Creator."

"Choose a blood cell."

I chose one of the red blood cells as it came rolling down the river.

"Come, we will fly to that cell."

We flew through the space toward it, and as we did, it became larger—larger than the man, larger than the planet the man was standing on, larger than the galaxy holding the planet, and then I could no longer see a blood cell. I could see the particles of matter that formed the cell. Between the particles was space. Flying through the space, we entered the cell.

Inside was a universe.

Galaxies of light swirled in the endless space.

"What do you see?"

"I see the Universe," I whispered. "I see Creation."

"What else?"

"I see order in the particles of the cells. But I do not see the Creator."

"What else?"

He was now growing impatient with me.

I looked around—I had already told him everything I could see—the beauty, the details. There was nothing else.

"Nothing," I said.

"What else do you see?" he demanded.

I looked around again, earnestly searching for a glimpse of the Creator, but he was still hiding. "I see that the Creator must have been here, I see what he has created, I see there is no end to it, no beginning, but other than that, all I can see is space."

"And what is space?" he asked.

"It's nothing. It's an endless void."

"Now open your own heart and receive the message I have been sent to deliver," he said softly, no longer angry, "that upon which we have flown, that which is throughout all of creation, that which you have referred to as an 'endless void,' it is the conscious mind of the Creator. It is the awareness. You have wondered if your prayers can be heard. Now you see that your heart beats within the awareness. Acknowledge its presence for the first time."

I awoke the following morning with a vague sense that I'd had a strange dream, but I could not recall any of it.

Later in the afternoon, I sat down at the computer to write a letter to Fred, who had moved again, and was even further away than before.

"Fred," I began, "I feel weird."

I noticed with my peripheral vision something moving in the tree outside my window, and turned to look at it. Sitting in the tree was an eagle. He was looking at me.

I had never seen an eagle like this before—it was speckled gold and black, and like the crow in the desert, his head was white. As I looked into his eyes, suddenly every detail of the night's journey into the Mind of the Creator flooded through me.

"Fred," I wrote, "I've seen where God is hiding."

It was a good opening sentence.

Then I wrote, "He's hiding everywhere so we'll be sure to find him."

—8—

The Great Awareness,
Aware of Being Unknown

I phoned Father Yosef after I finished my letter to
Fred, and told him that there was, indeed, a
Creator after all, and told him where he was
located. He thanked me for the call.

However, the quandary regarding the nature of
the Creator remained. I had seen that his eye
was certainly on the details of matter, that his
mind was surrounding each particle of matter. Yet nothing had
shown me whether that Conscious Mind—stretching off into
eternity, through me, through everything, connecting all of
Creation—was or was not filled with the judgment and jealous
vengeance so steadfastly reported.

Shortly after the dreamwalk into space, I was invited to
speak at another gathering, this time at the home of a rabbi.

This gathering was slightly different from the previous
ones. This time, not everyone in the audience was a Ph.D. On
this occasion, there was an undergraduate student who had
been invited. I remained, as I had in each previous gathering,

the person in the room with the lowest certificate of formal education.

There was another difference in this group of people. The men and women were from many different countries around the world—Holland, France, China, India, Canada, Jamaica, Aruba, and several countries in Africa to name a few. It was a room filled with a rainbow of colors and cultural backgrounds. Rainbow colors.

A room filled with a Rainbow.

I'm sure they did not know why I sat for a while and stared at them. On this day, as I looked into the faces of many nations, I finally knew the meaning of the Dance of the Midnight Rainbow. A rainbow cannot be formed from one color or two. A rainbow must be made of many, many colors.

I decided that I would tell this gathering the same thing that I had told the previous gatherings—nothing more. I would not tell them of my latest journey into the Universe, because the audiences seemed to have had enough trouble with the most simple messages. I was unsure how space travel would settle in the minds of people from cultures unfamiliar to me. It was too new. I would keep quiet about it unless someone specifically asked to hear more—something that had never been asked of me before.

I told them about the teacher's messages, and concluded the talk. The undergrad then raised her hand, and I acknowledged her.

"Is there anything more that you've seen? Have you seen anything recently that you can tell us about?"

That was my cue.

I then told, for the first time, the story of where God is hiding.

When I was finished, the room was quiet. The undergrad had her eyes closed, and I wondered for a moment if I had bored her to sleep.

She then slid from the chair that she was in onto to the floor, and lay down upon the floor full length. Putting her face into her hands, she began sobbing in hard, wracking sobs from somewhere deep within. Her clear passion caused my own eyes to tear, and I noticed that several other people were also fighting back tears.

When the girl was able to speak, she did so from the floor where she remained.

"I've never prayed in my life," she said between gasps, her face red and wet, but she did not seem to care about appearances at this moment, "I've never prayed because I never knew where God was." She took several more gasps and wiped away tears that were still coming. Then she revealed something else, something that gave a good indication that I was not the sole recipient of messages and suggestions.

"I had something else to do this afternoon," she said, "I had theater tickets that couldn't be refunded. But something told me to give the tickets away, because I should come here instead. So I did, and now . . ." she dissolved into hard tears again. "I've been waiting my whole life to hear this."

Her words nearly overwhelmed me. On the day that I first understood the meaning of the rainbow, I understood the meaning of the name that I had been given what seemed like a long time ago. I finally understood what I—a woman—was to be speaking about. I would not be speaking about anything of my own making, about anything for which I could stand proud and take credit as its author or creator. Neither would I speak like a scholar. I would speak simple words in a simple way. In speaking, there would be no preaching or tirades, there would be no academic lecturing, and no moralization or judgment. I would describe what I had witnessed, and nothing more.

The happiness in seeing small pieces of this puzzle finally fall into place was abruptly dampened as, once again, a few people in the audience wanted to do some dissection.

Various questions were brought up: "What does this all really mean?" I couldn't explain that. All I could do was tell the people what I'd seen and heard. One woman appeared to be particularly suspicious of me, which I noticed because she was glaring at me through squinting eyes. She finally raised her hand to speak.

"You look like you've had a terrible life," she said. She was a psychologist, not from the US. "It has been filled with tragedy—I can see it in your face," she said.

Ariel immediately spoke up. "I don't see that in her face, at all."

I wasn't sure what the psychologist was seeing, but I shrugged and answered, "No, I really haven't had a bad life. I guess my life's been pretty unremarkable up to the point when this all started happening."

"Then you must have had a terrible childhood?"

"Nope. I had a happy childhood. Lots of good memories."

"Are you saying that you have experienced no tragedy in your life, whatsoever?"

"No, I'm not saying that at all—we all experience tragedy in our lives. I grew up the oldest of four girls. In 1982, my twenty-six-year-old sister, Patty, died unexpectedly. That was a tragedy."

She had found her pay dirt, and now wished to focus on the death of my sister, and search for other tragedies that she knew were there and I was refusing to acknowledge. I did not wish to do this, however. I was suddenly weary of having the conversations turn to focus upon me, instead of the messages I relayed.

And, of all the incidents in my life, the one about Patty was the one that I did not want to talk about. If the conversation proceeded in that direction, we would no longer be focused upon the hiding place of God, we would be focused on Hell, because that was now the dwelling place of my sister.

Mercifully, other individuals tired of this public psycho-analysis rather quickly and pulled out their bibles. Searches were conducted for any sort of scriptural reference that might pertain to the new message I had just relayed, and in finding nothing whatsoever, a conclusion was drawn: Because nothing that I was saying had any scriptural basis, it was not really worth much.

I was asked again if I thought that the teacher with the messages was Jesus, and I responded, again—emphatically— no, that I did not know who he was.

Exhausted, I left, stinging from having long-buried

thoughts of Patty exposed, as well as from a growing sense of frustration regarding biblical backup.

As I approached my car, I heard a man call my name and turned around. He was a black gentleman, a tall, handsome man of regal carriage, elegantly dressed in white. He had been silent during my talk and its subsequent dissection. He had offered no comment. Now, as he stood next to me, I saw a hint of tears in his eyes. He spoke in a very quiet voice with a lilting accent, and I had to lean closer to him in order to hear his words.

"I, too, have seen the light of which you speak," he said. "It is real—it is all real."

Happiness shined through the clouds for a moment.

"I knew that someone would finally come forward and tell me that I wasn't the only person on Earth seeing this!" I said, smiling at him.

He had been reluctant to speak about his experiences because he, too, thought that he was alone in what he was seeing. We exchanged telephone numbers, both of us thankful to have found someone with whom we could discuss experiences with the light.

I arrived at home to find the house empty. Craig and the kids had gone to the mall. I sat watching the last afternoon rays of amber sunlight flow through the living room curtains, and thought about the events of this day's gathering. There were good things that I should have focused upon, but my mind kept flowing back to the humiliation and fear that the psychologist had brought me to feel. I couldn't shrug the feeling off. Her questions had brought me as close as I'd ever come to being forced or coerced into publicly telling the details of Patty's embarrassing deed. It had been too close for comfort. If word got out about my sister, I reasoned, no one would ever listen to anything I said again.

I sat there on that cool winter afternoon, alone with old memories of Patty that were still barbed enough to inflict raw, new pain, with the accompanying question, "Why?"

The shadows of evening surrounded me as I relived the details of the day we buried her.

There was much that I had been thankful for on that day.

I was thankful, first of all, that the burial service had been brief.

I recalled the prayer that a friend had spoken at the service. It, too, had been brief. The friend spoke the prayer because there was no clergy present at her grave site. They were not present, because my sister had died in a presumed state of the worst type of sin, that of despair.

Although the handwriting on the suicide note did not match my sister's handwriting, and although there had been no prior hints warning us of her intent, it was the official opinion that she had ended her short life with a .357 magnum blast into her own face.

The statements issued by those in charge made it clear that they were no longer awed by the dead, or horrified by death's details. These people had learned to approach the dead in a hollow manner, without emotion. In this state they could make official notes and then speak of the dead with casual indifference.

First, she was pronounced dead—irreversibly and undeniably dead. For my family, this was the hardest statement to believe.

My youngest sister, Colleen, was the first to be notified by telephone of Patty's death.

"That's not possible. I just talked to her an hour ago," she had argued, not realizing how much one's life can be changed forever in the course of one hour, or one minute for that matter.

Colleen then went to my parents' home to tell them that the fabric of their lives had just been torn in half. Colleen and my father flipped a coin. The coin would determine for them which person would telephone me. My mother was not among the candidates for this task because she had collapsed and could not stand up. The coin selected Colleen.

"That's not possible," I argued with her. She was crying hysterically.

"I'm sure there's been some mistake," I went on, trying to reassure my little sister, "everything is okay—they only think it's Patty—they must have the wrong person."

I continued my argument with her until my father got on the line and confirmed what Colleen had told me. The white buzz never came to save me from this one.

I do not remember how we told Carol—my other sister—
that her life too was now irreversibly shattered. I do not
remember anything else until I somehow arrived by plane at
the airport in Texas. I know that someone must have phoned
Carol, because both she and Colleen were there at the airport
waiting for me.

I remember being told by the Coroner, in his official capacity, that he had chosen not to perform an autopsy on Patty
because, "There wasn't any reason to do one—I could tell by
looking at her what she died from!"

Indeed. He could tell by looking at her . . . he could tell by
looking at her.

A professional from the mortuary phoned to say, "I sure
hope you folks are not going to want an open-casket, or a viewing."

In small and measurable doses, it began to sink in that not
only was it possible that she actually was dead, but also, that
she was unpresentably dead.

"Do you know what a .357 magnum is?" someone would
ask me, trying to drive the point of reality home in a dose much
to large to take.

"No," I answered.

"It's a cannon."

Patty's body was then placed in a pine box, and both the
box and the case were closed.

The worst of the comments, however, were the silent ones.
They lingered, following us all around in the form of coarse
and accusing looks from acquaintances, and from some of
those we had considered as our friends. Having died in a sinful
state, Patty had lost more than her life. She had lost her soul.
Her remains might have been in that pine box, but she was in
Hell, and this disgraceful situation demanded judgment and
scorn from the more pious on the entire surviving family.

I sat between my two sisters on that day in June, holding
them as they lay across my lap. Before us was a large hole in
the ground situated next to an equally large mound of dirt,
both mercifully covered by a green tarp of Astro Turf. I was
thankful for the tarp, thankful that I did not have to look into

the hole and become personally familiar with its cold details. And I was thankful that my parents had listened to me when I told them to stay home, that there was no need for them to come and witness this, that the social obligations demanding funeral attendance were as pointless and cruel as the judgment, and that a child's funeral is nothing that a parent should ever have to witness. They stayed home, walking the walk of the living devastated. I heard a sound from my mother's heart on that day that I hope to never hear again. I was thankful that they stayed home, because I would not have been able to hold the entire family in my lap on this summer day when the five of us were no longer a family of six.

Next to the mound and the hole, of course, was the inevitable box that they claimed contained Patty. It, too, was covered from view, and I was again thankful that I did not have to become familiar with its piney splinters. The pine box was covered by an ornate mahogany shell that would be removed at the final moment, and saved for another pine box funeral on another day. It had burnished brass handles.

We had stopped to buy three roses—yellow and pink Peace roses—on our way to this place. When we arrived and found the stage set for the final act, we placed the roses upon the mahogany covering, and sat down in the metal folding chairs that had been arranged to face the mound, the hole, and the box.

The prayer did not ease any of my numb grief at that time. Instead it was strangely disturbing, haunting, almost as disturbing as the friend's hands and voice which were shaking as he read the prayer from a black bible.

"Yea, though I walk through the valley of the shadow of death, I will fear no evil . . ."

The valley of the shadow of death . . . the valley of the shadow of death . . . My mind was now repeating words and phrases that were particularly disturbing although I was unable to feel any further torment. This pain was too big; I was numb.

. . . the valley of the shadow of death.

This valley sounded like a terrible place to take a walk. Why would anyone want to take a walk through this valley of shadows?

I sat in the living room of my home in Florida, rattled by the pain of these memories. I was so absorbed in my memories of that brilliant summer day, the day when I wore my favorite blue and white dress for the last time; the day when the web of our lives was ripped to pieces; the day when the green tarp covered the truth of the earthen hole, the mahogany covered the truth of the pine, and shadows covered her final valley, that I did not see my teacher arrive in the living room.

He touched me on my right shoulder, and I looked up into his face and his eyes. They were filled with pain.

"There can be no shadows," he whispered, "unless there is also the presence of light."

Then he left.

I called Father Yosef and asked him to come over so that we might discuss this. He came over right away.

"Of course," he said, as we sat in the semi-darkness filling the living room. "I'm not surprised that he would say something like this. He seems to be filled with compassion. He's suggesting that while man may have judged and condemned your sister, God would not."

"What?" I asked, this did not seem like the characteristic teachings embraced by priests, "I thought that 'condemning' was part of your job description."

"It's not part of my job description," he said. "Man has no authority over the relationship between God and humanity, and certainly has no authority to condemn a human being and end his relationship with God."

"Are you telling me that you don't believe my sister's in Hell?"

"Yes. How could a God of mercy and compassion send an anguished soul to be further tortured in a Hell? Of course she's not in Hell. If Emily or John fell down and hurt themselves, would you then beat them and punish them further, or would you try to ease their pain?"

"I would never beat them for any reason. Of course, I'd ease their pain. That's what mothers are for."

"So do you think that God's compassion is less godlike than that of a mother?"

"I'm not sure."

"We are God's children. Your compassion comes from Her."

Father Yosef left me in a state of spreading confusion. First he dismantled Hell, then he referred to God in the female gender—and compassionate, no less. Sometimes my talks with this priest left me totally baffled.

That night, I was awakened once again by a bright light shining in my eyes.

I opened my eyes, hoping to find my friend the teacher in my room, because I felt that maybe he might be able to answer questions regarding compassion versus vengeance. But he was not visiting on this night. Nor was it the eagle (and for this I was somewhat thankful, as I had not fully recovered from that rather harrowing trip). I saw what appeared to be an angel. I was immediately imbued with a sense of well-being and happiness.

The center of the angel's chest was luminous, and light streamed from the glowing heart outward into arcs on both sides of him. The arcs of light formed what might be described by any startled observer as "wings." His hair was gold in color, and his heart and wings were white. His face was radiant and lovely.

"Come with me, and I will show you something very beautiful," he said. "Will you come?"

He was not at all a "commanding" or demanding presence as the eagle had been, he was more quiet. This angel was more in the spirit of a dove. I felt very safe, and agreed to go with him.

In a moment, we were approaching an enormous glowing city made of crystal. We entered the city and I saw many other angels similar in appearance to the one I was with, gathering in the halls, palaces, and courtyards. Lights glistened and sparkled off the crystal walls with a growing intensity.

"Do you know where we are?" he asked.

"Yes. This is the house of all hope. This is Heaven."

The angel smiled, "This is a reflection of Heaven—a portion of the kingdom. It is a very small replica made in the image of Heaven so that it might house the song of the Creator."

"It's so large," I said.

"We're just in time," the angel said to me.

"In time for what?"

He raised his hand to his lips, requesting silence. I kept still, and after silence filled the city, I heard a beautiful solitary voice as it began to sing. The song echoed off the crystal walls throughout the city and the angels appeared to be over-whelmed with emotion. Some began to cry. Others began to sing.

"What is this sound?" I asked. "What is this song?"

"This is the sound of the Creator singing a love song to Himself."

"The Creator?" I was stunned. "He sings to himself?"

"Yes. He sings to himself frequently."

"Why?"

"Because no one on Earth sings to Him any longer, and so he comforts Himself with His own songs."

This was an unfathomable concept for me, bearing no like-ness to the concept of an omnipotent overlord. I stammered, looking for words, "But—well, why doesn't He just demand singing?"

"He would never demand such a thing. Doing so would compromise one of His gifts to you."

"What gift?"

"Free will. If you will not sing to Him of your own accord, then He will sing to Himself."

The voice rang through the crystal halls filling it with beautiful resonating echoes. I became aware that, within this house of all hope, there was not only the sweetest of all music, there was also great humility, innocence, and faith in love.

"It's all rooted in love and compassion, isn't it?" I asked.

"Yes. There is no part of creation that does not desire love."

I do not know why the song was being sung with words that I could understand. I would have understood this love song even if it had been sung without words, but these were the words I heard:

The River of Life
That runs through Jerusalem,
Your name is Man.

The River of Man
That runs through Me,
Your name is Love.

"This is so beautiful," I whispered. I could understand why
the angels were crying. "Does He know I'm standing here listening to Him sing to Himself?"

"Yes, He's aware of you."

"But, He's—He's humbling Himself. Isn't this humiliating
for Him?"

"Perhaps you might like to join Him in singing?"

"Okay," I said, "but if I start singing, will He stop?"

"No—He'll sing with you, and you will become a part of
His song."

The words were very simple, so I began singing as loudly as
possible—loud enough to hear my own voice echoing off the
walls—and, I hoped, loud enough for Him to hear me as well.

"That's very good," the angel said, laughing.

"Do you think He heard me?"

"Oh, yes. Undoubtedly."

At this point, my next awareness was that of being shaken
by Craig. I had been singing loudly enough to awaken him in
the living room, where he'd fallen asleep.

"I'm not sure what is going on," he said, "but I have a feeling you'd better write down everything you were just saying."

"Oh, could you hear the singing, too?" I said, my eyes wide
and wild. "It was God! He sings to Himself!"

Craig backed away quickly. He did not want to hear more,
but I took his advice and wrote down the words of the song.

The following day, I could not stop thinking about the
events that I'd witnessed on the previous nights.

Tears came to my eyes several times that day when I
thought about the beautiful sounds, the beautiful city of crystal. Tears came when I thought about the simple humility of
the Creator, the Awareness that was aware of being unknown.

Tears came when I thought about the gold and white angels and their exquisite wings of passion.

I went to the kitchen to look at the butterfly wings that the teacher had told me to gather, and stopped, dumbfounded, in front of the container. The butterfly wings were gone with the exception of one gold and white fragment.

At approximately two the next morning, I was awakened by a bright light shining in my face. I was at this point sleeping with a sense of anticipation hovering in the background of my dreams, and I awoke quickly, eager to see who was visiting on this night. I had many questions to ask.

It was the same angel who had visited the previous night. This time, the angel did not tell me that there was something for me to see. In seeming anticipation of my questions, he asked me what I would like to see. I immediately began to give him a list of everything that might be of interest.

"I want to know where that city is—where the replica of Heaven is. And what happens when we die, where do we go? And that city—I want to see the city of angels again!"

"Come with me," he said, laughing.

In an instant, we were approaching the crystal city where the Creator sang His beautiful love song. A song was in progress, the angels were crying, and I began to sing to the Awareness, hearing his voice and my own as they echoed together through the city.

"I wish that I could come here often," I said to the angel.

"You can come as often as you'd like."

"I can? Every day, then. I want to experience this every day."

"Then you may."

"You mean you will come and take me here every day?" I asked.

"You do not need me—you are invited to come here. This city belongs to you."

"But I don't even know where we are."

The angel smiled and gestured upward, toward the towering crystalline walls that seemed to extend into eternity.

"Behold the city of angels," he said.

Still smiling, he then gestured toward me.

"Behold yourself. We are now standing within an open chamber of your DNA. This is where the Creator sings."

I do not remember my trip back from the city. I only remember that the largeness of the smallness was so overwhelming, I could no longer endure what I was witnessing with my conscious mind. At this point, the lesson was compassionately ended.

The following night, I was awakened by the same angel who had returned to complete the list of questions I had given to him. This time we did not travel to the city. We traveled out into space again, but somehow the heavens looked different.

I watched as many stars of varying brilliance moved at different speeds, and from all directions, toward an enormous light in the center of the Universe.

"This is the Consecration," he said, "it is love undiluted and concentrated."

"And the stars that are moving toward it?"

"Those are souls traveling through the mind of the Creator back into the undiluted source of all love."

"Why are they different, and traveling at different speeds?"

"They move according to their life's actions. If they are filled with joy and innocence, then they are brilliant and move quickly to enter the Consecration. But, it is difficult to move quickly when one is burdened with weights. Negative acts and emotions—thoughts and works of anger and hatred—they weigh heavily on the soul. They cover the brilliance that each soul is born with, and they are difficult burdens to carry. As each soul nears the Consecration it longs for, it is cleansed and freed of its burdens by the love it approaches, but sometimes it is a long process. For this reason, it is very good to pray for those who have died, especially if they died carrying heavy burdens."

"You mean like my sister?"

"Anyone who dies with burdens will be helped by your prayers. You can help ease their burdens, cleanse their soul, and help them on their journey toward the Consecration if you fill yourself with love and pray for them."

Suddenly a brilliant flash sped past us, and traveled direct-ly into the Consecration.

"What was that?" I asked.

The angel smiled. "That was a child."

The beauty of that child's soul was unspeakable. All of Heaven seemed to take notice of its journey back into para-dise.

"There is only love and beauty . . ." I said, ". . . and com-passion?"

"Yes."

"But, what about Hell—what about punishment for sins?"

"As you've seen, 'sin' is its own burden."

"And Hell? Where's Hell?"

"Hell exists in the mind of man. You won't find it here."

"You mean that the Creator wants all of the souls to return to Him?"

"Yes. Each soul contains within it a part of the Creator—a portion of consecrated, undiluted love. Love seeks love out in the Universe, and when it finds love, it finds itself, and it finds God. He would not turn away a portion of Himself."

Out of curiosity, I asked to see what Hitler looked like, and was told that the souls were not known by spoken names, but by their actions.

"And my sister?"

"Her soul is filled with love, and is becoming brilliant. She is, after all, in very good hands."

The Universe seemed to be moving according to one par-ticular law, and it was not crime and punishment. It was, as the teacher had said, cause and effect.

On December 15, I turned forty. That night I was awak-ened yet again by a bright light shining on me. I opened my eyes and found my teacher, the being of light, standing there, smiling, waiting for me to awaken and look at him.

"Will you come with me?" he said, reaching forward with his hand.

"Yes."

I took his hand and there was a sensation of wind and light blowing through my body. In a moment, we were floating out in the Universe. The galaxies were moving according to the compassionate Awareness, the stars embracing planets, their planets holding moons. Each particle down to the atom was known and held by Space, the great Awareness.

"Choose," he said, gesturing outward.

I looked at him, wondering if we were going to repeat the journey I made with the eagle. He understood my confusion.

"Choose a gift for yourself," he said.

"A gift?"

"Yes—choose anything."

I realized that this was an important moment, and I was briefly thankful that my primary concern in life was no longer my nose.

"Anything?" I asked.

"Yes."

I thought about it for a moment, and said, "I would like to be a healer of people."

"Are you sure that this is what you choose?"

"I have been a healer of wild animals for many years," I said.

He nodded his head in agreement, "Yes, you have."

"So, if it would be possible, now I would like to be a healer of people."

"Are you certain that this is the gift you choose for yourself?" he asked a second time.

"Yes."

I felt no pain as I saw both of my forearms leave my body and journey by themselves out into the stars. My forearms became large, or perhaps I became smaller, it no longer really mattered. Size is merely a perception that has no bearing or importance. I saw stars entering the opened forearms, and then flow out of the fingertips in blue streams. The hands then cupped themselves, and were filled with a lake of blue light. Holding the lake in the cupped hands, my arms were then given back to me.

"It is done," he said. "There is a mystery to the gift that you have chosen for yourself."

"There is?"

"Yes. It is a great mystery. The gift that you have chosen is given to you only while you are giving it away. Give it freely so that you may receive it."

I then found myself in my bedroom with both arms extended up into the night air. There was a blue haze surrounding my forearms and hands.

The following day, I asked Father Yosef if we might go for a walk so that I could describe the latest events to him. He agreed to join me, and we went for a walk at the site of the ancient burial mounds. It was there that I told him of my new gift.

"The problem is," I said, "I don't believe in 'healings.'"

"That's okay," he said, "it doesn't matter."

"What? How am I going to be able to do healings if I don't have any faith in them?"

"Faith healings are not dependent upon your faith," he said, "they happen because of God's faith."

Sometimes, he had a remarkable ability to remove obstacles from my path.

"Then, the healings will actually have nothing to do with me, or my faith?"

"That's correct. You'll just be the empty cup that God's going to fill."

That night I was awakened by Emily crying. I got up and went into her room.

"What's the matter, honey?" I asked, sitting down on her bed, next to her.

"It's my legs," she cried, "they hurt."

She was having the leg cramps that come in the night during children's active growing cycles. I decided to try my new gift on her.

Standing up, I wondered if there was supposed to be some sort of ceremony to be performed prior to the actual "healing." I had not been given a training manual. I clapped my hands together, rubbed them a few times simulating the warm-up I had once observed a magician perform, and took several deep breaths. Then, holding my breath and filling myself with as much strain and personal intent as possible, I placed my palms on her legs.

The entire room lit up.

She and I were both so startled that I stopped holding my breath, gasped, and pulled my hands away.

The room became dark again.

I placed my hands on her legs, and the room lit up. I took them, away and it became dark. Dark, light, dark, light, dark, light. I completely forgot about fortifying my intent as I watched this, amazed, again and again.

Emily's eyes were wide and her mouth was open. "Mommy, what is this?"

"Don't be afraid," I said, "it's God's light. He's making your legs feel better."

I decided that Craig should see this, and ran out to awaken him.

"You've got to see this!" I said.

Reluctantly, he came into Emily's room. I knew that it wouldn't work now, of course, but when I placed my hands on her legs, to my amazement, the room lit up.

I did this several times so he could see the light, dark, light, dark phenomenon.

When I finished my demonstration, and the room was dark again, he said, "I'm sure it's nothing—just static." He bent over Emily, and placed his hands on her. The room remained dark. I put my hand on her and it lit up.

If I had not been so intent upon the demonstration of "my" new abilities and had remembered that they actually had nothing to do with me, perhaps he might not have felt so slighted. He walked out of the room and said, "I don't know what it is, but whatever it is, I'm sure it's not what you think it is."

I would have probably said the same thing if the situation had been reversed.

Absorbed in the visual entertainment, I had completely forgotten the original purpose for being there, but Emily's legs had apparently stopped hurting, and she went back to sleep.

Several days later, John came down with a nasty bug. He spiked a fever of 102, and after several hours of non-stop vomiting, we decided to take him to the pediatrician to be monitored for dehydration. While I dressed John, Craig took Emily for a brief walk in the park because she had been cooped up in the house all day.

I did not feel that my gift would be of use in a situation as serious as this, but once I was alone with John, I decided to try it out, just in case. I placed my hands on his head, on his stomach, on his legs—not knowing where the virus or bacteria might be hiding—and he immediately fell into a deep sleep on the floor. In approximately five minutes, he awoke. He was completely well. He got up off the floor, went into the den and began jumping on the sofa.

When Craig and Emily returned after being gone for a total of ten minutes, this was how they found him.

Craig was, for the very first time, visibly stunned. "Did you do one of those 'healings' on him?"

"Yes."

"I guess maybe something is going on here, then."

It was one of the rare times that he seemed to acknowledge the presence of something very strange indeed.

For the most part, he was more comfortable remaining the person of logic and reason that he'd always been. It would be several years before I would come to understand that his healthy skepticism was not only a normal human response, but it was the precise lesson that I needed to experience during the time that we spent together.

—9—

Transition:
(Let's Call the Whole Thing Off)

Having seen all this, I now felt a burden of my own that was somewhat different from that of sin. It was a powerful and unexpected sensation that seemed to come out of the blue, leaving me feeling very anxious.

What had started out as a rather entertaining encounter with numerous Indian spirits and their traveling companion, a teacher from space, was now getting way out of hand.

Just as Craig had predicted on the day of the awakening, it was now not only merely taking over my life, but a quick before and after comparison of myself revealed that it had taken over my life—completely. Immediate countermeasures were needed.

I decided that it was time for all of this to stop, so that I might return to being a normal person once again.

Adding to my personal discomfort was the sense of isolation and new questions about heresy. The more I saw, the more it continued to oppose traditional teachings. In earlier times, the talks I was giving might have earned me a spectacular and fiery exit from this life.

I spoke to one final gathering of people. When I was told by a member of this group that it was not possible for me to be seeing and experiencing what I was seeing and experiencing because personal knowing is not permitted according to scripture, I canceled further speaking appointments, frustrated to the core.

I alone believed everything that I had seen. How could I not believe what I was personally witnessing? I alone felt relief in knowing that judgment was something that mankind had reserved for itself, and that the Consciousness of the Universe was one of compassion rather than vengeance. And, I alone could not take any more.

I was astonished, astounded, and confused. I felt out of sorts. I had not just seen and heard enough, I had seen and heard way too much.

Father Yosef was off doing some missionary work in Belize, but I called him on the telephone to voice my complaints. He answered on the first ring.

"I've seen enough," I said after relaying the latest events to him. "I don't want to see anymore."

"What do you mean?"

"I would like this to stop now. I've had enough, and I don't want to see any more visions. I want it to stop."

"Weren't the visions given to you out of compassion, to answer your own questions?" he asked.

"Yes, but now I want it all to stop."

"To stop?" he said, and then he yelled at me. "I have never heard of anything so ungrateful! Don't you realize there are people who would die, give up their lives, to be able to see what you're seeing?"

"I have died!" I yelled back. "My life as I knew it is gone! I want it back! I don't want to see anything else, and I don't want to see any more lights!"

"That is a defeatist attitude!" he yelled from another continent. Then he calmed down. "Look, you are just going through a period of transition. Yes, your life has changed, and yes, you are uncomfortable with it. But that's only to be expected with anything that's new. This won't last. You'll feel all right with it soon. I promise."

"How soon?"

"I don't know, maybe a few weeks, maybe a few months."

"And then will I be normal again?"

"Do you mean will you return to being the person you were before this all happened?"

"Yes," I said.

"No," he answered. "You will never be able to go back to being that person. That person no longer exists. This is the new you."

I hung up in his ear, in protest of the worthless advice he was giving me, and called Fred the Medicine Man. Basically, I gave him the same complaint, to see if he might know of some herbs or chants that would return me to my old normal self—the person I was prior to discovering that God was singing love songs in our DNA, and prior to all the lights.

Fred was far worse than Father Yosef, and not at all sympathetic. He laughed.

"Make it stop? Whaa-haa-ha!!! Oh, that's good! Haahahahahahah. You can't make it stop!" He was laughing so hard that I was sure there were tears rolling down his cheeks. I had seen this sort of laughter erupt from him before.

"There must be something that I can do!" I said.

"Nope," he said, he was actually gasping for breath, "it's only going to get worse," he added, barely able to get the words out before being overcome once again.

This was not what I wanted to hear.

I hung the phone up on Fred, exactly as I had with the priest.

Overwhelmed by the burden of feeling like a stranger in my own life, and feeling very real grief for the loss of the woman I had once been and would never be again, I went to my room while the children napped that afternoon and cried over my state of personal unbearable anguish and solitude. I didn't feel any better after my cry, though, and did not feel better the following day.

Instead, I felt worse. I felt dizzy from the strangeness of my own life. The depth of my sense of isolation grew to a stupefying degree. In the days that followed, I began experiencing episodes of horrifying panic in which my entire limbic system seemed to be screaming, "Run for your life!" Each attack required me to use every shredding fiber of will to resist doing just that.

One day in February of 1989, while taking an otherwise peaceful drive down to St. Marks, I heard that clarion call so powerfully that I stopped the car, jumped out and—following its orders—began running. After about fifty feet, my rational mind was permitted to speak a word or two above the din being caused by the panic-stricken limbic system.

"What exactly am I running from?" Like the jackass wearing the stick with a carrot suspended from it, I was, of course, carrying it all with me.

In early March, there was another powerful limbic insurgence, this time while taking a lazy, glass-bottom riverboat ride with my mother.

Because she is my mother, and therefore familiar with my normal appearance, she immediately recognized that I was in a state of difficulty. My eyes, as well as the cords in my neck, began to bulge. Sweat poured down my face and I prepared to jump overboard.

"You're having one, aren't you?" she leaned over and whispered, politely.

"Mm hmm," I nodded, gazing longingly at the water.

"You're not going to jump, are you?" she whispered, shaking her head in a motherly "No, no, no."

I wasn't able to talk, so I shrugged a "maybe."

"Don't jump, okay? You'll be all right in a few minutes."

I don't remember the rest of the trip, but when we docked I was still onboard. I made my way quickly to the restroom, where I became ill.

This convinced me that I needed professional help, and so thinking that this was a job too large for any one single professional to handle, I sought the assistance of two psychiatrists and a psychologist. In their offices, I took and then re-took what seemed like every test and personality inventory known to man. Most importantly, though, I talked. I told them what I had tried to tell Fred and the priest—that I had seen too much.

The tests indicated that I was not insane, that I was not delusional, and—to almost everyone's surprise—that I was telling the truth about what I had seen. Something had happened. The first psychiatrist sat at his desk the day the test results came in, and he wept.

"Will you tell me more?" he asked.

I agreed. I returned to his office and, taking my time, I told him everything. Sometimes, both of us wept over the simple messages of compassion.

He prescribed two temporary medications in order to stop the horrifying panic attacks, and they worked immediately and very effectively.

The second psychiatrist wanted to hypnotize me in order to find out more details, particularly about Judas.

Because I was previously told by the teacher that those details were not to be discussed, I did not permit the hypnotic investigation.

The psychologist wanted to come to my house and stand in the area where the teacher had stood, which I permitted.

I was given a tremendous sense of relief by those gentlemen.

But, still, I felt like a stranger in my own life. The sense of isolation continued to grow.

Several days after I learned that I was sane, the fragrance of the teacher filled the room, and several white stones fell onto the floor. He looked at me with his eyes of compassion.

"I feel like a stranger," I said. I was crying again.

He put his hand out toward me.

"Take my hand," he said, quietly, "and I'll show you that there are no strangers in Paradise."

I took his hand, and drew overwhelming comfort from the one source I told Fred and Father Yosef that I hoped to never see again. It was a confusing time, very troubling.

"Come with me," he said, "we will go for a walk."

We walked out into the front yard. It was cool day, but the pastel signs of spring and renewal were beginning to appear as life began to stir and awaken from its winter nap.

He drew my attention to the remains of a small drama that had involved the entire universe sometime during the summer of the previous year—the summer when I had planted the field of corn, and traveled to the desert. It seemed like an eon ago.

Clinging fast to the fence post with fleshless stick legs was the dried, tan shell of a cicada nymph. How the fragile shell had remained there for so long, as though waiting for the teacher to come and find it, remains a mystery.

A drama began to unfold in my mind, and the teacher was quiet, as though he might have been watching the same drama unfold.

On the first day of the growing season, the first day warm enough for the earth to catch and hold the sun's heat within her black and moist soil, the time of the quickening came. Life stirred within the warm loam, awakened by the hot call to exist. On such a day, the call had beckoned the cicadas to come up from the ground where they had slept in dark silence for seventeen years.

I remembered well the sounds of that summer, the droning buzz and hum of the cicadas. They had been a part of the summer's love song. The serenades of the birds had mingled well with those of the peepers and other hopeful lovers sharing the treetops. It seemed that everything was calling out to be noticed, as though aware that to pass this way and never know love is the only real sin.

The cicada would have heard her call on such a day. She would have crawled up from her chamber of darkness beneath the surface of the Earth, and out into the light she had never before known.

She then would have journeyed across the yard in search of something, not knowing quite what it was that she was seeking, but searching nevertheless.

Discovering the fence post, she had climbed up several feet, feeling satisfaction in being just a little closer to the sun. Having gone the distance, she had perhaps sat and rested, waiting for the unknown. And the unknown came to the cicada. It came and it split the full length of her life open, parting her shell in what surely would have appeared to be a death blow.

But I knew that this drama unfolding in my mind was not about death. It was about the unending journey of life.

The unknown had not killed her, it had opened something for her—unlocked a door that would lead her to her freedom. With the shell that had once contained her now opened, the new cicada emerged.

She must have pulled herself ghostlike and pale from the spent shell, assisted in her birth into a new life by only the sun, who then dried the tears and birth fluids from her—gently, carefully—very carefully, because here rested an unmistakable work of God.

Her wings would have elongated as they dried, and her paleness gave way to fluorescent colors and fancy patterns created by the mind of the Creator, the Awareness who had never once in the cicada's seventeen years of existence in darkness— never once—stopped thinking about her, never once stopped waiting to hear her sing.

Fully dried, the cicada would have then flown to the tree-tops to meet the lover who was calling to her, waiting for her.

Her empty shell would be left behind, clinging fast to the post long after the life it had once contained had flown away.

In time, the shell might be discovered by a little boy or girl in search of mysteries. It might be added to a collection of treasures by someone unaware that they held in their hands only a shell, and that the real treasure was elsewhere singing love songs.

The Earth was dancing to the song of life. It was a song from eternity, a necessary song, necessary in order to strengthen the vulnerable ghostlike soul as it is beckoned to come forward and stand in the light—as it is asked to know love.

I looked up at the teacher, who was no longer looking at the shell of the cicada, but was looking at me.

"The cicada who once lived in the darkness, is now living in the light." I said. "She cannot return to her old shell, because it can no longer contain her."

He smiled.

He had shown me all of this without speaking a single word.

I had found comfort from my loneliness a year earlier sitting in a corn field. The corn's needs were a reflection of my own, and I saw that the corn was my sister.

Now I drew comfort from the journey of the cicada. I saw in her journey a reflection of my own. I was not alone. I had never been alone.

As a child of the Universe, once again, I was surrounded by relatives.

As I waited for Father Yosef's prediction of comfortable acceptance to occur, I was often drawn to hold in my hands the mysterious white stones and the pottery that continued falling out of the air in and around the house.

Emily watched me as I reached into the Lakota box one day, and retrieved a handful of stones.

She sat next to me on the couch for a while, watching me without comment or question as I cupped the stones with both hands. I assumed that she was lost in her own thoughts during this quiet moment. But I was wrong.

"I know what they are, Mommy," she said after many minutes had passed.

"The stones?" I asked.

She nodded her head.

I should have known that she would understand their meaning—she had probably always understood their meaning.

"They are stepping stones to God," she said.

—10—

. . . By Any Other Name

 During the month of April in 1989, the teacher's visits in the daytime suddenly became more frequent and I sensed a very subtle uneasiness in the air. Sometimes I would look up from reading a book or working on a piece of crochet to find him standing there in silence, staring at me. I would wonder how long he had been standing there without speaking, and why.

Other times, he arrived with a desire to ask questions and obtain opinions regarding the various activities in which humans sometimes busy themselves.

One afternoon as I sat in the living room reading a book about man's bizarre search for the fabled Holy Grail, I looked up to find him watching me. He was smiling that afternoon, which was good to see.

"What is the 'Holy Grail'?" he asked.

"Well, I'm not sure. I think it's a cup."

"Oh, then it is a container?"

"Yes, maybe—a vessel of some kind. I'm not sure."

"Why does man continue to sift through the dust in search of such a cup?" he asked.

"I don't know, it would probably be something of great value. Worth a lot of money."

"It won't be found in the dust," he said. "If you wish to find such a cup, then look into one another's eyes."

The following afternoon, he returned.

"Why do you fast in my presence?" he asked me. I had been fasting several days a week from all food; it was something I was doing frequently.

"Because it's good to suffer," I explained, "it makes us more worthy to be in the presence of God." This was another lingering lesson that remained, in spite of all that I had seen. It had taken its roots during childhood classes about the joys of martyrdom and, therefore, its roots ran deep. He laughed out loud. He was about to do some pruning.

"The Awareness does not create your flesh hoping that you will mortify it. It is good to fast joyfully sometimes, but it is also good to have a joyful feast. While you are of flesh, you are not expected to deny yourself all that has been created in the physical realm."

"But you told me to fast."

"Fast, but not to extremes. Feast, but not to extremes. The laws of cause and effect extend to both. Partake within reason and according to self-control. The most important element, is the joy.

The following day he returned, singing a love song. It was a song about people.

> You are all that is sacred
> Called forth from the past
> To stand in the present
> And you hold in your hands
> The future.
> You are called
> To sit
> In the place of honor
> At the Table of the Great Feast.

Other beings found their way here during that very busy month of April, as well, some imparting strange messages that I still do not understand.

The Love Song of the Universe

One night I was awakened by a man shouting, "Rameses knew!"

I opened my eyes to see a tall, muscular, older gentleman with shoulder-length white hair. He was rather scantily clad, wearing a white garment that covered his right shoulder, was clasped at the waist and flowed to the floor, but the left side of his chest was exposed. In his right hand was a large gold-colored staff, and at the top of the staff was a gleaming trident.

His voice was very loud. He repeated his original announcement: "Rameses knew!"

(He pronounced Rameses, "R-r-r-r-AHM-ess-eez," trilling his R.)

I said, "Rameses knew what?"

"The Secret of the Triad," he answered impatiently as though everyone else already knew about this and I was the last to hear it. "I am here to give you the mathematical secret."

"Well, thank you very much, but I think you might have the wrong person," I said, "I don't know anything about math."

"Nevertheless, I am here to give it to you. I will repeat it as necessary. You will need to write it down." He said that it had to do with the perfection of the number three.

The thought has since occurred to me that he might have been saying something that only sounded like "knew," and I might have completely misunderstood his actual meaning. He might have been saying, "gnu," or "nu," or "new."

His formula consisted first of the geometrical design of a triangle containing three circles within it, arranged in another triangle. The center of the three circles—the area where their perimeters met each other—formed yet another triangle. The mathematical equation consisted of a triangularly-shaped, long-division cryptogram of numbers, all of which were divisible by three.

He said that the pyramids were not constructed as burial chambers, but were constructed as a sign that could be seen from a great distance. The sign indicated that knowledge of light was present here. He said that the triangle is a universal symbol for the language of light.

He left, and I've never seen or heard from him since.

Very soon after his visit, another visitor came with an exceptionally loud, male voice. I did not see him, only heard him as he shouted at me, seemingly through a megaphone at approximately three-thirty one morning. I had fallen asleep on the couch in the living room.

"Go get a pencil!" he screamed getting right down to business without any sort of greeting or introduction.

I fell off the couch and then jumped to my feet. Following his orders, I ran through the house in search of a pencil—not a pen, but a pencil. If I'd located a pen, I would have undoubtedly been sent again in search of a pencil.

He wished to talk about space travel.

He said—still shouting—that in certain quadrants of what we call "deep space," there are areas of anti-matter that have been artificially created. He said these areas contain extreme magnetic fields, and are used in space travel to "skip" from one quadrant to another without the passage of time. As one approaches the magnetic field, he explained, light and time are absorbed by the dense core of this field, and if the polarity of the vehicle is reversed at the appropriate time, the vehicle would "skip" from its current location (point A) to its destination (point B). Since time and light were being absorbed, he screamed, at least a portion of the distance would be covered without the passage of time. This was travel beyond the speed of light. Travel beyond the speed of light is not possible using combustion propulsion—but is possible using magnetic fields.

He hollered as well about two-dimensional portals that link different areas together without time or distance. Because I have no background in mathematics, I had some difficulty understanding much of this, and so he took time to explain it simply enough that a child might understand it.

He said that there is such a portal located in Central America and it is linked to an area in the U.S. He said that if a person in Central America wanted to see what was on the other side of this portal and put his head through it, the lower portion of his body would remain in Central America, while his head, having gone through the portal, would no longer be visible in Central America. His head would emerge from the side of a mountain in a US mountain range—the location of the portal's other side. "No damage done!" he shouted. (With the exception, I thought, of the damage done to the poor observer who might happen to be walking by either location during the experiment.)

The next visitor was from Africa. He was black, and attired in beautiful robes printed with exotic earth and foliage designs, mingling with the patterns of wild leopard. On his head he wore a turban that appeared to be made of silk, but unlike the robes, the silken fabric was plain and bore no designs at all. The man spoke no English, but greeted me quietly—softly—in a language that I did not understand. The room was charged with an atmosphere of quiet elegance. I have no idea of his identity, but he was breathtaking to behold. I believe that he just stopped by to say hello.

I was awakened next by a living staff of light, floating through the hallway similar to the way in which a shimmering hydra or jellyfish might swim through the sea. At the top of the staff were nine arms or tentacles, each terminating in an orb of light. When it first entered my bedroom, its nine arms were closed, but then—as it felt secure in my presence—it opened them revealing its core. It was quite beautiful, a beacon of light and consciousness in the dark night. It did not communicate with words, but with emotion. I was fascinated by its fluid motions and at ease with it. It expressed a desire to enter my children's room and look at them, and I permitted this, sensing no maternal fear in such a visit. I heard it singing a strange but beautiful song to them—a water song, or a Song of the Staff, or that of a cetacean—and the song had no words, only melody. The following night the strange living staff of light returned, this time with what I believe were its own offspring. The offspring were not staves yet, but were small glowing spheres, each bearing a replica of the large staff within. They were, perhaps, small ideas of hopes and joys not yet fully formed. The veins sparking within them contained the same colors and patterns as those in the arms of the staff, and this led me to believe that they were related.

The following night, I was awakened by a bright orange light. A large sphere was in the room, and inside it was an eagle at least six feet in height. The eagle's feathers were made of orange flames and his feet were outstretched, his talons opened as if ready to grasp his prey. He began moving slowly toward me, fierce talons glistening. Out of fear, I raised my left foot in order to keep him away. He withdrew his talons, closing both feet into balled eagle-fists, and he gently pressed both fists against the sole of my raised foot. Then he left.

Several nights later, the being of light returned to talk about space travel.

I assumed he meant space travel referring to journeys through the Mind of the Creator. But, no, he too wanted to talk about vehicular travel through space. He seemed to enjoy science.

He suggested that the reason we were having some difficulty "getting off the ground," was that we were creating our vehicles in the same manner that we had created our version of "God." We have been creating internal combustion engines in the image of ourselves. At some point, he specifically mentioned the Bussard ramjet, which prompted me to take another trip the following day to the State Library of Florida. (The library was playing an increasingly important role in helping me understand what was being said to me.)

He talked for several hours on the subject of our affinity with internal combustion, and suggested that it would be much more efficient to use a method of propulsion that did not require the digestion of fuel. Specifically, he suggested magnetic propulsion. He also suggested that it would make more sense to launch flights from orbiting satellites rather than terra firma, thus eliminating the enormous effort of thrust required to escape a full gravitational field.

His observations always seemed to make sense.

While trying to determine what, exactly, a "Bussard ramjet" was (it is a theoretical manner of space travel, in which a huge ship with a huge open maw funnels in, or "ingests," hydrogen particles while traveling through space, and uses them as the fuel for nuclear fusion—thus, it eats as it goes), I came across many other subjects that initially seemed to be unrelated, yet were in fact all related by a common character- istic: heresy. It is a word that can be used for just about any sort of new, or nonconforming idea.

While I was gripped in my life's most powerful desire to learn and seek the truth—to read the research on subjects I'd never dreamed of before—a new development occurred.

In the final days of April, 1989, visitations from the being ceased abruptly. I did not see him for several days and I began to suspect that he was contemplating departure.

On the last day in April, however, he returned, and awak- ened me to talk again about mankind's state.

"Will you come with me?" he asked.

"Yes."

We were in space, and I saw the enormous light in the cen- ter of the universe.

"What do you see?" he asked.

"That is the center of the universe," I answered, somewhat proud that I was now able to easily recognize different areas of deep space.

"Yes. It is yourself," he answered, quietly.

My pride vanished as I was immediately plunged into con- fusion once again.

"But I thought that was the center that I had seen before—the Consecration," I said.

"You are, after all, created in the image. You are—each of you—the center of your own universe. It is for this reason that you are meant to seek the truth with your own eyes. Because you each see the Universe from a different perspective, you will each have a different view of the same truth. Seek the truth yourself, and with opened eyes.

"If you build a clock made of glass and stand one person in front of the clock, and one person behind it, the person stand- ing on one side will see that the hands of time move only for- ward. The person standing on the other side will see that they move only backward. Both may argue that only their view is the correct one, but each would be basing their argument on what he alone has perceived: a fragment of the truth. Each would need to view what he is perceiving from different perspectives in order to understand that one cannot see the whole truth from a single vantage point.

"You are—each of you—filled with sacred potential. You are made from ancient particles of creation, and you have each been given sacred and compassionate gifts. You have been given the gift of memory so that you might create your future well. Remember that it is a tool of creation, not a tool of self-torture. Remember that the past is not a suitable dwelling place. Dwell in the present and place hope in the future. You cannot change the past, but with each moment you can change the present and each change effects the future of the Universe.

"You have been given the gift of free will. Remember that you are responsible for your own actions."

He now brought me into a beautiful garden that extended out into eternity.

"Is this the Garden of Eden?" I asked.

"This is your garden," he said. "You have each been given your own garden. Tend your own garden, and tend it well. You will be known only by the harvest of your own garden. You will not be known by the harvest of your neighbor, or by the harvest of your ancestors. Nor will you be known by the harvest of the leaders whose paths you follow. You will not be known by the good works of others, nor will you be known by the burdens others choose to carry. You will be known only by the harvest of your own garden. Tend it well."

There was a small, nondescript bird with brown feathers eating berries in the garden and the being stopped for a moment and he looked at her.

I did not know who this sparrow was—or more correctly, I did not remember who she was—nor did I know why she was there in my garden.

A conversation began to unfold in my mind. It was a conversation that had not yet taken place between a Native American holy man and myself.

I told the holy man stories that he might like to hear about wild animals—stories about the eagles, the bears, the beavers, and the deer that I had cared for—the important stories. He listened, and sometimes he laughed as he heard how the magnificent animals retained the nobility of their character while guests in my house and yard.

"But," he said, "you haven't told me the real story, yet. There was someone else that you cared for."

Having taken care of about twenty thousand wild birds and animals, I had no idea which story he wished to hear me relay next.

"No," he said, picking up the root beer float I made for him, "you might have thought that it was the eagle who was most important—or the bears, or the beaver, or the deer that you took care of. But it was a little one who was really the most important."

"Who?"

"It was the sparrow with the broken wing who was the most important."

This particular story would take me a moment to recall.

"How did you know about the sparrow with the broken wing?" I asked. I hadn't mentioned her.

He, however, was apparently able to see my thoughts.

"She was a messenger," he said. "And she came to you before the eagles, the beavers, the bears, and the deer, didn't she?"

"Yes, she was first. But how did you know this? And what was her message? I don't remember receiving a message from her."

He laughed.

"Oh, the message wasn't meant to be given to you, it was meant to be given to someone else."

"Who? Who was the message given to?"

"It was given to Grandfather."

"To Grandfather?"

"Yes. When you fixed her wing, you gave freedom back to her. What happened next?"

"She flew away," I said.

The holy man pointed up to the sky as though he was watching the little bird making her journey. Somewhere in his old eyes, in his sight and gifted vision, I knew that he was seeing this story unfold. He waited patiently as he watched the sparrow fly to her destination and deliver her message.

"She flew all the way up to Grandfather," he said, "and showed him that someone had stopped to help a sparrow."

He continued looking past the sky, and into a distant land that was filled with good stories and the grandfather of his ancestors.

"And so that is why you can tell stories about the eagles, the beaver, the bears and the deer today," he said, "because someone paid attention to the story of a sparrow."

This conversation about the sparrow I was now looking at in my garden, would take place three years later, in 1992.

My thoughts returned to my garden. I heard children laughing nearby in the garden. Their laughter was familiar to me—it was the laughter of my children. Not far from the sparrow in the berry patch was a cicada that, having gone the distance, and having passed through its moment of metamorphosis, was singing.

Its summer song blended well with the laughter of the children.

There was a corn field in the garden, and clouds filled with Indians. There were wildflowers and sage and purple cone-flowers. Near the field of corn was a bush of yellow roses. Several butterflies bearing colors that only the Creator might convincingly intermingle fluttered around the blossoms.

Overhead, an eagle was soaring, screaming its own love song so that all might hear it and know it.

Between two citrus trees, their boughs bending with sprays of blossoms fragrant with promise, I saw the black and white weaver spider sitting on a brand new web of faith.

This was a garden that had been filled with many gifts.

"Remember that the most seemingly insignificant parts of creation are deserving of respect: they are sometimes the greatest of teachers," he said in a near whisper, now looking down, his hands clasped behind his back as we walked through the garden.

"Remember that the Creator sings in all that is created, and that you are a part of all that is created. The Creator is a verb, and the name of the verb is Love.

"Remember to set aside a portion of one day of the week to begin a healing of the earth of which you are a part.

"Remember that control, for the most part, is an illusion. There is only one power and force over which you truly have control, and it is your own free will. You alone are responsible for your actions.

"Remember that you may choose to walk your own path. If you choose a path of light but stop to pick up burdens along the way, then even a path of light will become heavy.

"Remember—all that you see is a reflection of all that you are, or all that you might be. The Earth is a reflection of the condition of humankind. Humankind is a reflection of the condition of the Earth.

"Remember to be cautious with your thoughts and your words; they are tools of creation.

"Remember cause and effect.

"Remember that one person speaking alone in the wilderness can bring about little change, but one person speaking alone within a multitude can bring about great change.

"Remember that the past is not a suitable dwelling place.

"Remember the butterflies."

"You're going to leave, aren't you?" I asked.

"Remember the Indians."

"I don't want you to leave!" I said.

"Remember that there is nothing more important than love. It ignites wonders to behold. It, too, is a tool of creation. It creates itself, and respect, and joy."

"Please don't leave me," I said.

He did not answer. He stopped walking and looked directly at me, seeing me. Smiling, he held out his hands to me, palms up, and I grasped them.

"Remember all that has been given to you, and that while you might only hold it in your hands for a brief time, the gift is yours to keep forever."

"But I don't want you to leave," I said, "I think I'm in love with you."

"Remember me."

I phoned the priest the next day to inform him of the latest messages, and of my suspicions.

"I think he's either left, or he's going to leave," I said, feeling a heavy tear run down my face.

"What makes you think that?" he said.

"He asked me to remember him."

The priest was quiet for a moment, thinking, then he replied, "Maybe he doesn't mean it the way you are taking it."

"What do you mean?"

"Maybe he wants you to try to remember who he is."

"I don't understand."

"Never mind. It was just a thought. How would you feel about his leaving?"

"Terrible. I've fallen in love with him. I think I'm going to continue to feel wonderful because he has altered my whole life. But I would miss him terribly. He showed me how connected I am to everything, that I'm never really alone, that I'd greatly underestimated my capacity for just about everything—even love. But I don't want him to leave, I want him here."

"In your hand, so to speak."

"Yes." It seemed selfish of me, but that's what I wanted.

"I have a feeling that he's not going to leave. I don't think that this has anything to do with departure. I think it has to do more with arrival. I also think there's something that you should read now," he said.

"Okay," I said, "what?"

"The Gnostic Scriptures."

A tidal wave of horror and suspicion washed over me. The word "Scripture" could only refer to one dreaded subject—a subject now presenting new frustrations in my life.

"Does this have anything to do with Christianity?" I asked.

"No," he answered, "actually it doesn't."

Nevertheless, it sounded ominously religious, and I hoped that after having placed so much trust in Father Yosef for so many months, that he was not about to dishonor the promise he had made to me when we first met.

"This is not an attempt to convert me, is it?" I asked.

"No, not at all. Are you familiar with the term gnosis?" he asked.

"No."

"It means having personal knowledge of something. I think you should obtain a copy of the Gnostic writings. They are ancient documents that were found hidden in the Nag Hammadi desert, and in caves in Qumran. They contain some information that you might find very interesting."

"Why?"

"Just try to have an open enough mind to read through them."

I told him I'd think about it.

After several days of thinking, I decided to take the risk. Accompanied by the two children, I paid another visit to the State Library to locate a translation of the Dead Sea Scrolls.

Upon our arrival, the front door of the building opened inexplicably as we approached it. The next door we approached—the elevator—also opened inexplicably.

A trip to this library is not to be made, of course, without a visit first to the chamber of the mastodon—the museum that is located in the eerie, dimly lit basement. The mastodon stands as a very fitting, long-dead but still proud sentry of bones at the dark doorway. He welcomes the curious to come and see the museum's wondrous relics. One never knows what treasures will be found there. We have seen old shipwrecks, Tarzan's loincloth, and a mechanical shark from Jaws.

We took the complete tour, including a visit to Granny's Attic where good children who have been careful not to touch anything of wonder can then play with selected old stuff hands-on, compliments of a grateful museum staff. After playing, we left and approached the main elevator.

As we neared it, the door opened again of its own volition and John, in a bit of a rush, let go of my hand and ran ahead of Emily and me. He boarded the empty car by himself. A look of horror came to his face as the doors immediately closed and John was launched into a journey to parts unknown.

Reality set in quickly. John took what must have been a very deep breath and then exhaled it in a most memorable and lengthy scream. I listened helplessly to this sound as it echoed through the metal elevator shaft, reverberating through the floors, halls, and mastodon bones in this otherwise quiet building. The bitter taste of panic rose in my throat. My son's one-note wail grew faint and low in the distance, in accordance to the Doppler effect (which I had recently read about), and then—with great relief—we heard his scream become louder and louder as he was returned immediately to the basement by the invisible doorman.

The door opened on its own and John ran out and into our arms. After a brief reunion in which we reviewed the reasons why we should hold hands regardless of how old we are, we calmed ourselves and rode—together—to the second floor.

The suites and vaults of the library are nearly always quiet and devoid of patrons, and this day was no exception. As we approached the elevator leading to the warehouses, its doors also opened. We stepped into the car, and it began our ascent to the floor that house religious books.

The area containing religious material generated by man (and an occasional woman) was nearly overwhelming. We walked up and down several aisles as I tried to choose an appropriate book before I noticed a book that was lying on its side at the end of the aisle. It was unshelved. I walked to that book and picked it up. It was entitled, *The Gnostic Scriptures,* translated by Bentley Layton (Doubleday, 1987), and it contained his translations of the ancient texts. It would do, I shrugged.

Nearby, also unshelved, was *The Nag Hammadi Library,* a tome containing more translations of Gnostic writings, with James L. Robinson as general editor (Harper San Francisco, 1990). The oddness of the title appealed to me, so I selected that book as well, and we returned to the elevator. Once again, the doors opened strangely as we approached.

Back down on the second floor, I checked the books out and we went home. The kids decided to play out in the front yard, and I deposited both books—unopened—on the sun porch, and watched TV.

Several days of notable quietness passed, and finally, on the evening of May 16, 1989, the teacher returned, awakening me with his light. I sat forward in the bed waiting for him to speak, but he did not say anything. He simply stared at me for a long while, and then left.

The following night, the same thing occurred. He stood near my closet doors and stared at me. There was something in his eyes, a great pleading, a sadness perhaps, a loneliness. I found the pain in his eyes unsettling.

On the morning of May 18, 1989, I phoned Father Yosef, who was now back in town after another missionary trip, to describe this unusual behavior and ask his opinion.

"He seems to want something from me," I said, "but I'm not sure what he wants. He looks very sad and it's about to break my heart."

"Maybe he's waiting for you to ask him who he is."

"No, I already did that, remember? It was a long time ago."

"No you didn't," the priest said, "you asked him his name, and he told it to you. He also said that you wouldn't understand it. This time ask him who he is."

"Okay, if he comes back tonight, I'll ask him."

He came back that night.

I lay there in my bed watching him as he stood looking at me in silence for the third night in a row. Rising up to lean upon my left elbow, I asked, "Who are you, anyway?"

A look of relief came over his face. This was, indeed, exactly what he was waiting for. He approached me and placed both hands on my shoulders. Bending down over me, he put his head against mine, and I smelled the sweetness of his fragrance and breath. This was a tender moment and I thought that he was going to kiss me, but he did not have that in mind. What he had in mind was to give me the answer to my question.

With his head against mine, and his mouth touching my left ear, he spoke softly, slowly, in one of his whispers.

"I am the Silence and the Word," he said. "I am the Silent Voice of the Enlightenment which has no Words. I am the Word of Deliverance."

Stunned and horrified, I pulled away, out of his hands, and looked up at him. "Oh, no," I said.

A look of deep anguish clouded his face, and he slowly rose

until he was standing. Looking devastated, he began slowly backing away, never taking his eyes off mine. And then he was gone.

The following morning, very upset, very angry, I called Father Yosef. I felt as though I had been "tricked." Somehow he had crept into my life posing as a spaceman—and I never suspected a thing. I repeated the Teacher's words for the priest.

"That's who I thought it was," he said, quietly.

"What? You mean to tell me you knew this and didn't say anything?"

"Well, I suspected, but I didn't know. Besides, it wasn't my place. If I had said anything, you wouldn't have listened to a word he said."

"But he tricked me! He let me believe that he was a man from space!"

"He is," the priest said.

"What do you mean?"

"Space—you were shown that Space is the conscious mind of the Creator!"

"How long have you known?" I demanded.

"I began to suspect right after you told me about the fish."

"Then you knew it all along! Look, you know my feelings about this—you know that I hate his teachings—" I screamed into the telephone.

"It's not his teachings that you hate," he said, interrupting me, his voice matching mine in its anger, "it's what man has turned his teachings into that you hate!"

He was talking in circles.

"I know what I hate and what I don't hate! I told you that I didn't want anything to do with Christianity—or him!" I shouted, and then repeated what I'd just said for good measure, "I don't want anything to do with him!"

"Well, I'm not telling him to leave," Father Yosef shouted back, "if you want him to leave, you'll have to tell him yourself!"

There was a brief moment of silence as we both seemed to be in search of something powerful and stinging to say next. My face felt hot, flushed with anger, and confusion. I was now facing a rather large decision. If I ever saw him again, I could tell him to leave—to get out of my house. Or I could attempt to accept him in spite of his identity.

"Have you read the books I told you about yet?" he asked, voice still raised.

"No!"

"Well, I suggest that you start reading—now!"

Father Yosef very rudely hung up the phone before I could respond.

I went out to the sun porch where the books were still lying, unopened, and began reading.

The first book I opened was *The Gnostic Scriptures*, a translation of the ancient texts by Bentley Layton. I did not start in any particular place, just opened the book and skimmed over a few pages with half-hearted interest, not understanding most of what I was plowing through, and not really caring one way or the other.

"I cannot believe he did this to me," I repeated to myself, as the night's horrifying revelation replayed itself in my mind.

Then the book fell open to the "Secret Book According to John," specifically, the Poem of Deliverance, and my eyes passed over references to beings of Light. In that one brief reference, my full attention was captured. While I couldn't understand some of the religious jargon, Beings of Light I could understand fully.

> Again I returned for a second time.
> And I traveled, coming into the beings of the Light . . .
> . . . Yet a third time I traveled
> . . . and I entered the midst of their prison,
> Which is the prison of the body.
> And I said, "O listener, arise from heavy sleep."
> And that person wept and shed tears, heavy tears;
> And wiped them away and said, "Who is calling my name?
> And from where has my hope come, as I dwell in the bonds of the prison?"
> And I said, "It is I who am the forethought of the uncontaminated Light . . .
> And I who am leading you . . .

Arise! Keep in mind that you are the person who has listened;
Follow your root, which is myself, the compassionate . . .
. . . I have told you all things, so that you might write them down and transmit them . . ."

The Apostle John spoke quietly to me on that day, whispering messages in written words across a sea of centuries. Beings of Light were traveling to visit other Beings of Light—human Beings of Light—awakening them from sleep, transmitting messages of compassion to them, messages of help and hope meant to be written down.

The words flowed through my mind like a liquid balm, an ointment. Singing a familiar love song, John's words calmed for a moment the turbulent storm of confusion raging within me. These were words that had been written nearly two thousand years ago, and yet they were familiar. According to the writer, it was not at all out of the ordinary to for humans to be visited by Beings of Light two thousand years ago. Light, Light, Light. There were references to the Light everywhere—but I had never heard about any of this prior to that moment.

The pages turned, touched softly by a breeze or a breath— or a hand that I could not see. I saw an unusual word at the bottom of page 120 of *The Gnostic Scriptures*. It was a reference to the sign of the fish.

Strange memories began to stir and the memories produced strange questions and wonder. Fish, the sign of the fish. The unusual connection to fish had been in clear view since day one of this entire experience. I telephoned Father Yosef in near hysterics.

"Please come over and help me through this," I said.

He was apparently waiting for my phone call. The priest came over immediately carrying more books.

The first of many corrective measures about mistaken identities was about to be taken.

High tide was about to occur.

This time, the tide would bring with it a cleansing flood, a good deluge that would wash cloudy misunderstandings away from once-clear and powerful teachings.

—11—

The Hidden Scriptures:
Let There Be *Gnosis*

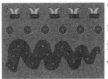"Fish," I said to the priest, as we settled onto the couch in the sun porch, each of us holding a stack of books. "Please tell me what you know about this 'fish' reference."

"Think back to that first night you saw him," he said, "when he told you that there was something more important than what was upon your nose."

"Yes, he said there was something else more serious that was in need of my attention."

"Right. He was telling you that what you needed was right there under your nose—he was standing there in front of you! And when you asked him what it was you needed, he told you."

"Fish."

"Right."

"But, I don't understand. Why did he tell me to eat fish?"

"He didn't."

I quickly reviewed the words of the conversation between

the Being and myself on the night that I was finally able to see him in September.

"He never told you to eat fish," the priest said, quietly, sensing my confusion, "he told you that you needed fish. When he told you this, you were the one who said you would get on it right away by eating fish and seaweed. You told me that he laughed when you said this. No wonder he laughed. He was telling you that you needed him."

"But I hate him!" I said, somewhat startled at my own rage. "I hate his judgmental teachings, and—and his contempt for women!"

Of course, this was not really the true cause of my anger—I'd never seen or heard the first hint of any contempt or judgment coming from this Being, this man from the Light I had come to know. My anger was due more to my state of shock and confusion. Nothing about the man I knew seemed to conform with standard doctrines attributed to him, or established in his name.

Maintaining a professional, cool steadiness, Father Yosef looked directly at me and said, simply, "I don't think you hate him at all. At least, that's certainly not what you told me."

There was a long pause. Still looking directly into my eyes, the priest said, "You told me only a few days ago that you're in love with him."

"I'm in love with him—but not him!" I stammered, not quite sure how to explain this emotional morass, and embarrassed because hot tears were now welling in my eyes, threatening to betray my personal state of disturbance.

"As I have said," the priest said, looking down at the book in his lap and away from my exposed emotions, "I think that what you are hating is a mistaken identity about this man—this Teacher—as well as teachings attributed to him in error. What you're hating is the inaccurate characterization that has been created over the centuries by mankind. You're not hating him, you're hating what people have invented about him."

"I hate all of this," I said, now sounding as though I were trying to convince myself rather than the priest, who had just made a very good point.

He turned the pages of Gnostic writings and pointed to something incredible. It was a strange composition, filled with opposing and paradoxical thoughts not unlike my own in this particular hour. It was a poem about viewing the truth from two vantage points, about love and hatred, about how easy it is to mistake the identities of others. Written with Gnostic androgyny—unbiased gender equality—a divine, human paradox had been sent to cry out to human minds that were open to new thought. The title of the poem was, "Thunder, Perfect Intellect," and the words—perhaps written by a man, perhaps not—were being spoken by a woman.

The priest's fingertips touched the page just below a single line that was somehow—impossibly—addressing this very moment.

The line was a question being spoken by one identified as the first and the last, and its simplicity was poignant: Why do you love me and also hate me?

Father Yosef and I sat in silence for a while, reading, and pointing out sentences to each other as we read the fascinating details of personal encounters with the near-indescribable Beings of Light.

The ancient encounters were once held to be the most desirable and treasured of all life experiences. I knew why. The effect upon the human being is universal. The Light is something that every cell in the body recognizes instantly—while the conscious mind then struggles to comprehend and explain what it is witnessing.

Two thousand years separate my own account and the ancient writers' accounts with the Light; years during which the original knowledge and written descriptions of such encounters have been all but purged from the Earth. Standing in silence in the midst of those many years without Light, however, is the indestructible truth. While mankind might have burned books, and judged as heretics those who follow the Light instead of traditional teaching, the Light itself cannot be extinguished. A timeless divine gift, it remains available for all, offering a direct connection between the human individual and the divine giver of the gift. It is this connection that requires no intermediaries, and it offers the constant and unchanging messages of truth and hope for which humanity has always hungered.

The ancient descriptions of the encounters were identical to mine.

The Light of the badly misunderstood christ illumination—the untouchable, divine christening—is unchanged.

The messages conveyed through the Light are unchanged.

And the man, the Being from the Light who was now the object and focus of my full attention, was described in perfect detail in the books on my lap. He, the Teacher, is unchanged.

His personal makeup is unchanged.

Questions from those who met and witnessed him were unchanged.

What is he, this man who is flesh one moment and Light the next? Setting all names aside, what, in the name of Heaven and Earth, is he? According to the Gnostic writings, this very question was also being asked by baffled witnesses two thousand years ago.

Is he but one of the celestial emissaries who has come here again and again to show us our true human potential? Is he a messenger sent to ask us to try to remember our own divine origin? Because his messages are timeless, unchanged, and forever speaking of the endless life of the soul, is it perhaps time, at last to stop referring to him in the past tense?

One question seemed to lead to another.

With some humor we noted another of his personal preferences that also remained unchanged. While he had been known by many, many different names, salutations, and titles—possibly dating back even longer than a mere two thousand years—there was one title in particular that he did not wish to be given.

He did not wish to be referred to as "master." (Gospel according to Thomas 13, *Nag Hammadi Library*)

The ancient writings held many good surprises and affirmations.

I went into the bathroom to retrieve a box of tissues. Returning, I placed it on the couch between the priest and myself. I would need the entire box on this afternoon. My state of shock was profound.

In the Gnostic writings, it became clear that, not only did the Teacher repeatedly encourage individuals to go within and seek the luminous truth individually, but with order and balance he acknowledged and established the equal status of the female in this call to come and know.

There were no suggestions or teachings of disrespect or contempt for the female attributed to Jesus in these ancient scriptures, nor was there any demand for female subservience. Quite the opposite was true. The rabbi did not merely invite all who had been divinely inspired and illuminated to speak of their visions, he reminded them that, having been divinely inspired, they were then divinely expected and commanded to speak and teach, whether male or female. There was to be no exclusion based upon gender. The instructions calling for gender bias and female submission are in New Testament letters attributed to Paul—the only apostle who was not a disciple of Jesus, and therefore was not present while he was teaching. (See 1 Corinthians, 11:3, 7, 9; 14:34, 35; 1 Timothy 2:11, 12.)

Stated repeatedly, and serving as unquestionable example of his revolutionary stand on gender equality, the Gnostic scriptures maintain that among the disciples surrounding Jesus, his most beloved companion was the one named Mary.

In the Gospel according to Thomas, we found another interesting teaching that struck chords of sense and sensibility. This was the unabridged teaching regarding the act of "seeking" the truth.

Jesus said,

> "Let one who seeks not stop seeking until that person finds; and upon finding, the person will be disturbed; and being disturbed, will be astounded." (Gospel according to Thomas 2.)

The teaching goes on to say that after being astounded, that person will finally come to terms with what they have discovered, and they will find peace and composure. They will know the truth, and personal knowing—gnosis—is the key to eventual peace and composure.

Father Yosef tapped the passage with his finger. It was an important one.

"This is a compassionate warning about the rather difficult period of transition that one sometimes goes through after finding the truth," he said.

The messages coming from people writing two thousand years ago seemed to contain timeless instructions needed by all humans seeking change and spiritual growth. We noted also that the Teacher did not refer to his mission as "Christianity," but simply as, "The Way." Humble simplicity was at its core.

According to the Gnostic writings, the disciples were told to give the instructions for growth and change to others. In doing so, they were to be gracious, compassionate, and above all—above all else—they were to be nonjudgmental.

They were to teach others to seek personal acquaintance with the Divine, and to not stop seeking until they had found it.

There were to be no elite titles of rank or status. All were to be equal. There were to be no bizarre, manmade rules or rituals that might cause protest, separation, suffering, or division. The gifts of love and healing were to be given freely to others, and the disciples were not to accept or amass riches in exchange for them—nor were they to be too picky about the food offered to them when they were guests in people's houses.

(What goes into your mouth is not half as important as what comes out of your mouth, he told them. [Gospel according to Thomas 14, *Gnostic Scriptures*])

Jesus seemed to have great insight into the human psyche, and knew that excess rules would lead to factiousness, while simplicity and love would assure cohesiveness. He told his disciples to keep the rules simple, and to add nothing to what he established (see the Gospel of Mary, Fragment 9, *Nag Hammadi Library*.)

Father Yosef left late on that afternoon.

"Stay with it, okay?" he said, opening the kitchen door and stepping out onto the stone porch.

"Yeah," I said. He knew that I would "stay with it," because the battle was already over. It had actually been over for hours.

"Thank you, Father," I said.

"Oh, it was a pleasure," he answered, smiling with exaggerated mirth—the entire ordeal had presumably been anything but a pleasure.

"Don't tell anyone about this," I said, "or about me, or about you-know-who."

"Don't worry," he answered, shaking his head, "I won't."

A day that began in outrage was turning out to be a good day for all concerned parties, after all.

As the afternoon grew into early evening, a sense of great calmness settled upon me. Having read the old words of wisdom, I knew that this was the promised sense of peace and composure as recorded in the Gospel of Thomas. The truth had been discovered, and now, in gnosis, peace would be forthcoming.

Gnosis. My experience finally had a simple name. There was peace in knowing its name, and knowing that what I had experienced—a simple gnostic illumination—was not unique, that it had once been well-known by human beings before its details were hushed and eventually forgotten. And, there was also a hint of peace in knowing that what I'd witnessed was indeed happening "according to scriptures." It was conforming rather nicely to the lost scriptures of John, of Mary, of Thomas, of Philip, of James—scriptures hidden away in a cave for safekeeping.

At some point, I felt compelled to trace the root of the word "ballast" which seemed to be another aspect of the original teachings of the rabbi—balance, and stability. They seemed to be close relatives of compassion, and of cause and effect. I opened a tattered, old dictionary. There, under ballast, I found:

1. substance that improves stability
2. something that gives stability, especially in character

And to my utter amazement, I found—

3. gravel or broken stone.

I looked at the Lakota box that held some of the Teacher's ballast, and another wave of confirmation and understanding washed over me, bringing with it a new question and a new sense of awe. How did the Lakota Grandfather know?

I put the dictionary and other books away, and sat in the living room, thinking.

The afternoon sun was sending low and long shafts of golden light through the windows. Craig and the kids would be home soon from their afternoon at the park, but now, in utter stillness, there was time to savor the enormous breadth of what appeared to be a plan unfolding slowly and patiently, and with great awareness.

The teachings of a man from the Light first drew crowds of listening people not because they feared Hell if they didn't listen to him, but because his teachings made them feel good about themselves and filled them with hope, love, and peace. He was teaching gnosis. He was telling people that they—*they*—were the children of God, and that they, being of divine origin, could experience the gnosis that was their birthright if they would only go within and seek it themselves. He was teaching full, individual knowingness, because with it comes a personal relationship with the Divine Universe.

But his most profound teachings from the Light—that we are divine in origin—were banished, and in time, good memories faded.

No longer able to think of the emissary himself except as someone of the past, no longer knowing his real messages, no longer able to remember even our own origins, we lost The Way and our sense of personal inner goodness. Gnosis gave way to confusion. The Awareness would again become unknown and unapproachable. It would be known only as a malignant deity to be feared, or if at all possible, appeased.

But while mankind might have interrupted the divine plan while it was in progress, interruptions are only temporary setbacks.

Divine countermeasures were taken.

As the second millennium began to create a rosy hue of dawn on the horizon, the last of the surviving Gnostic writings—scriptures secretly hidden away in caves for the better part of two thousand years—would be mysteriously re-discovered, just in time for that long-awaited millennium.

—12—

Can We Try Again, Please?

On the night that I first came to accept the unfolding identity of the Teacher—the night that I was able to accept a truth that would have knocked me off my feet had I not been lying down when he, the rabbi, delivered it to me—he visited again.

As I walked out of the bathroom at approximately eight-thirty, he was standing in the hallway. He was smiling and radiant—luminous.

He must have been silently present and vigilant during my intense day of research. He must have seen it all, because there was an unmistakable look of very human relief on his face.

His right hand was raised in a gesture of peace and greetings. His left hand was at his midsection. Not one to harbor grudges, he did not appear to be at all resentful of my earlier claim that I hated him.

I was so startled when I opened the door and found myself unexpectedly face-to-face with him, that I accidentally walked through him, something I'd never done before.

I heard a rush of winds and the love song, and felt every atom in my body scatter outward, showering small sparks into deep space. I fell inward and outward at the same time—scattered everywhere—exploding, imploding—my atoms laughing, singing. Thoughts became mingled, and as I found myself standing inside his consciousness, I felt fearlessly safe, and loved.

Songs were everywhere, filling space, echoing through the crystal chambers, and endless corridors of DNA.

This was where I wanted to stay. But as I stepped through and emerged on the other side with a loud bang—an explosion similar to the one that occurred when the young native man touched my arm in the front yard—my consciousness returned abruptly from space, my thoughts became my own again, and I found myself standing in the hallway with my back to him.

Stunned by what I had just experienced, I turned to look at him. His back was to me. He turned slowly to face me. I saw that he was dressed differently now, and that he was laughing quietly—apparently unoffended by my rude blunder of having somehow stepped through him. In fact, he looked as though he might have enjoyed it.

Facing me, still smiling, he looked directly into me, into the chambers that he had opened with those eyes of his many months earlier.

He now wore a dark red robe over one shoulder of his white garment. A staff was in his right hand—a strange staff, the top of which was glowing. Resting across his shoulders was a young sheep. He was dressed as the ancient yet timeless archetype of the shepherd.

If he had ever dared to appear in this manner before this day—the first day that I could tolerate his identity—his love song would have fallen upon my closed heart and mind, all because of a two-thousand-year-old misunderstanding and a mistaken identity.

Knowing this, he had been content to be perceived as someone from space. And truly he was just that.

He was a man of many names, too many for a human to utter at one time. I knew some of his names and signs now, and could speak some of them, although not all at once as he had previously done. But the names uttered by mankind were not important. Called by any name, in accordance to his philosophy, he would be known by the fruits of his works.

"I love you," I said.

"The Son of Man does have a place to lay his head," he said, "he rests it upon the sheep that he has found and carries on his shoulders."

I tried to remember every detail of this moment so that I might not ever forget the beauty of it all—his hair, his eyes, his exotic fragrance of myrrh and spices, the rich colors of his robe, the light that was still singing. I studied him carefully and he allowed me to do this—to stare at him and take everything in, etching it all into my mind.

There were no scars marking him—none—and this was perhaps reflective of his philosophies and teachings. He was not dwelling in the past. He was standing in the present.

Then, he disappeared.

The following night while I was standing in the bathroom looking into the mirror, he returned. A flash of light reflected into the mirror and I saw that he was behind me. I turned to look at him.

"I want to go with you," I said.

"You can't come with me now," he said. "There is something that I wish to ask of you, and if you choose to do it, it will be necessary for you to remain here."

I knew immediately what he was going to ask. He was going to put me to the test, and ask me to try and keep all of this a secret. Quite frankly, I was more than happy to oblige.

"Okay," I said, relieved, "listen, you don't have to worry about anything—I won't tell a soul about you, or any of this. I won't ever mention it again."

He laughed. I was misinterpreting his intentions once again.

"Tell others everything that you have seen and heard," he said, raising his arms and spreading them out wide in the shape of a huge, full circle.

"What?"

"Tell others," he repeated, smiling.

"But no one will believe this!"

"You are not responsible for what others believe," he said. "You are not being asked to bear that responsibility. Nor are you asked to try to convince others to believe what you are going to tell them. You are only asked to tell them what you have seen and heard as a witness."

"But what if I accidentally tell something that is meant to be a secret?"

"Nothing has been told to you in secret, except for the Yehuda story. You will not bear any burden of secrecy, because the secret that was spoken to you was removed from your memory."

"But—well, this is terrible," I said, not wishing to have to go public with this. I was already familiar with that frustrating crusade. It had been a difficult enough endeavor for me when I thought he was just a visitor from space. "I don't want to have to tell people about this!"

He embraced me lightly, barely touching me, but his hands felt strong, and I wondered how I could have walked through him the previous night. Tonight he seemed to be a man of warm flesh, of bone, and of blood. A sense of fortification welled in me, possibly something similar to that which heartens the cicada as she crawls out of darkness and prepares to go her distance for the Light. As I stood there with his hands upon me, something unfolded within my mind. It was a small drama that involved the entire universe a short time ago, this particular drama occurring just after Thanksgiving. I saw in lucid detail the whole story as it unfolded, without words, in my mind.

On a winter afternoon, I watched as a young girl of little wealth gave away theater tickets so that she might come instead to join a gathering of people.

I watched her.

It hadn't been easy to give away those tickets—she had saved for them a long time. But something—someone—had whispered a suggestion to her on that day that if she would come to this meeting and listen, she might hear a message being spoken to her, personally.

She normally wasn't one to listen to such ethereal whispers, but on this particular occasion, she felt oddly moved. She gave her tickets away and arrived at the home of a rabbi in time to join a group of people, and to listen for something. She did not know what she might hear.

I watched her listen, and I listened to myself speak to the group.

When I finished speaking, I heard her give me a predetermined cue to continue speaking, and so I spoke about the hiding place of God.

And then, I watched her lie down upon the floor in front of the rest of us, unashamed, and weep tears of passion—not because of anything that I had done, but because of a message that she heard. It was a message being spoken to her, personally. It was a message that another consciousness, one of great compassion, knew well that she was in need of hearing.

With the tickets, she had taken a necessary first step, and having done so the Awareness then took all other steps necessary to carry her away in a dance of passion. It had gone the distance for her.

Such is the love of the Awareness.

Such is the importance of just one person.

And, what if there is just one more person who is willing to take a necessary first step. What if there is just one who is waiting for a personal message . . .

What if there was someone else waiting to hear this? What if the girl had given her tickets away, but there was no one willing to relay a message to her? It was a simple message after all—"Greetings."

These were not questions imposed upon my mind, but they were questions of my own asking. I had never witnessed passion revealed so unmistakably, so clearly as on the day that I saw it happen; when a young woman heard for the first time the song of the Universe, and discovered that within the song, her name was being called.

The "what ifs" then took a dark turn. What if there was no passion on that day—or on any other day? What if the Awareness remained aware of being unknown? And then, I saw people placing their beliefs in horrifying predictions because they didn't know any better. They didn't know that thought is a form of energy. They didn't know that sadness and turmoil are only in our future if we put them there—if we cause them to be there.

I began to see a terrible . . .

He moved his hands to my shoulders holding me at arms' length, interrupting my thoughts. I looked at him, and another "what if" replaced my dark ones.

What if we were being given a chance to start all over again . . .

I remember taking a deep breath when I heard that.

"Will you come forward for me?" he asked.

"Yes," I answered.

I would come forward, and I would tell others.

I would tell them as best and as simply as I could so that they might hear everything. Then I would write it all down so that they might read it as well, while they—we—create the future.

By 2000, the indigenous peoples who were traveling in the Teacher's company included not only Native Americans, but indigenous from all continents, islands, and regions. I witnessed spectacular arrivals, including a visit one night from numerous natives of Australia, with a surprise appearance by entities held to be mere myths—the Lightning Brothers. They are not myths at all. They are real.

I continued to reflect in awe on all that had happened here, and all that was continuing to happen here, and I wondered—not for the first time—why the teacher remained surrounded in his travels by native peoples of the world.

What was the meaning of this great connection? Are they the only ones still able to see? Are they the only ones who never abandoned gnosis? Have they returned to be our rightful teachers? Have they kept sight of something that societies born of governments and cultures can no longer see?

Still seeking the wisdom of the priest I was first sent to find years earlier, I sent an e-mail to Father Yosef and asked him his opinion on this question. What is the meaning behind this very grand connection between the ancient natives and the

Teacher, I asked him. Why did the Teacher return surrounded by them?

Father Yosef responded as he had once before, with a suggestion of something for me to read.

It was not secret scriptures this time, but it was something that had been selected by early church fathers to remain in the New Testament during the time of the great scripture selection, synods and councils. It was a portion of the fourth gospel, the Gospel of John, and it was available for all to see.

Once again, the words of John spoke quietly to me across a sea of centuries.

Father Yosef's message read as follows:

John Chapter 4, verse 23

Yet an hour is coming, and is already here, when authentic worshipers will
worship the Father in Spirit and truth. Indeed, it is just such worshipers
the Father seeks.

Perhaps, then, that is the answer. Perhaps he wishes to be among those who still hold in their hearts the awareness of old and sacred truths.

Or, perhaps, we might never know the answer. Perhaps, until the hour is right for us to receive the answer, until the coming hour is here, it will remain an unanswered question.

Epilogue

On the day that I concluded the manuscript, ending it with an unanswered question, I celebrated.

I was suddenly filled with a desire for new books, for more knowledge. I decided to walk to the bookstore and find something good to read!

It was a pleasant two-mile walk. A hint of early autumn was in the afternoon air. The kids were in school—high school, now—and so I was unrushed in both the walk and the leisurely selection of a good book. After arriving at the bookstore and looking through its many stocked shelves, I selected three paperbacks that appeared interesting. One dealt with ancient history, pyramids and Mars; one dealt with gardening; and the other focused on current events.

Arriving at home, I picked up the book about Mars and pyramids—the gardening and current events could wait—and dove into it. I read only as far as page eight, however, before running across something I'd never heard of: *vesica piscis*. There was no clear explanation given for those two words, other than that they were terms dealing with geometry.

Although geometry and mathematics have never been areas of interest to me, I felt as strangely compelled to look up the term vesica piscis as I had been to search for root meanings of the word "ballast."

I went to the computer and ran a search for *vesica piscis* on the Internet.

In a moment, the results of the search flashed onto the screen as headings and titles of many websites dedicated to *vesica piscis* were listed on page after page after page.

The page titles flowed like fragments of a powerful, heralding message. Words such as "ancient," "sacred," and "cosmos" were used in the titles and headlines—and then I saw other words, words like "christ consciousness"—christ, referring to an essence, a state of being, an evolutionary process—and I saw words describing perfect balance and unconditional love.

Vesica Piscis, I read on the computer, is the vessel of the fish . . . held by some to be the sign of the awaited coming of the christ consciousness . . . a coming in which the Word will be made flesh again . . .

The descriptions were hauntingly beautiful.

From the many sites, I picked a page at random and began looking at the beautiful images of the vesica piscis, the geometrical designs of harmonic balance known as sacred geometry.

Circles overlapped circles within the images, creating again and again a pattern of almond-shaped fishes, and in many of the drawings, groups of four fish were joined as though in a kiss, endlessly forming the cruciferous shape of a four-petaled flower, or a cross—the X of the ancient chi rho. This cross was the perfectly balanced cross of the fish, a symbol never meant to suggest an instrument of death. It was meant instead to be a symbol of divinity, of perfect balance, of life, Awareness, and of a peace that is long-promised.

I scrolled down to the next image, and what I saw caused me to catch my breath with a sudden start. I stared, frozen in a timeless moment of awe, at the design now in front of me; a design that explained, without words, the unanswered riddle of the connection between the Teacher and the Indians.

Displayed on the computer in front of me, was a *vesica piscis* design that looked exceptionally familiar.

It was the sacred design painted on the Lakota box.

The question of "why" was now suddenly answered with quiet dignity, and complete silence. The answer did not come in words, but through images.

"This is unbelievable," I said under my breath. And it was. It was all unbelievable. Everything that I might have once held to be impossible was happening with a casual grace, while this most profound plan continued to unfold as unrushed as my afternoon's walk had been. It was all unbelievable, and yet, it was all true, undeniably true. It was real.

Finally understanding the role of the native spirits in the plan, I began to understand the roles of others. It is perhaps due to the massive, unseeable scope of the plan that I had been only able to see small fragments of it until this hour, when the pieces of the puzzle fell into place, making perfect and logical sense. It was previously unseeable because it is the biggest of all big things—it was too big to be seen.

The indigenous people, the native ones, have been carrying the ancient promise of the sacred coming in their own consciousnesses, for centuries. Old teachings of balance and harmony, and old teachers aware of the truth were never meant to be forgotten. Those who dwell in the spirit world are a living portion of the balanced, unfolding plan.

With those of the spirit world already taking their places as the great coming begins, the rest of the invited participants are now being awakened to take their places as well.

Those who are of flesh and dwell in this world, at this hour, are the ones now being awaited. We who are of flesh are the other living participants of the balanced, unfolding plan.

Our names are being called, one name at a time.

Like the box that came here empty so that it might be filled, we as individuals are the vessels who can now be filled until we overflow with the promised, sacred consciousness.

Dictus a deamos presidio proximo anomi contestae didymous non sequitor arani tu quoum segundo a mundo . . .

In 1988, I heard the Teacher whisper baffling words that sounded like these after he inadvertently startled me one night. That was the night when he awakened me by whispering into my ear, and I awoke to find him bending over me, his head against mine. I was so startled at his nearness and presence that I screamed.

Eleven years later, while discussing this with my daughter, Emily, tears suddenly welled in her eyes, and a look of awe and insight came over her.

"Mom," she said, "I think I know the message that he was giving to you that night."

"You do?" I asked, amazed yet at the same time not surprised that she would understand his messages very well, "What do you think he was saying, darling?"

"He's back, and he's standing closer than you might think," she said.

—Mary Sparrowdancer,
Woman Two Man Speaks,
follower of The Way

About the Author

Mary was born on Narragansett Bay, in Rhode Island. She and her children, John and Emily, her mother, and her sisters are among the few remaining descendants of the Narragansett First Nation of American Indians. The Narragansett Nation, like other First Nations, were once great in this country.

Although her background includes studies in clinical laboratory medicine, she has devoted a large portion of her adult life to providing free humane care for orphaned and injured wild birds and wild animals, with her primary goal being the restoration of their freedom. She has cared for an estimated twenty thousand birds and animals ranging from black bears, bunnies, and frogs to eagles, owls, and one rather nondescript, but important, little sparrow. She credits her parents with instilling in her a profound respect for the freedom and dignity of all living creatures.

Mary lives in Florida with her children, where she focuses primarily upon the rights of human beings, the call for a new global compassion, and the perspectives as outlined by the Being of Light. She invites readers to visit her website at www.sparrowdancer.com.

Hampton Roads Publishing Company

. . . for the evolving human spirit

Hampton Roads Publishing Company
publishes books on a variety of subjects including
metaphysics, health, complementary medicine,
visionary fiction, and other related topics.

For a copy of our latest catalog,
call toll-free, 800-766-8009,
or send your name and address to:

Hampton Roads Publishing Company, Inc.
1125 Stoney Ridge Road
Charlottesville, VA 22902
e-mail: hrpc@hrpub.com
www.hrpub.com